ADVENTURE, ROMANCE AND WAR
IN THE FAR EAST

The Iris Hay-Edie Diary

Copyright © 2015 by Justin Wheeler
Published by Ediciones Ibéricas
Edited by Ingrid Johannessen Wheeler and Justin Wheeler

Based on *The Diary of Iris Hay-Edie Johannessen* © 1997
Edited by Ingrid Johannessen Wheeler
Library of Congress Control Number: 97-77867

ISBN: 978-84-7083-972-6

Table of Contents

FOREWARD   11

PROLOGUE   13

MY EARLY YEARS   15
Stories of Kashmir   15
My parents life in India   16
Early years in Cornwall   18
The South of France   19
Château de l'Aiguetta in Eze Village   24
Nice   28
Back to the Château   29
St. Aygulf   40
Monte Carlo   43
The "Season" in Paris   48
Learning something useful   49

RUNNING AWAY   55
Escaping my Mother   55
London   59

VOYAGE TO THE FAR EAST   69
Hong Kong at last   76
Canton (Guangzhou)   84

A TRIP AROUND THE WORLD 89

Voyage to the States 89

France 95

Steamer via Calcutta 97

Madras 98

Calcutta 99

The Garden City and Pagoda of Rangoon, Burma 100

REIDAR 103

Can it really be True Love? 104

Reidar's leave 111

Engaged at last! 114

My trip to Shanghai and Peking, China 117

Hong Kong with Archy 122

Reidar returns from his leave 125

Our first home together 125

Reidar's beginnings 127

The wedding 133

John "JoJo" is born 138

JAPAN RISES 141

Lake Chuzenji, Japan 142

Shipping picks up in Hong Kong 151

The Battle of Shanghai 154

Hong Kong becomes the busiest port in Asia 155

The Great Typhoon 157

The Japanese "Rape of Nanking" 161

OUR NEW FAMILY AND HOME AT SKYHIGH 163

Europe revisited 163

Reuniting with our brother Vean 165

The Norwegian family   168

Back in Hong Kong   172

Skyhigh   173

Saigon, Manila and Singapore   175

War in Europe and the German invasion of Norway   177

Ingrid "Ingeling" is born   178

THE BATTLE OF HONG KONG   **185**

The Eve of War   185

The Japanese invasion of Hong Kong begins   186

Hong Kong is surrounded   192

The Japanese land on the Island   199

The Japanese bomb us at Skyhigh   201

Hong Kong forces wear thin   204

Hong Kong falls to the Japanese   214

The Surrender   215

Occupied Hong Kong   218

Japanese atrocities   219

Wallem and its ships are battered   223

Internment for the enemies of Japan   224

A Persian New Year celebration   228

The stress of close quarters   230

Skyhigh in ruins   232

When will we be interned?   233

The new normal   235

Our plan to escape Hong Kong   241

OUR ESCAPE THROUGH CHINA   **243**

Macao   244

How Opium controlled China   253

Farewell Macao   262

Our walk through China begins	264
The road to Kweilin	266
Kweilin (Guilin)	282
Flight to Chungking	296
Over China and The Hump	304
Calcutta	307
INDIA, KASHMIR AND BEYOND	**309**
Nortraship	309
A train to Rawalpindi	310
Upward to Kashmir	313
Kashmir	314
Climbing Handibal	318
On to Bombay, our new home	322
Bombay (Mumbai)	323
School in Poona	325
A "third" honeymoon in Ceylon (Sri Lanka)	327
Joining the St. John's Ambulance Brigade	336
The Indian horse races	338
Leopard's Den, Kashmir again	340
Dancing at Nedou's Hotel	343
Bear hunting	347
Camping on the slopes of Domercote	355
Bombay again	359
Reidar shares a drink with Clark Gable	361
The Allies gain ground against the Axis Powers	363
Anniversary celebration	363
Bob's suicide	364
Voyage to England	366
V.E. Day	366

OUR RETURN TO HONG KONG   369

The fall of the Japanese Empire   369

Hong Kong is liberated   370

EPILOGUE   377

AFTERWORD   385

For the free spirits in the world who are not afraid to take another step forward.

Foreward

This story is unique in many ways. It is based on the diary and memoir written during many decades by Iris Hay-Edie, a free-spirited Scottish girl who grew up in the glamorous French Riviera during the 1920's living in unusually grand residences, but who unfortunately had a horrible relationship with her mother.

Her life was full of adventures as she ran away from home and travelled around the world almost constantly. Later in Hong Kong, she and her Norwegian husband Reidar Johannessen built a business, had two children and lived in the house known as *Skyhigh*, the highest home on the island with spectacular views that decades later broke the world record for the most expensive property sale.

Her diary gives the reader an interesting glimpse of what it was like in the remote colonial Far East in the 1930's, then during the Japanese invasion of China in World War II, and later experiencing its growth as a region that is now so important to the world economy.

After Reidar's death in 1970, she later remarried, but chose to live by herself at their home in Jamaica where she would be visited regularly by her family and friends. She was the spiritual foundation of the growing family, and made a lasting impression on others who knew her.

Her outgoing and positive personality, mixed with her love of nature and world cultures, can be experienced in her delightful anecdotes and often humorous stories.

She was also a very dedicated photographer, and apart from a large amount of photos and Bolex films that were lost during the war when her home was bombed by the Japanese (with her in it), her photos and postcards from the past add an extra dimension of interest to her story.

In the late 1990's when Iris was in her nineties, her daughter Ingrid decided to compile her diaries into a private edition book that would be available to her family. We all found it fascinating and passed it on to friends who seemed to feel the same way.

Finally, another twenty years later, my mother Ingrid and I jumped on the project again with the goal of expanding upon it by adding more detail about the people and places that she encountered on her adventures. Much additional information was gathered from family records, Ingrid's brother John, the internet, as well as references from Anthony Hardy's book *Typhoon Wallem*, a very interesting history of Wallem & Company where Reidar worked for 33 years in Shanghai and Hong Kong.

For Iris' grandchildren and great-grandchildren who knew her, this book will serve as a reminder to them of her wonderful personality and charm, and also provide an understanding of our family history during a enchanting era when colonialism and its accompanied formalities were considered so important. Today this type of lifestyle has almost disappeared, but it is certainly interesting to read about and wonder how it must have been.

Justin Wheeler
Iris' grandson & Editor

Prologue

Iris Hay-Edie Knapp was born in Cornwall, England, in September 1909. Her father, Charles Hay-Edie, worked most of his life in the Far East as the managing director of the Alahabad Bank in Calcutta. Meanwhile, her mother Jessie Nimmo, of the Scottish Bartholomew family who were "Royal Cartographers" for the King of England and renown for their maps and atlases, chose to raise their three children in England and later in the South of France.

The parenting was done at a distance, with very little personal attention and following strict Victorian era social morality of the British Upper-Class. Iris and her two older brothers were sent to boarding schools when they were only a few years old, visiting their mother only on the holidays. Unfortunately they never experienced a happy family life together, and tension between Iris and her mother became unbearable for her. So she ran away from home and never turned back.

Nearly a century later, after an extraordinary life spent in many far away lands, and having experienced times of loneliness and longing, poverty and wealth, a World War, true love and a broken heart, Iris looks through her old photographs, reminiscing as she types notes into her diary while sitting at her desk at her home in San San, Jamaica, overlooking a dense rainforest and the turquoise waters of the Caribbean Sea.

MY EARLY YEARS

Stories of Kashmir

I like to think that the beginning of *Me* was in Kashmir. That might explain my great love of mountains. Anyway, my mother used to tell us so often about her visits to Kashmir in those long ago and far away days, when, after the train journey from Calcutta lasting several days – complete with servants, food, bedding, etc. – one travelled days by tonga drawn by bullocks. She told us about the carpets of blue and yellow iris flowers that stretched endlessly across the Vale of Kashmir. She thought they were so lovely that she determined to call her next baby *Iris*. I was eventually born in Cornwall and christened *Iris Primrose Hay-Edie*.

Iris, Archy and Vean

I wonder how far back one's memory is supposed to go? My first recollections, between two or three years old, were of a nursery with a fireguard around the fireplace upon which nappies hung to dry. I also remember being put into a cupboard to sit on the pottie and being made to stand in a corner when I had been naughty. My next clear memory is being left at a boarding school in Penzance, Cornwall, where I stayed for nearly four years with my older brothers, Archy and Vean, while our parents were in India. I was only four years old.

My parents life in India

Calcutta 1910. Photo taken by my father after Sunday breakfast at the Tollygunge Club. My mother is second from the right.

When I was very young I never saw my father for years on end, as he was working in India, and it was the custom to stay away for several years before going on "home leave", which could last for the best part of a year at a time. In those days it was not possible to fly and the sea voyage to India took nearly a month. My father was Number One of the Alahabad Bank in Calcutta, and he and my mother lived there in an enormous house with innumerable servants, as was the custom then.

They led a very social life, and Mother used to love telling us stories in later years about the large and very elaborate dinner parties they gave with many courses and, of course, halfway through the dinner, after the entree, a sorbet would be served "to cleanse one's palate" before the main course. Every occasion was always very formal and evening dress *de rigueur*. There would be a servant standing behind every guest's chair, and if there were not enough in the hostess's own household for this purpose, then each guest brought his or her own servant.

She told us of one near calamity when the *kitmagar* (butler) came and told her, just before dinner was to be announced, that the *punka* (a cloth fan) over the dining table had got stuck somehow and would not function, which would be disastrous in that heat. She moved over to one of her faithful young admirers, always at her beck and call, and whispered to him the predicament and could he help? He readily agreed and assured her he could easily fix it, but he would have to get up and step on the long dining table, which was covered with a fine white damask tablecloth. He removed his shoes and stepping gingerly between the silverware and crystal, he carefully managed to disentangle the curtain of the *punka* and get it moving again. My mother was infinitely relieved and grateful, until she saw to her horror and despair, large sweaty footprints down the center of the table!

She also used to tell us exciting stories about going on big game hunts for tigers, riding on an elephant, as guests of a *maharaja*. The camping arrangements were so elaborate that even a four-poster bed was transported for their benefit into the jungle.

During the hot summer months most of the wives and children would go up to hill stations, such as Simla, Darjeeling or Kashmir, but when the children reached schooling age they were nearly always sent away, or left at home in Europe, mostly because of the climate and also due to the lack of educational facilities. When the mothers stayed with their children, leaving their husbands alone for lengthy periods, the separation often led to broken marriages.

Early years in Cornwall

Cornwall, England, 1914. The early years vacationing in Cornwall were happy and carefree, and our little house was charming. It was called The Bungalow. It was built on a high cliff overlooking the sea with Godrevy Lighthouse far out, the Carbis Bay Beach below and St. Ives in the distance.

Our days were spent on the beach, digging sand castles and exploring pools on the rocks where tiny fish had been left behind by the tides. There were also lovely picnics up on the moors at Tren Crom, amongst the great Druid stones, and tramps through the heather. Sometimes we came across shafts from the old copper mines, covered over with ancient wooden planks. We used to push stones through the cracks and listen for the sounds of them striking rocks on the way down and finally hitting the bottom far below.

Mummy told us stories of the German submarines lurking in those waters, as we were at war then, and about smugglers and spies who used to hide in the many bays of that coast. She also told us that spies had come into The Bungalow one night to signal out to sea from her sitting room upstairs, but that she had called out from her bedroom next door that she had a revolver that she would use if they did not get out. Rather alarming tales for small children!

We had a maid who came with a tiny baby. One day the maid was out and Mummy had to go down to the train station to meet Vean, who was arriving from school. She felt we could not leave the baby completely alone in the house, so I was left to look after it, at only five years old. The baby was screaming its head off, so I went into the room to see if I could do anything about it, and tried to lift it off the bed to comfort it. But as I tried to sit down with it in my arms, it wriggled so much and slithered onto the floor, landing on its head and naturally bellowed louder than ever. I was quite desperate then and started to shout at it, hoping I might drown out the noise it was making by making more myself. I marched up and down the passage outside the door of that bedroom shouting at the top of my voice, telling the baby to be quiet and hoping I was frightening it as much as I was frightened. I was also worried about the fall onto its head, although it did not look any different.

The combined noise we were making must have seemed like bedlam when my mother returned. I have always wondered whether that poor baby ever did suffer any permanent damage. It also made me think about how very dangerous it was to entrust a baby to a very small child.

The South of France

Nice-Côte d'Azur, 1916. When I was seven years old I went to live in the south of France. My parents had bought a very attractive, medium-sized villa at Cap d'Ail, which they named *Villa Iris.* I stayed there with my mother alone to begin with, as my father was still in India. He returned on Christmas Eve, and there was great excitement the day before because of a terrific storm in the Mediterranean. We kept thinking of how terrible it must be for him to be on board ship on such a stormy sea. All was well, however, and we had a very happy Christmas, although we never had any tree or decorations around the house, or sang any carols, or did anything particularly Christmassy, except opening some presents.

Years after, my brothers and I used to reflect that if only our mother had been content to live in that pretty house, our lives would probably have been a great deal happier. But she was not content. She wanted a bigger house and she also wanted my father to leave India for good. He, of course, would have to work for a bigger house, so it was a difficult situation.

One time she took an overdose of sleeping pills, and the whole household was in turmoil because she could not be roused one morning. I was dispatched up the hill to fetch the local French doctor. I ran all the way, crying with fright and anxiety, but by the time I got home again with the doctor, she had just awakened. After that my father must have agreed to come back again from India as soon as possible, because he retired when he was only 42.

Postcard of Cap D'Ail and the Eden Hotel

In the meantime my mother had her eyes upon a very large and fine villa further up the hill. It was a little way back from the big *Eden Hotel*, which was a most fashionable resort in those days, but I don't think the position was nearly as nice and private as down nearer the sea where *Villa Iris* was. The new house was called *Villa Perle Blanche*, but my mother renamed it *Castel Blanc*!

It was a beautiful villa, originally built by the Lumiere family who invented the cinema, with an enormous pillared hall running the whole depth of the house, a sweeping marble staircase leading up to another great hall upstairs, four enormous bedrooms with their own large bathrooms. The stairs then led up to the roof terrace where two nice rooms were built in the turrets with bathrooms added later. The sitting room and dining room were enormous, and downstairs the servants' "domain" was also vast.

Castel Blanc, Cap d'Ail. Our home from 1919-1939.

There was a nice garden with a great many orange and tangerine trees. Once I had a brilliant idea that I was sure would overjoy my mother, as she always used to take an "infusion" of verveine or camomille after dinner each night, adding a little orange flower water. So, when she and my father were out at the Casino in Monte Carlo one afternoon, I set to work, with the help of a maid we had, and stripped nearly all the trees of their blossoms. We had a big laundry basket full, which I proudly led my parents to on their return, as a wonderful surprise. I was the one who got the surprise when I saw their reaction! I got such a severe scolding, and found it difficult to understand why they were so angry with me. I had thought my mother would be so happy to see all those picked orange blossoms, which could be just boiled up and made into "Eau de Fleur d'Oranger"!

My younger brother, Vean, and I had a governess while we were there. She was an elderly spinster relative of Father's, extremely plain looking and angular, with a red nose and shiny red hands, all bony. I am afraid we made her life pretty miserable, and I don't think we learnt very much from her. Eventually she left because she couldn't bear us any more.

Casino de Monte Carlo

While Mummy and I were living there and Daddy was still in India, she used to go to the *Casino de Monte Carlo* almost every afternoon. While she was gambling, I would be left sitting at the Café de Paris, at a little table all by myself, trying to make my ice cream last as long as possible. The waiters all knew me and kept an eye on me. I was never bored as there were always plenty of interesting people and goings-on to observe. Also I had a book with me, or else my crochet work, and it was very pleasant to sit in the sunshine watching life go by.

Sometimes I would be left at the cinema where I saw many exciting films with Pearl White as the heroine, but it was very tantalizing because the film would always end with Pearl in some terrifying and seemingly hopeless situation, just about to be put to death by the villain, or else facing a situation "worse than death"! One time she was thrown into a pit full of writhing snakes; another time she was left lying, bound and gagged in a pool that was slowly filling up; and another, she was trapped in a burning house, etc., etc., and I was left in suspense for a whole week wondering how she could possibly escape.

I wished that when I grew up, I too would be an adventurer and travel to the farthest and strangest places.

There was an orchestra at the cinema, of course, as the films were silent, and I used to enjoy the varied music as it was adapted to the action of the film. There was an usher who used to conduct me to my seat and who was always very nice and friendly, until he started to become too "friendly" and tried to do some horrid things, which simply terrified me. I was only eight years old and I was too frightened even to tell my mother; also I was afraid she would stop me going to the cinema. So I avoided him whenever possible or else told him, very politely, to keep his hands off me.

Quite often, especially if it was raining and I couldn't sit outside the Café de Paris, Mummy would take me into the Casino with her and leave me sitting in the Atrium with my crochet work. I found that most fascinating, watching the elegantly clad ladies and gentlemen coming in, and sometimes after half an hour or so, the same ones would walk out again. I always observed their faces very carefully, wondering whether they were going to commit suicide or not. Having heard so many tales from my mother about the terrible happenings after people had lost all their fortunes, I found it an absorbing pastime trying to detect who had lost money and who had won.

There were many beautiful clothes and jewels to be seen, but there were also the old women, who looked like hags, dressed in the most peculiar and often tatty old clothes, with floppy hats covered with lace, flowers and feathers. Mummy told me about these old women, who earned a pittance by just occupying a chair at one of the roulette tables the moment the Casino opened. Then when the place filled up, they would cede their chair to some wealthy-looking person and expect a good tip for it. Many of the *habitués* of the Casino looked like characters out of a play, or a book, almost too exaggeratedly peculiar. I came to know many by sight, and could never really make up my mind as to whether they had suicidal tendencies or not.

At one time Mummy had an ardent admirer. She must have had many as she was very lively and attractive then, but this particular one was most persistent. He used to arrive at the villa with flowers and boxes of delicious cakes from Vogade, in Nice. I thought he was a very nice man. But suddenly Mummy decided she didn't want to see him any more and we went through a period of staying home in the afternoons, behind closed shutters to make it look as if we were not there, and the servants were instructed to say, whenever he called, that we had gone away. After some days we dared to resume the drives in to Monte Carlo again and all went well, until one day we met the admirer walking along the road to our villa. He exclaimed joyfully and held up his hands as he stepped towards the carriage, but Mummy called out to the *cocher* to drive on "Vite, vite, n'arrêtez-pas," so the old boy whipped up his horses and we swept on, nearly knocking over the poor admirer, who was left standing in the road looking very bewildered. After that we never saw him again.

Château de l'Aiguetta in Eze Village

While Mummy and I were living at the *Villa Castel Blanc* on our own, Daddy being still in India, we drove up to the old village of Èze one day in the carriage to visit a gentleman by the name of Tennyson who lived in a château up there, which he was evidently thinking of selling. Why my mother should have even thought of buying another place, having only changed homes such a short time previously, from the small *Villa Iris* to the large *Castel Blanc*, was amazing. But then she explained afterwards that it was all for Daddy's sake! She wanted him to have something to do after he had retired from India, and with a large property with a lot of land there would be plenty to keep him occupied "running the Estate".

Anyway, I always remember the drive on that beautiful sunny afternoon, sitting in the open carriage and slowly being taken higher and higher up the winding road through sweet-smelling pine forests and olive groves. The hillsides of gray rock were carpeted with fragrant herbs, thyme, rosemary and lavender, and the wonderful view of the blue, blue Mediterranean was sparkling far below. It was all so countrified and natural then, with hardly any traffic and very few houses on our way.

When we reached the square at Èze Village we left the Moyenne Corniche and took a narrow unpaved road that led up to the Grande Corniche. Halfway up was the Château, and we turned into the drive, which wound its way up through lilacs and overgrown trees, almonds, peaches, and masses of rambling roses sprawling all over the place. It all looked deserted and uncared for. *Château de l'Aiguetta* loomed above us looking like an ancient castle with crenelated turrets, gothic-style windows, balconies and terraces of all sizes and shapes formed by the "stepping-back" of the building on the upper floors. The whole thing was the colour of old weathered stone, hung with thick creepers. It seemed like something out of a fairy story.

Château de l'Aiguetta

This strange atmosphere of unreality persisted as we stood in front of what we took to be the main entrance and pulled on the chain of a large bell hanging there. But it seemed as though the place really was deserted. Not a sound or sign of life anywhere. However, eventually we heard the sound of a door opening in the distance, and saw a man beckoning to us at the end of the long arcade that ran the whole length of the front of the Château. The man was evidently Mr. Tennyson's major-domo, although we thought he looked somewhat scruffy. He led us through a massively heavy wooden door with gigantic iron hinges and lock on it into a narrow passage and stairway made of red earthenware tiles, which spiraled up inside one of the round towers.

We found Mr. Tennyson awaiting us in his library, a fine, long room with gothic windows, filled with fabulous antique furniture, and the walls lined with hundreds of wonderful looking volumes. He was a nephew of the Poet Laureate to Queen Victoria. A very fine looking man with a big white mustache and gray hair, but he looked as if he had just woken up from a sleep. (We discovered afterwards that he had been having one of his drinking bouts for a few days. We also learned later that he was an erratic character and had been mixed-up with Oscar Wilde and Frank Harris and "The Black Douglas". In fact he was persona non grata with the British Government and not allowed to return to England.)

He had built this Château on very ancient foundations and kept adding to it as the mood took him and his finances allowed. He used to gamble heavily at the Casino at Monte Carlo and when he had lost a great deal of money, he would come up to the Château and shut himself in for days or weeks and just drink. Tennyson explained that he had meant to build a ballroom over the terrace and a billiard room on the upper floor, but that he had lost so much money at the Casino that he had to stop all work and decided he must sell the place.

He also owned another villa further up the valley, where his mistress lived with the illegitimate daughter she had borne him. The mistress was very much against his selling the Château, as she considered it should become the property of herself and her daughter. So there were difficulties right from the beginning. My mother in after years used to say that she was a witch and had put a curse upon the place! I could believe it.

When my father returned from India and found he was the owner of this amazing place, I think it must have been a considerable shock to him, particularly as we still had the very large *Villa Castel Blanc* at Cap d'Ail. That villa was always supposed to be sold after the Château was bought, but that never happened. My mother also tried to rent it out for the season, but without success.

The Château must have been a tremendous expense constantly, and I shudder to think of the money they must have poured into it over those ten years. The entire central heating had to be installed, electricity and plumbing all over the building overhauled, several new bathrooms added, and the telephone brought all the way from Villefranche, many miles away below on the coast. Judging that there were not enough rooms for servants, my mother had two extra ones built on the roof and an extra bathroom installed in one of the top turrets.

Also, a cottage with four rooms was built at the back of the Château to house more staff.

To begin with, we started off in grand style with a 10 person staff including a chef, kitchen maid, two housemaids from the village, a Russian butler, a Russian chauffeur, as well as four men working on the grounds.

We also had a Model-T Ford car in which the chauffeur took the chef down to Nice to do big marketing. There was one particularly steep part of the road on the way back, which I remember always had to be tackled in reverse, as the car just couldn't manage it otherwise.

The first man we had to drive it got confused over the gears as he was trying to turn the sharp corner out of our drive on to the road to Èze. He wanted to reverse, but the gear he used turned out to be forward, and the car shot forward and fell into a small ravine on the other side of the road. Fortunately the chauffeur was able to leap out before it went over. We all rushed down the drive to view the ruins of the car, which lying about ten feet below the road, upside down, but didn't seem to be damaged much apart from a crushed windscreen. As luck would have it, a cart was coming up from the village delivering our coal, and the horse, somehow or other, managed to pull the car out of the ravine. When it was set the right way up again, it was driven down to a garage to get the windscreen fixed as if nothing untoward had happened.

Life was fairly normal for me in those days because I was usually away at a boarding school in Nice, which I loved. Archy was at Harrow and Vean at another school in England, and we only came home for the holidays.

There was always plenty to keep us busy on the property, even though we seldom had any friends to visit, and Archy was inclined to get bored after the first few days. He was not as amenable as Vean and I were when Mummy decreed that we should water the garden, morning and afternoon, far off by the tennis court and along our boundary by the road. This meant carrying heavy cans of water for long distances over and over again. In fact it took hours, and Archy invariably got fed up and didn't see why he should spend his holidays working instead of enjoying the interesting things to do on the Côte d'Azur.

Afterwards, when he went to a college in Switzerland, he was allowed to bring a friend home for the holidays. He must have been 17 or 18 at that time. One day Mummy asked them to help chop firewood from some trees the men had felled in the woods. It was a very hot summer's day and they got very thirsty. So Archy brought out some wine to quench their thirsts and by the time they were called in for lunch, they could hardly stagger up the stairs, and their behavior at table—which Vean and I thought hilarious—decidedly horrified our parents.

Nice

At my school in Nice, the Institut Masséna, I seemed to be a great favorite with the headmistress, Madame Canaguier, who was also the owner. There were girls of many different nationalities, Greek, Italian, Spanish, Portuguese and some from South America, but to begin with I was the only British girl, and there were no Americans.

My best friend there was a very sweet and pretty Russian girl, two years older than I. Maroussia had been brought to the school several years previously by her father, who had then disappeared, and neither she nor the headmistress had ever seen or heard from him since.

In consequence Maroussia was treated as a glorified servant, being made to work very hard at all kinds of tasks in the school and look after Madame Canaguier, and, chiefly, after her rather revolting little Pomeranian dogs. But Maroussia was very talented and was just about the best pupil in the school. Also she played the piano beautifully and could dance very well. We became such close friends that we used to call ourselves sisters, and she poured out her heart to me over the years that I was there. Her life was far from easy although Madame Canaguier was really very fond of her.

My mother used to go for a cure each summer, not necessarily to the same place or for the same cure, or because of her doctor's recommendation. However, one year it might be Aix-les-Bains, because it was so well known, then the following year it could be Vichy, as that, too, was very fashionable and a lovely place. Then it was Plombières, and another time La Bourboule. We would stay at the best hotels. I would act as combined lady's-maid-companion to my mother and generally enjoyed myself quite well, as she was not so difficult then as she became later.

Anyway, while at Aix-les-Bains I got an attack of appendicitis, and had to be operated upon in a hospital in Chambéry, a town not far away. I still remember so clearly the heat of that summer, the nuns who looked after me, and my father coming almost every day to see me, and to sit and play piquet with me.

I was in hospital for three weeks, and then my parents took me to Lausanne, Switzerland, and I was left in another boarding school there. Archy was still at La Villa College in Lausanne then, so I did not feel abandoned and very soon was happy as ever.

Archy used to come and take me out on Sundays, and we would have lots of fun going for walks, or boat excursions on the lake, or to the cinema, and then going to a patisserie and stuffing ourselves with terribly rich and creamy cakes. One day we went for a lovely walk up in the hills behind the town. I had on my best dress and shoes. The path led us near a small river and I couldn't resist hopping from rock to rock to try and reach the other side, but alas I fell in! My return to school, soaking wet, with scraped and bleeding knees, squishing shoes and irate brother, was somewhat ignominious.

Back to the Château

Èze Village, Nice, 1923. After a year in a boarding school in England, I was fourteen when I went back to the Château again, and my mother was becoming even more temperamental. She seemed to be always complaining about something or other, and finding fault with everyone and most of all with me. Ever since I could remember she had always been delicate in health, so she had everybody, excepting Archy, who refused, running around her in circles trying to save her any undue exertion. I was treated like a slave at her beck and call all day long and getting into great trouble if I was not immediately in attendance. From five o'clock each morning I would bring her early morning tea in bed, until the last thing at night when I had finally seen her to sleep.

There were times when night after night she would call me into her bedroom, because she could not sleep, and I would have to stand at the foot of her bed for ages listening to her complaints and tales of woe. Mostly they were against my father, saying how cruel and callous he was, telling her she must not spend so much money on the houses or be so extravagant over her clothes, because he could not afford it anymore. Even her summer visits to cure resorts he called extravagant, when he knew how important it was for her health, etc. etc. And, of course, all she had done was generally "for his sake".

No wonder I was thankful whenever I was allowed to escape back to the Institut Masséna in Nice. But my mother kept sending for me at odd times, so that my schooling was very disrupted, which obviously meant nothing at all to her, as long as I could be brought back to attend to her needs. I never had a complete term there, always arriving after the term had started or leaving long before it had finished.

Vean was at school in England then, at Rossal, so sometimes I was left at the Château on my own, when my parents occasionally went off on trips or spent time in Monte Carlo, where they had by then rented a small flat. But at such times they would arrange for Fifine, one of the little maids from Èze Village, to come and stay overnight with me, so that I would not be nervous.

Fifine was a very pretty, vivacious little brunette, and we got along marvellously together. I was too young to realize at that time that she was evidently also getting along marvellously with Serge, our Russian butler. We both slept then in an enormous room at the top of the house. I slept in the gigantic old four-poster bed while she had a small bed that had been moved in especially for her. We used to talk for ages after going to bed, and she would tell me all the gossip from the village and about her own family life.

One night we were talking about how creepy the Château was at night. So we dared each other to run the next night through the top floor rooms, then two flights down the "Red Staircase", along the gallery behind the library, drawing-room and dining-room and up the great marble staircase, back to our own room again, just to show how brave we were—all without putting on any lights.

When the time came the following night I started off first, full of determination not to let my jitters show! Fifine followed a little way behind me, but I ran much faster than she did. As I was running along the gallery and passing under an Egyptian hanging that covered one of the archways, I was seized by a pair of arms, and I screamed in wild terror. I was quickly released and ran, panic-stricken, along all the rest of the gallery and up the marble stairs.

By the time I reached our room, I realized that it must have been Serge and that he must have thought I was Fifine. She eventually reached our room, and said how terrified she had been too and that she had scolded Serge severely. But he had just laughed. She must surely have told him of our plan beforehand.

When the weather was bad I would curl up on a window seat in the library and read some of the amazing books that were part of Tennyson's vast collection. He had asked permission to leave them there until he found room for them in one of his other residences. They were fascinating and so beautifully bound. There were great tomes of French and English literature, so big and heavy that I could hardly lift them out of the lower shelves. I remember pouring over the *Crimes Célèbres* and *Les Amours de Napoléon Bonaparte* and *Le Marquis de Sade* and such like, as well as great volumes of Edgar Allan Poe and Arthur Conan Doyle and many, many others. There were also stacks of novels in Tauchnich editions in a separate cupboard, together with stacks of copies of *La Vie Parisienne* and other such magazines, through which I rummaged with great interest, and often considerable amazement and disbelief!

Serge would be cleaning the floor or polishing some of the beautiful antique furniture and so we would talk about what his life was like before he became a refugee from the revolution. He worked in an office then. Now he had no family or friends, and the future seemed a blank for him, he said. He planned to kill himself when he reached the age of forty.

Our Cossack chef, on the other hand, was of quite a different character. When he was, literally, full of spirits—it was the custom then for each member of the staff in a household to be allowed a bottle of *vin ordinaire* daily—he used to leap onto the big kitchen table and perform Cossack dances. Sometimes he had knives in his mouth, held by the tips of the blades between his teeth, while squatting down on bent knees and kicking out his feet. He would shake his head in different directions and the knives would come flipping out all around him. All the staff stood around clapping and cheering him on, as we children did too. But of course our parents were not there at such times.

He was a marvellous pastry cook and used to make wonderful *eclairs* and *napoléon's cakes* and many other fancy things, really much too professional for our needs, and eventually he got a job in a fine restaurant in Monte Carlo.

Our devastatingly good looking Russian chauffeur was the son of a former general in the army of the Tsar, but at that time he was making a precarious living in Nice as a cobbler. Alexis left us after a while to become an instructor at a driving school in Nice. We heard afterwards that he had married a very wealthy American woman who had been one of his pupils.

One day, when I was at school, the chauffeur came to fetch me in the car to go home. I noticed that the linen seat covers, which were usually spotlessly white, were very rumpled and stained with blood. When I asked Jean why this was, he seemed very vague and mumbled something about having been to the *marché* in Nice. Some of the baskets with meat and chicken had made stains, which he had not had time to clean.

But when I got home I learnt the real reason. Serge had shot himself with my brother's revolver, and Jean had just taken his body to the morgue. It was a great shock to everybody. I remembered how he used to say during our long talks in the library that he was going to commit suicide when he reached the age of forty. And he did. I was very sad.

The Château was a rather gloomy place to live in, especially later when Vean and I were there so much on our own. There were five floors altogether, counting the foundations, which consisted of several massively built vaults and cellars of different sizes with walls that measured over one meter thick with tiny windows that faced onto the long gallery outside. The Red Staircase was cut right out of the rock at that end of the building. It was all so dark and mysterious in that part of the building that I always felt rather frightened when I had to go there.

One evening my father asked me to fetch a special bottle of wine from the big *cave* (cellar) where all the wine was stored. The switch for the electric light was placed far from the door, so I had to cross a long way in pitch darkness, which made me very scared as I imagined all sorts of horrible things there. When I switched on the light, there was a sudden scurrying sound all around the walls and then complete silence and stillness. To my horror I saw dozens of enormous rats all around on the shelves and wine barrels, motionless as if riveted to the spot and all staring at me as if they were going to spring upon me in attack. I was so terrified that for a moment I could not move. Then I made a dash for the door to get away. It was a nightmarish experience and forever left me with a feeling of repulsion of rats.

There were archways and long corridors hung with Indian and Egyptian wall hangings, antique spears and arms, and a high-backed oak chair with a horrible-looking iron hook protruding high up in the middle of the back, which Tennyson told us was for garroting!

The rooms were furnished with beautifully carved furniture, French, Italian, and also Queen Anne cupboards and a very long dining table. I am sure that many of the pieces should have been in museums. But all these rooms had very low ceilings and small gothic windows with stained glass windows, so that I found them rather dark and depressing, particularly as the wallpapers were in dark colors to look like tapestry. The beautiful Persian carpets that my father had collected, while he lived in India, looked most fitting in this setting.

At the end of the main gallery was the library and the spiral Red Staircase with its red tiles and terra cotta walls. Ascending those stairs was my mother's suite with a large entry hall, sitting room and rounded balconies. The view was glorious from there down the valley towards the old village of Èze perched on its conical mountaintop.

My mother's bedroom

The bathroom was built into a turret and at the other end of the bedroom was a large alcove with a huge marble fireplace. Her bed was supposed to have belonged to one of Napoléon's mistresses. I came to know that bedframe very well, as I spent so many hours standing at the foot of it.

There was a lovely set of Louis Quinze furniture, an amazing Gobelin tapestry with glorious soft colourings and design, and inlaid marquetry commodes and tables that I spent hours polishing and that I came to appreciate the beauty and amazing artistry of those pieces.

From Mummy's bedroom a door led down some steps into my bedroom. It had a fascinating small four-poster bed with a mephisto's head carved in the canopy overhead. There were two tall gothic-style windows opening onto a nice terrace. This looked across the valley to the bridge leading to Èze Village and the rocky cliff below.

The Château with a view of Èze Village in the background

I loved to climb up that mountain with the dogs and make my way through the fragrant shrubs and herbs that grew amongst the rocks. When I got to the end of the promontory, I would sit perched on the edge of the cliff, day-dreaming and looking straight down onto the cars that passed hundreds of feet below.

My father's room was a lovely big bright room with a very fine terrace having the same lovely view down the valley to Èze Village and the blue Mediterranean Sea beyond.

In our early days at the Château, when Archy and Vean were there for the holidays, and Mummy and Daddy went off for a few days to Monte Carlo or to the Villa at Cap d'Ail, I would sleep upstairs in Daddy's room to be near the boys and not feel frightened. But despite their proximity, I was terrified and used to lie awake in that big four-poster bed, with the bedclothes pulled over my head, watching the hands on the illuminated face of the clock I had taken to bed with me. They advanced so unbelievably slowly, and I would listen to the various strange and frightening sounds of the house in the interminable darkness of the night.

I could hear footsteps coming down the Red Staircase and pausing in the passage outside the bedroom door. The ancient wardrobe creaked and cracked as if somebody was inside it. I was too petrified to run to my brothers' room and ask to stay there with them. I still remember vividly the agony of those nights. But what surprised me was discovering that both Archy and Vean felt nervous too, and thought they had heard footsteps coming down the Red Staircase in the night. The handle of their door had been turned and the door left slightly open, although they were both positive it had been properly shut when they went to bed.

After my stay in England with the Turnbulls from the boarding school, my parents asked them to come and stay with us at the Château to coach us in English, literature, history and grammar. Vean was then at home too, and Nancy, their daughter, joined us in our studies. To begin with all seemed to be going well, as long as our parents stayed away.

Then Mr. Turnbull also started to feel that there were some strange things happening at times, such as their bedroom door frequently being opened at night, even though they had locked it before going to bed. To begin with, they even thought that Vean or I might be playing tricks on them, but soon realized that this was far from true. He found it very difficult to be unable to put a normal explanation on these peculiar happenings, especially after we had told him about our experiences. After a few months, the Turnbulls left and went back to England.

Iris, Archy and Vean with a few of their mother's dogs

That summer Vean and I spent about three months on our own at the Château. We had no friends and nobody came to see us. It was peaceful and there was always so much to keep us busy in the garden and also in the house, especially we had the dogs to look after. At one time we had *sixteen* Alsatians of all ages and *nine* Pekinese (Mummy's special breed)! Also we had chickens and rabbits and bees. Only two men worked permanently on the grounds then, so Vean was kept busy with the vegetable terraces, the fruit trees, vines and olives, as well as all the other innumerable trees and shrubs that Mummy had had planted all over the park, all which needed watering during the long, hot summers.

On the 14th of July, Èze Village held a *Fête* in the village square. A large tent was put up, and there was music and dancing. We received a formal invitation from the Mayor of Èze, much to our dismay! Neither Vean nor I felt at all socially minded, but we thought that as we were the only so-called "gentry" living in the district, in the biggest house around, we had better make an appearance. So we put on our best clothes and walked down to the village.

When we arrived the Mayor came out to greet us and lead us to places of honor. The proceedings started with the band, all local talent, striking up the Marseilles, with tremendous fervor and deafening noise from the brass trumpets and other instruments. Then came a speech from the Mayor, which seemed to go on interminably, while everybody perspired plentifully in the heat of the tent. Finally the wine was poured and the party really got going, but Vean and I managed to slip away quickly, not fancying being caught up in the dancing!

Sometimes, when I was out at night with the dogs, I would look up at the great dark mass of the Chateau looming above me and think what a gloomy place it was and I dreaded going back into it.

Once I saw a light go on in one of the turret rooms and wondered what on earth Vean could be doing up there at such a time of night. But when I asked him about it later, he said he had not been up there for days!

One evening as we were standing in the hall at the foot of the marble stairs, saying goodnight to Jean Figuera, the new chauffeur, who was going back to his home in the village, we heard steps coming down from the top floor. We all stopped talking and stared at each other in amazement, wondering who it could be, as only Vean and I were sleeping in the Château at that time. Vean had Hadji, our beautiful Alsatian dog, with him, and started to go upstairs to see who it was. But half way up, the dog, with its hair bristling and staring eyes, started growling and barking. He suddenly broke loose from Vean's hold, dashed down the stairs and out into the night. Vean decided not to investigate any further, and Jean hurriedly took his departure!

As the years went by, although I was still nervous at nighttime in the Château, I was not afraid of going out in the darkness with nature all around. I quite often used to go down the valley, right under the great high bridge, where there was no path on such a steep hillside. But I knew my way so well and could make my way over the rocks below the south face of the village to my special little lookout place. This was a very small ledge of rock, just over the edge of the cliff, and completely invisible from the village in the daytime. There was a drop of over a thousand feet to the main coastal road, the Route du Littorale, with Èze-sur-Mer far, far below.

I would sit mesmerized watching the headlights of cars driving along and wondering, when I grew up, if I would ever find myself bowling along that famous road, on my way to the Casino in Monte Carlo, or to the high lights of Nice? What would my future hold?

I would sit on that lonely perch for hours, even after the thrilling spectacle of the sun rising out of the sea was over, as it climbed so rapidly up into the sky. And once I saw mountains on the horizon, where I had always only seen the blue Mediterranean before. I was amazed and thought I must be seeing a mirage. But when, in great excitement, I told Carlin, one of the old village men who worked in the garden, he said that on very clear days it was possible to see the mountains of Corsica. I was very thrilled to know I had seen those mysterious mountains on that faraway island, and Corsica seemed such a legendary place. I lived so much alone then, in a sort of dream world, half-real, half-imaginary, telling myself stories in which, of course, I played the principal part myself.

When our parents came home again, my heart sank. I would hear the car turning off the road and onto our driveway, far below, and would run down to meet them at the entrance, thinking "no more lovely freedom, just work, work, work!" I was her slave. I washed her silk underclothes and ironed them so carefully, and mended the long runs in her silk stockings, picking up each stitch with a fine crochet hook. I mended the ancient tapestries that hung on walls and the Gobelin tapestry carpet that lay on the floor. I was at her beck and call day and night, waiting on her hand and foot, literally. Yet despite the way she treated me, I adored her and would do anything for her unquestioningly, even to being nasty to my brothers and father when she filled my head with stories against them.

My father was a dear, wonderful man and I know he loved me very much, but he was far too weak with my mother and let her get away with all sorts of extravagant whims and, in later years, with her heartless behavior towards Vean and me.

St. Aygulf

By this time my parents had acquired a holiday villa along the coast at St. Aygulf. It was a charming, out-of-the-way little village at that time, away from any main road, set amongst pine trees, eucalyptus and mimosas. The villa was a two-story, unpretentious, small house set in a large garden that was a jumble of mimosas, geraniums climbing all over the place, fig trees and large gray cacti.

A wide gravel path led to the lovely beach of St. Aygulf where we went swimming every day. There were never many people around in those days, and the sand was so fine and clean. The beach stretched for about two miles until the river at St. Rafaël. At the back of this beach were lovely sand dunes and completely wild and natural, with no houses or roads.

The drive used to take several hours from Monte Carlo or Èze over the Esterelle mountains, or around them on the coastal road from Cannes. I used to love those drives and spent the time absorbing the beauties of the scenery and dreaming my dreams. When I was sent on ahead with the maid to get the house ready for my parents, we travelled by train to St. Raphaël then had to change onto the little train, which went to St. Tropez, stopping at St. Aygulf on the way.

Postcard of the coastal trains

I loved the whole atmosphere of that place. It was so simple and bright after the darkness and gloom of the Château and the grandeur of the villa at Cap d'Ail. There I felt in my element, particularly when my parents were not there.

I would get up in the very early morning when the sun was just making a lovely golden glow on the horizon and run down through our garden already fragrant with the perfume of mimosa and flowers. I then climbed over the gate and onto the rocks to perch on the furthest point out over the sea and watch for the fishermen to come by. They would let me climb into their boat, and then we went rowing over the mirror-like water towards the enormous glowing orb of the sun rising majestically over the horizon.

The sea was fairly shallow for a long way out and the water was so clear, that I could see the rocks below us, and the men could spy their quarry, mainly octopus and sea urchins. Leaning over the side of the boat, with a pole that had a combined spike and hook at the end, they would spear these creatures. Up would come a wriggling mass of snakelike limbs that would be unhooked and thrown into the middle of the boat. However, if they missed there was no second chance. The creature would send out a cloud of inky liquid making it impossible to see anything and it would make its escape. I was not too happy at times sitting amongst all those wriggling, slimy and revolting looking creatures, often trying to attach themselves to my legs and feet. The prickly sea urchins were not much better.

The men used to urge me to try eating a sea urchin (*oursins* to them), which I did once. I was ashamed to admit I had not tasted one, as they considered them a delicacy. But I found it horribly squishy and salty and I made such a face that they all roared with laughter at my reaction.

But what I loved most of all was to run along the beach at night when there was moonlight and never anybody around. I used to run and run along that beautiful soft sand, playing games with the gentle waves as they whispered in and out in the shining path of the moon. Then I would go and lie amongst the sand dunes, still warm from the day's sunshine and sometimes fall asleep. It was so beautiful.

One evening when my parents were there, they had one of their miserable rows. It made me desperately unhappy when this happened, which was all too often. We frequently lived through periods of dark gloom when my mother was always cross and criticizing everything that I or Daddy did, or didn't do. But this particular evening the bitter words were even more cruel.

I finally took refuge down in my room. My bedroom had been the laundry room before and used to be accessible only from the garden, but now there was a small passage cut through the thick wall leading to it. With a coat of whitewash on the walls, a chair, table, and a mattress on the old wash tub, it made an adequate bedroom for me. I was only too thankful to be a little removed from my parents and able to go out into the garden without them knowing. I valued my privacy, however small the space, far more than comfort, and I had plenty of experience of sleeping in strange accommodations in various places.

That night I was dreadfully distressed and in a flood of tears. I felt that the atmosphere at home was becoming more and more miserable and unbearable, and I longed to find a way out. Although there was a storm blowing, I went out into the garden in the blackness. The wind was howling and heavy rain beat against my body. It was exhilarating and exciting. My misery seemed swept away by the fury of the elements.

As my eyes became more accustomed to the darkness, I decided to look at the waves from the rocks at the end of the garden. It was a most thrilling sight, watching the gigantic masses of water hurling themselves against the rocks upon which I was perched, just out of reach. I was soaking wet, of course, and quite cold, but loving the excitement of sharing so closely Nature's wild mood.

Suddenly I heard my father calling me, and when I reached him, he clutched me with trembling hands and shouted above the roaring wind: "Do you know what your mother said to me? She hoped you had gone out to drown yourself!"

Monte Carlo

The Château was finally sold to the Casino of Monte Carlo, or rather the *Société des Bains de Mer de Monte Carlo*, as it was called officially. The plan was to make a country club of it with a golf course and tennis courts, the latter of which were already there.

I, then, had to stay with my parents in the flat in Monte Carlo or else at the *Villa Castel Blanc* at Cap d'Ail, which they also were hoping to sell. During the day the maid and I would do housework and keep the place in a state of perfect readiness to be shown to any prospective buyer or renter. Most went away with no follow-up. I felt sad for my father about this, knowing how worried he was over the bills that kept constantly coming in.

With my parents outside the Casino

Then came the time when my parents went out to Ceylon (*Sri Lanka*) to meet Archy, who came from Hong Kong to join them there. I was left staying on my own in the flat in Monte Carlo to look after my mother's little Pekinese dogs. I was eighteen then and used to go to the Monte Carlo Country Club to play tennis, which I enjoyed very much but never became very good at. However, I made some friends and started to lead a more normal life than the one of solitude that I was accustomed to.

The secretary of the Tennis Club of Monte Carlo, a Russian called Vladimir Landau, was very nice and friendly, and used to play in the Monte Carlo Davis Cup and other tournaments.

I met another Russian called Basil Davidoff, charming and cultured, and lots of fun to be with, but not a penny to his name. He was employed as Bailiff by Madame Balsan, formerly the Duchess of Marlborough. They built an enormous château on the other side of Èze Village from where our *Château d'Èze* was situated. Mummy was furious when she heard they had called it *Château d'Èze* also. The only explanation was that when Tennyson owned our château years before, it had been known as the *Château l'Aiguetta*, but Mummy, of course, wanted something grander.

When living in Monte Carlo on my own, I used to go out quite frequently in the evenings with Basil and Vladimir. Also, there was a young Austrian couple, whose parents owned the enormous *Eden Hotel* at Cap d'Ail, close to our *Villa Castel Blanc*. It was a very lovely and fashionable hotel in those days.

So I suddenly was introduced to smart little restaurants and nightclubs, which was a great thrill for countrified little me. The place we went to most was a nightclub called *The Knickerbocker*, where there were wonderful Russian dancers doing Cossack dances with knives in their mouths, just like our Cossack chef used to do.

I think the others, who were all so sophisticated, must have been amused at my great excitement and enthusiasm at going out to these places. The men always treated me with courtesy and never tried to take advantage of me. In fact, although Basil did ask me to marry him later when we met again in Paris, his advances went no further than kissing my hand! His father had been in a high-up position in the Court of the Tsar, and Basil loved music, operas, and ballets and knew them all by heart.

One evening after they had dropped me back at the flat, I didn't feel like going to bed at all. There was a full moon and Mont Agel with all the other lovely mountains was illuminated so brightly. It seemed such a sad waste of so much beauty to just go to bed and sleep, so I decided to walk up the funicular railway, which started near our flat, and walk to La Turbie, a little Roman town high above Monte Carlo.

1000. - Chemin de Fer à crémaillère de Monte-Carlo à la Turbie

It was after midnight when I set off, having changed my dress and shoes (women never wore slacks or shorts in those days). I had a feeling of excitement to be going on such an adventure. It never dawned on me that it might be dangerous. I just thought it was probably illegal to walk up the funicular tracks, but who was to know as it was the middle of the night.

It was the most glorious night. As I climbed higher and higher the carpet of twinkling lights along the coast seemed to spread out further. I could pick out the rock of Monaco, the Palace and the Oceanograph at the end. Of course, the Casino at Monte Carlo was brightly illuminated. It was all so magical, that I never felt tired. The aromatic herbs under my feet wafted up the most wonderful fragrance in the warm summer air. The rocks and wild bushes of the mountainside were illuminated so clearly in that brilliant moonlight.

When I came near to La Turbie, I thought it better not to risk going any further, although I would have liked to go on to the ancient tower that was built by Julius Caesar. I perched on a rock and stayed a very long time, just dreaming and thinking about life.

During the days, I used to love going down to the harbour and walking along by all the fabulous yachts that were tied up there. Each one was more enormous and more glamorous than the other. I would stand and gaze at them, picturing the fabulous lives of the wealthy people who owned them. I wondered if I would ever marry someone with a gorgeous yacht and go sailing all over the world!

My mother, in a somewhat reckless and expansive mood, had said that she and my father would give me the old Lorraine-Dietrich car. It had been parked in the garden at St. Aygulf for many months already and would doubtfully be used again, since we no longer had a chauffeur.

I decided to go by train to St. Aygulf, taking a mechanic with me from the garage we used. We also took tools and a new tire, as I thought that since the car had been resting on blocks all these months the tires might have suffered from lack of use. We arrived at the *Villa Les Agaves* around noon and it didn't take long to find out that the car was in decidedly poor condition. It needed a lot of work before we could make a start on our drive over the Esterelle mountains to Monte Carlo.

The mechanic was very good and worked hard for many hours, but still looked doubtful when we finally set off on our journey. It was already late in the afternoon as we started climbing over the Esterelles in the rain and approaching darkness.

The first thing that stopped working was the windscreen wiper, which made it very difficult to see, of course. I had to keep leaning out of the window and was soon very wet. Then came a puncture. We were thankful for the new tire, as we had already used the spare tire before starting.

We managed to get through Nice, still in pouring rain, and up to the Grande Corniche. We thought there would be less traffic, and it would be easier to drive with no wipers. But then, alas, we had another puncture just before La Turbie, with no extra tire to change. It was about ten o'clock by then and still raining heavily. We were many miles away from any garage, or indeed any house, and there were no cars coming our way at that time of night. What to do? There seemed no alternative but to drive on with our flat tire, even though I realized that it would ruin the rim of the wheel.

It was a miserable end to the whole venture. We slowly bumped the rest of the way down from the Grande Corniche and into the garage in Monte Carlo, where they gazed in horror at the car. I left it there, feeling like a criminal and wondered, as I walked back to the flat in the rain, what my parents were going to say to me when they returned from Colombo! As my mother had said she would give it to me, my main thought now was to fix it somehow and then sell it. That would take care of the large bill that would inevitably be forthcoming from the garage!

The "Season" in Paris

1929. On my parents' return, I was sent to Paris to live with a French baroness and her husband in their very fine *hôtel particulier* in the Rue de l'Université.

The Baronne Reille was a charming and vivacious person who loved life and activity. She and the Baron had five children, who were all married, excepting the youngest son, and he was engaged to be married shortly. The Baronne felt very lonely in her large, empty house with no young people around anymore, so she had decided to have two English girls to live with them, whom she would take around Paris and launch into society.

I knew my mother was wondering what to do with me at this period of my life at 20 years old. It was not the custom then for girls to be trained for any job in the future, as they were just expected to get married. She would have liked to have me "Come out" (as the expression was) with a "Season" in London, and be presented at Court as she had been. However, not living in London themselves, my parents were unable to afford the enormous expense of having me launched by one of the titled ladies who do this for debutantes. So she evidently hoped that by staying with the Baron and Baronne Reille for some months, I might acquire some high society polish and, possibly, find a husband!

I don't know if I gained the polish, nor did I find a husband. I did discover though that my mother had been more or less negotiating with the Baronne about a marriage for me, with a young Count. I had met him at a ball at the Cercle Interallie, and he had evidently become smitten with me.

During an interval between the dances, I had caused the Baronne great consternation by allowing this young man to take me to have some orange juice, instead of rejoining the row of chaperons sitting along the wall keeping a strict eye on their charges. I was told it was very incorrect to go out of the ballroom with a young man unchaperoned.

The Baron traveled a lot by car all over France, as he had numerous private companies to look after, including a very big steelworks and foundry in Alès (towards the southern part of France). Once they took us to stay a few days at the lovely old château they owned there. We visited the steelworks, where rails for railway lines were being made, which I found absolutely fascinating to watch. The great cauldrons of red-hot metal being poured into molds; the noise of clanging machinery overhead; the roaring fires in the great ovens; and the tremendous solid masses of red-hot metal being pushed through machinery that turned them out into ever thinner strips until they became rails.

The Baron also took us to see the battlefields at Verdun, where so many thousands of Frenchmen had been killed during the 1914-1918 war, and where he himself had fought. He showed us the remains of the trench where he had dug in. The battlefield still looked like one, even so many years later, with the scars partly covered by grass and a few sad-looking, stunted trees. Deserted and desolate, it was truly a depressing place.

After a few happy months staying with the Reilles, I went to live with my parents, who had returned to Paris for a short while. The Baronne asked us for a lunch in the Bois de Boulogne one day, and on the way driving back, I heard her and my mother discussing the possibility of my being married to the young Vicomte de Courtivron. I was not consulted. But the issue never really reached an alarming state for me, because I knew that I would be expected to bring a substantial dowry to the marriage, which we would not be able to afford.

Learning something useful

It was decided that I should start learning to be a secretary— to keep up with modern times. The Baron agreed that I could come and begin as an apprentice in his private bank under the tutorship of his elderly private secretary, who was a very nice person. She showed me how to cut coupons and do all sorts of little odd jobs around her office. During the two-hour lunch break I would go and have lessons in shorthand, in French, of course. When I had mastered this eventually, I was so pleased with myself that I wrote my diaries in this shorthand. Now, alas, I can no longer remember how to decipher them!

Life in Paris on my own gave me the feeling of a wonderful adventure. I worked at the Baron's bank each day from nine in the mornings until five in the evening. After that I was free, with no parental supervision. I was able to go where I liked, when I liked, and return to the flat at whatever hour suited me.

Often I stayed on in Montparnasse until it was too late to get a metro back to the Champs de Mars. As I never had enough money to pay for taxis, I would have to walk a very long way home. I generally walked along the Seine embankment. It was so beautiful to see all the lights reflected in the gently flowing water and those from the bridges like sparkling diamond pendants.

Inevitably I was sometimes accosted, but only once did I feel I might be in real trouble. I could not get rid of my follower, and I did not want him to see where I lived. Fortunately a taxi came by and I quickly jumped in and drove as far as my money would take me. By then I was fairly near home and my follower far away. But it did teach me a lesson, and after that I always tried to be in time to catch a bus or metro home at nights.

My friends there were two young American artists, who had each won a grant to study art in Paris for two years. Each one had a studio with enormously high and rather dirty windows, facing north. They were tremendously enthusiastic about painting, each in a very different way, and would work for many hours on end with no time for food except in the evenings. We would generally meet at some modest little restaurant for supper and the bill was always shared meticulously, as everybody was always hard up.

Then we would go and sit at the Café Le Dôme, and they would talk endlessly about art and artists, paints and materials, etc., while I would try to absorb their "words of wisdom". We all drank coffee and made it last an incredible length of time, seldom ordering another.

Sometimes I would be there on my own, and although I felt very embarrassed to begin with to be sitting at a sidewalk café alone, I soon got used to it, as there were so many other girls on their own too. I think most of them were foreign students or would-be artists. I always had a book or paper with me, so that I could appear absorbed in reading. This was also a good way of avoiding unwanted attention.

In the daytime, when I was not working at the bank, I used to wander all over Paris exploring, only going into the museums and places that were free. I took cheap tickets on the buses and *métros*, and travelled far and wide. It was all fascinating and exciting, even though I was so much on my own.

Sometimes I used to go to the Bois de Boulogne very early in the mornings, because one could get a "worker's" ticket for half-price, if it was before 7 a.m. I would be able to hire a little single skiff and would enjoy sculling on the lovely lake in such a beautiful setting.

Looking back now, I cannot help thinking it was amazing that my parents let me live in Paris on my own like that. It was long before girls became as independent as they are today, when it is the usual thing for them to leave home and live their own lives. But I was so thankful to be on my own.

I met a lovely American girl called Carol Chandler when I was in Paris. She was studying singing and was obviously very well off, as she lived in a very select small hotel on the left bank. She had the most glorious copper coloured hair, which fell in luminous waves around her shoulders, and a pale, transparent skin like the most delicate porcelain. I was enchanted by her looks and her sweet character. We became good friends and saw a fair amount of each other, although it was impossible for me to keep up with her style of living. Through her I met a British doctor who was a widower with two daughters, aged six and twelve.

Doctor Lightstone, in his forties, loved dancing and he also loved to be surrounded by attractive young women. He had a house in London and sometimes used to come over to Paris and take Carol, or me, out dancing—which was of course a tremendous thrill for me.

When he heard about the situation with my parents and my longing to get away, he invited me to stay in his house in London for a while until I got organized. He had a living-in nurse for his youngest daughter who, alas, was mentally retarded, and a governess for the elder one, so I would be chaperoned properly!

All this gave me the hope that I really could and should leave my parents, especially as my mother was becoming more and more impossible to live with. She was always either against me or against my father. When one was in favour, the other was worse than in the "dog house". Two things I remember her shouting to my father in a fit of crazy rage against me: "God help the man who ever marries Iris!" and "I never want to see the sight of her bloody face again!" So I vowed to remove myself as soon as it was possible.

Finally my father decided it was best for him to stay on his own in the flat in Monte Carlo, while my mother came to Paris. Of course I was no longer able to work at the Baron's bank when my mother was in town as I was expected to look after her.

One day Basil Davidoff, whom my mother had met in Monte Carlo and liked mildly, because he had such perfect manners and was wellborn, telephoned and asked me out as he was visiting Paris for a few days. This came as a surprise, almost a shock, to my mother that a young man should wish to take me out. She spent so much of her time criticizing me in so many ways: I was so plain looking, so clumsy and awkward, and did not know how to behave in society; I would never make a successful hostess, as she had been in India; in fact it would be amazing if any man would wish to marry me, etc., etc.

However, she agreed that Basil could come to the flat after dinner that evening at eight o'clock and take me to a nearby sidewalk café for a coffee—but I MUST be back by nine-thirty at the very latest.

All went as agreed and I was back in the building by nine-thirty. I had a key to the flat but when I tried to unlock the front door, I found she had put on the door chain inside. It was impossible for me to open the door more than a tiny crack. I spent from half-past nine until close to midnight sitting on the stairs leading to the upper floors, getting up and ringing the doorbell at intervals and trying to call my mother. Fortunately Basil had left me at the main entrance door to the building and knew nothing of my dilemma.

I realized what must have happened. My mother had put the chain on so that she could check on the time I really did return;

then she had gone to bed and fallen asleep—quite probably having taken a sleeping pill as she often did. So there was nothing for it but to wait until she woke up or heard my calls.

Eventually she heard me and came to open the door. Of course she screamed abuses at me for getting back so late, after I had promised to be back hours ago. It was no use me trying to tell her that I had been sitting waiting outside all that time, or asking her why on earth she had put the chain on the door. She was quite out of her mind with anger and accused me of all kinds of things. She said she had sacrificed her own happiness in life because of us children. She had given up the man she really loved in order to keep our home from breaking up. I was so distraught by then and amazed at all she shouted at me that I turned on her and shouted back, "I wish you had left us then. You have made all of our lives so terribly unhappy."

That evening I planned to run away.

Running Away

Escaping my Mother

Paris, France, 1931. The next day, I was able to telephone Carol and tell her that I was planning to leave within the next few days—the moment I could make my getaway without my mother knowing. I asked her if she would telephone to Dr. Lightstone to find out if he really meant his offer to me of shelter.

She wrote back to me the next day—telephoning would have been too risky. My mother always picked up the second earphone and listened in on my conversations. Carol said he would welcome me any time, and to let him know the time of my arrival, as he would send his car to meet me at the station.

But it was not to be so simple. When I was out the next day shopping for food, my mother must have gone down into my so-called "bedroom" and seen my suitcase all packed in a cupboard. She opened it up, removed my passport and a five pound note I had been saving for my travel. She didn't say anything when I came in, but when I went downstairs she locked the door at the top of the stairs, so I could not get up again. I was almost in despair, but there was nothing I could do at that moment.

So I set to work to finish painting. The paint on the walls, ceiling and stairs had become very dark and dingy looking down in that little basement. So my mother thought I should paint it light primrose yellow, which I agreed to. It would certainly help to brighten the premises. I had already started and thought I might as well finish the work instead of sitting moping and fuming. I painted for hours with never a sign from my mother, even though she knew I had no food there.

I realized it was late at night, but still kept on painting as I felt too frustrated to try to sleep. Suddenly the door at the top of the stairs opened and mother came down in her dressing gown, looking quite wild. I climbed down from the ladder and she literally flew at me, clawing at my face and throat, screaming abuses at me for wanting to leave and accusing me of many awful things. It was terrible. The more I tried to reason with her just seemed to exacerbate matters. Eventually she left and again locked the door at the top of the stairs.

Next morning, after waiting some hours wondering whether she would make another appearance, or give me some food, I decided I had to make some sort of move. There was an unused back entrance into the pantry, off the kitchen where I slept. I was able to get the lock working again and opened the door, letting myself out that back way. Then I thought I would just go into the front entrance of the building to find out if by any chance she had gone out, as I had heard no movements in the rooms above. Leaving my suitcase with the concierge at the entrance, I went and cautiously opened the front door of the flat. I was prepared for a battle royal with my mother, but to my intense relief, she was not there. I immediately put the chain on the front door, so as not to be disturbed suddenly by her return, and set to work hunting for my passport. To my joy and relief, I found it very quickly. I was out of the flat again in a flash, jumping into the first taxi I saw, regardless of expense! I decided I would go straight to the Gare du Nord station and wait there until the train left for Le Havre.

I telephoned Carol, telling her what had happened and that I was on my way to England. I asked her to please tell Doctor Lightstone I would be arriving the next morning early at Tilbury Docks on a ferry, the cheapest way possible to cross the Channel.

It seemed an interminable time to wait for the departure of that train. The minutes dragged by, and I was becoming more nervous, thinking that my mother might well come storming along the platform to stop me going. My ticket had been in my passport and she might have found out when the train was leaving for Le Havre.

As the last five minutes were ticking past and I was beginning to feel more relaxed, I suddenly saw Carol running along the platform, obviously looking for me. I jumped down from the train to meet her, frantically wondering what had gone wrong to bring her there. She called out to me, even before reaching me: "Iris, you mustn't go!" Then she poured out the tale.

Doctor Lightstone had telephoned her an hour previously, saying, at all costs, she must stop my coming to his house. My parents had been on the telephone to him in London, threatening to sue him for enticing me away from home, saying they would have him—and me—arrested. It was all so dramatic, and I was in such a state as the train was due to leave in one minute. Carol said: "You can't go". But I just called back to her, "There's no time to get my suitcase off, and I'm going anyway."

There was a great whistling from the engine, and the train glided off with me aboard, somewhat breathless and stunned.

I had a few hours of sitting on the hard wooden seat of the third class, in a dirty carriage full of smuts from the smoking engine, and looking out onto the rather dreary flat countryside of northern France in the late autumn. Darkness was rapidly enveloping the whole scene. Plenty of time for thought and for trying to work out some plan for my immediate future.

I decided that my mother must have either overheard my conversation with Carol—asking her to find out from Doctor Lightstone whether I could go to his house—or else she must have read Carol's little note in reply. She had a nasty habit of reading all my letters. And I remember once coming in and finding her taking a mirror to the blotting paper I had been using. In those days one wrote with a pen dipped in ink and then had to blot it afterwards, so that often the writing would show up clearly in reverse.

Well, now there was definitely no going back, but the question was where to go once I got to London. I only had a total of £7 in my purse! I knew I simply had to get work somehow—what kind of work was a different question. Apart from rather slow French shorthand and even slower typing while looking at my fingers all the time, I had absolutely no training in any useful work. And I was in no position to pay for lodgings without a job.

The only person I knew in London, apart from Doctor Lightstone, was dear Mrs. Bowie, whom I had not been in touch with for a long time. I decided that I would go to her and ask if I might stay with her for a while until I could find some work.

LE HAVRE. – La "Columbia" Courrier de Southampton. – LL.

The trip across the Channel was quite bad. There was a storm blowing and the noise of the waves crashing against the sides of the ship as she pitched and rolled on the turbulent black sea was quite deafening. The place was crowded with Italians travelling with many babies and children, all crying and wailing, and also innumerable parcels, and baskets full of salami and onions, etc. As the movement of the ship increased, everybody became sick.

The atmosphere was unbearable, and I just had to escape to the outside deck at the stern of the vessel. There were no seats on that portion of the deck, only the outlets of ventilators, bollards, and winches and coils of rope. But I was so thankful to be out in the fresh air. Although it was wet and cold, I resolved to stay out there all night if I could just find some place to curl up in.

After exploring in the darkness I found a large coil of rope at the foot of an unused steering wheel. I couldn't understand what it would serve for at the stern of the ship, and it kept jerking one way or another as the ship was tossed about by the waves. Anyway, I curled myself into it and eventually fell asleep, despite the cold wind and drizzle.

What I did not realize then was that all the smoke that belched from the funnel was blown directly overhead and was showering me with black greasy smuts. The steering wheel kept bumping my head, but I was determined to stay on there rather than go downstairs again.

London

We finally arrived at Tilbury docks the next morning. After retrieving my suitcase, I was just deciding to take a train nearby into London, when a uniformed chauffeur approached me a bit hesitantly. (I don't wonder because I was looking so dirty and a bit lost.) He asked me if I was Miss Hay-Edie. When I said, "Yes", he told me that Doctor Lightstone had sent him to drive me to wherever I was going to stay. He also handed me a note from his boss. In it he said he was so sorry for what had happened, but realized after my parents threats that it might lead to terrible trouble for him if I went to his house now. But his car was at my disposal to take me to London. I was grateful for this anyway because every penny saved was important, but I couldn't help feeling a little incongruous and more scruffy than ever stepping into a fine Rolls Royce!

Mrs. Bowie, although taken completely by surprise at my sudden arrival on her doorstep, gave me a very warm welcome. But I was shocked to find her much changed in looks and appearing really ill. I told her my whole story. She was sad to hear about my mother's behaviour, but said she quite agreed with her about me going to stay at Doctor Lightstone's house. She said I would be more than welcome to stay with her, as I would be a great help to her with the two children. She said she was ill and suffering a lot of pain. She had seen a doctor, but he was not able to help her much apart from giving her painkilling pills. As she had no household help living in, she would be very happy indeed to have me there.

During the next few weeks I did all I could to help her with the children—seeing they had breakfast and got off to school in the mornings, doing housework and cooking and shopping for her. But her suffering seemed to increase and at night I could hear her moaning in her bedroom next door to mine. I used to go in to see if I could bring her anything or do anything to help. Sometimes she asked me to help her to turn over on one side or the other. She was in so much pain she could not manage on her own. It was heartbreaking to see her suffering so greatly, and I insisted on sending for her doctor, although she did not want this.

After his visit I begged him to tell me what was wrong with her. But all he said to me—which was so obvious—was that she was very ill and that he was going to have her taken to the hospital straightaway.

I went with her in the ambulance to the big hospital by Paddington Station. When I had seen her settled in a bed, in a great ward full of patients, I tried to be encouraging and told her not to worry about the children. I would be there to look after them and the house until she got better and could leave hospital. I promised to bring her, the next day, a few little extra things that she found she needed.

But next day when I went into the ward with the things I had brought, I saw a curtain around her bed, and the nurse ran over to me to prevent me pulling it back. She told me Mrs. Bowie was dead.

I felt completely stunned. I just couldn't believe it could happen so quickly. I had been talking to her only the day before. I felt overwhelmed with grief and utterly at a loss. She had been so kind to me, so helpful, and she was such a sweet person— and she suffered so terribly. It was the first time I had experienced being so close to a death.

I walked out of the hospital in a daze, tears streaming down my face, not knowing or caring where I was going.

Returning to Hampstead and having to break the news to the children, trying to comfort them, and look after them for the next few days, all on my own, was quite a responsibility. The emptiness of the house and thinking all the time about her death, weighed heavily upon me, and, of course, the poor children were heartbroken.

I used to go into her room and look at her dresses and touch the things on her dressing table and in the drawers, but I always put everything back exactly as I had found it, as if she might come in and find it untidy. She had relatives in the north of England and her brother had telephoned to say he was arranging to come and take the children as soon as possible and organize everything else. He was grateful for my presence there until he arrived.

In the meantime I was trying to resolve my own problem of where to live. Shortly after I arrived in London, I had been to visit Doctor Lightstone in his very nice house near Marble Arch, overlooking Hyde Park. I had met his daughters and the governess and nurse, also his very special girlfriend. Her name was Betty Pelly-Fry. She was a few years older than I, very attractive, with a lovely mouth that curled up at the corners and was always ready to laugh. She had such a sweet and gentle temperament one could not help loving her. Everybody thought Doctor Lightstone was going to marry her.

At this time, when she heard of the predicament I was in, she suggested that I might find a room in the boarding house that she lived in. She said that it was very nice and in a good locality nearby at Gloucester Terrace. If I could possibly afford it, that would be wonderful, but I had been trying to find some work, answering innumerable advertisements so far without any luck, as I was not qualified in anything.

Betty telephoned me the next day and said there was one tiny room available in her building, right up on the top floor. It would cost twelve shillings and six pence a week! I was so thankful I just said "Yes, please, take it for me".

The five flights of stairs to climb was nothing, as I was only glad it was not in a basement. The room was so small it could only just fit in a narrow bed, a chair, and a small table—no cupboard or chest of drawers to put clothes in. I had a small wardrobe trunk, which was the custom to have in those days of train and ship travel, and my suitcase and any other odds and ends were shoved under the bed. The room also had a nice big window looking across Gloucester Terrace and rooftops. It had a little gas ring upon which I could boil water for my tea or coffee, or make scrambled eggs and all sorts of other culinary inventions. The bathroom was two floors down, but that did not worry me at all. I was so thankful to have such a nice little room at such a reasonable cost, and it was a great comfort that Betty was living in the same house, so that I did not feel so lonely anymore.

London Bridge

It was, of course, absolutely necessary that I should earn some money. The few pounds that I had brought with me to England had already gone, and I was literally counting my pennies. I had sold some dresses—for a pittance, I thought—and hated the way the woman at the secondhand dress shop fingered each dress and made disparaging remarks before offering me just a few shillings that I simply had to accept.

I trailed all over London to answer some of the advertisements I thought might possibly lead to some work I could do. Once or twice I found myself in some rather odd places being offered rather peculiar jobs. One was down in the London dock area, in a very dilapidated building, up flights of stairs, in a room piled high with packing cases and cartons of clothes. I was then asked if I would model corsets! I said I did not think I had quite the flair for that. Thank you very much!

I went to theatrical agencies and to film agencies, and there I managed to get work as an "extra" sometimes. The pay was a guinea each day, which I thought was wonderful, but it was very tiring. One had to go out to the Studios at Elstree and then just wait around until being called. Sometimes that did not happen, and then there was no pay.

The agents would tell you what sort of clothing you were expected to wear for the crowd work, or whatever scene you might be needed for, and if you were called you had to go and make up quickly. The make-up consisted of smearing a whitish paste all over one's face like a mask and then picking out one's eyebrows and eyelashes with heavy mascara and outlining one's lips with thick brown lipstick. Then the mask effect was complete. I could not recognize myself, but I suppose it all came out well on the black and white, silent film.

To begin with I found it all fascinating, and I enjoyed looking at everybody and the workings of the scenarios with the actors, directors, photographers, etc., etc. The excitement of being actually involved—even in such an insignificant way—behind the scene in the Movies! But eventually my very, very faint hope that one day some Great Movie Magnate might offer me a starring role in his next production finally fizzled out. I had to admit to myself that I was not really cut out to be a star. For that one has to be self-assertive and confident in oneself, able to mix and talk easily with all kinds of people and enjoy crowds—all of which was completely opposite to my nature. I was much too shy.

IN THIS HUSTLING AGE one sport at a time is not exciting enough for some folk. For instance, these Colnbrook bathers are indulging in archery in a speed-boat!

A racy photo shoot for the newspaper!

At Christmas, Doctor Lightstone asked Betty and me to come and stay for a holiday week at his house in Bognor, on the English Channel. We drove down there with him and his daughters in his Rolls Royce. He had a nice house there, too, quite large, which was a good thing as we were many people staying there, including Betty's youngest brother, Jimmy, who was a year younger than I was and who had a job in the city with a big tea firm. We all had a lovely carefree holiday and lots of fun just going for walks and running on the sands, despite the cold winter weather. Being young and very unsophisticated, simple things suited us very well.

Back in London again, Jimmy came to live in Gloucester Terrace, too, and had a room at the top of the house next to mine, but bigger. That was useful, because we all used to congregate in his room and use it as a sitting room. Jimmy used to play his guitar and sing, and he had a nice voice. We had a portable, wind-up gramophone that gave us lots of enjoyment, as we had no radio then.

We used to cook scrambled eggs, or sausages, and have toast and tea, or coffee for supper. Nobody ever even thought of alcohol of any kind, and if we had, we could never have afforded it. If we were feeling like going out on a spree—very occasionally—the big treat was to go to Lyons' Corner House, big and crowded and inexpensive; but that was very seldom.

As Jimmy was a tea taster, he was sometimes able to bring back from his office little sample packets of different kinds of teas. Some of them were truly very fine blends, and they gave me a lifelong taste for good tea, especially Darjeeling.

Jimmy was also very helpful in finding me some jobs at a time of dire need. One was at an enormous air exhibition at Earls Court, where Jimmy was exhibiting some of his model airplanes. I was to watch the stand, and he spent hours explaining to me what I should say to people who came asking questions about intricate points. I tried my best to remember, but I have a feeling that some went away with somewhat muddled information.

Jimmy was later to have a very fine career in the RAF during the Second World War. He led a squadron of bombers on raids over Holland and Germany, and was subsequently decorated with the DFC. Later he became Air Equerry to King George VI and lived in Buckingham Palace—which was referred to as "Buck House". Then he became Air Attaché to the court of the Shah of Iran, in Teheran, and then as Attaché again, in Australia.

The Horse Show at Olympia

Another was a job at the Horse Show at Olympia stadium. I rode on top of an old-fashioned carriage that elegant ladies and gentlemen used to ride to the races, to the Derby at Epsom, or to Ascot. It was very fashionable in Victorian times, and the ladies were all dressed up in their frills and furbelows.

In between the exhibitions of jumping and horsemanship, there came a show when several of these fine old carriages, drawn by teams of six beautifully matched horses, all bedecked with shining harnesses, the driver and grooms in smart red uniforms, and elegantly dressed ladies sitting on top, came sweeping into the arena, one after the other. The horses cantered at great speed and the drivers exhibited great skill in guiding their teams as they went several times around the arena.

It was a spectacular scene. The building was gigantic and the arena so vast. All around it sat thousands of spectators in the audience, row upon row rising in the background towards the dim heights of the lofty roof.

I was thrilled to be perched on top of the carriage at such a height and going at such a speed, all dressed up in a bustle, mutton chop sleeves and a saucy little straw hat with flowers on the rim. I also had a parasol, small and frilly, with a long shaft. All very pretty, but highly impracticable when sitting on the very edge of a narrow bench as the carriage hurtled around the curves at each end of the stadium, with only a tiny, low railing to keep me from sliding off the end as we swept in grand style past the Royal Box, with the King of Spain watching as a guest of the British Monarch. I got paid a guinea a day for this job, too, and there were two shows daily, afternoon and evening. It was lots of fun.

During all the months I had been in London, I had not had any communication with my parents. But I had been writing quite frequently to my dear brother, Archy, who was then working with a shipping firm in Hong Kong called *Mackinnon Mackenzie Shipping Company*. They were agents for the large fleet of vessels belonging to the *P&O Company*.

I had written to Archy all about the happenings at home and about my final departure from Paris. He had written me back full of sympathy and indignation at the way I had been treated by our parents, particularly by our mother. We both felt she must have been suffering from some strange malady to behave in the way she did.

However, he said he very much wanted me to come out to Hong Kong and live with him there. I could surely find some job there in the secretarial line, even though I was so inexperienced, because there were so few girls available for such jobs. As I mentioned before, it just was not the custom for girls to work in those days.

I was tremendously excited at the prospect of going out to Hong Kong and waited with considerable impatience for him to make the arrangements for my ticket out there. Poor Archy, he had to borrow the money from a good friend first. Then all the bookings and other arrangements had to be done by post, which generally took at least three weeks to a month by sea mail, as airmail did not exist then.

At one time my finances were so low that I had to sell my wardrobe trunk. Jimmy, always helpful, helped me to carry it along Praed Street to the secondhand shop. Once again, one guinea was all I got for it. But, being young and full of high spirits—and hopes—I never seemed to get too depressed about the situation. Something was sure to crop up sooner or later.

We had so much fun doing the simplest of things, such as going for walks on the weekends all over Hampstead Heath,

Kew Gardens or Windsor Forest, and flying Jimmy's model planes on Wimbledon Common.

We went to a marvellous Military Tattoo parade in the country. Troops of different regiments in their colorful uniforms, highland kilts swaying to the tune of the bagpipes, thousands of soldiers marching from distant points of the countryside, all converging to the green valley in front of us.

It was past midnight when the show was over and we piled into the car and drove back to London. By then we were very hungry and decided to have a midnight snack at the nearest Lyons' Corner House, just to top off our wonderful evening, though we had spent most of our money on the trip. I shall always remember the look of complete mystification on the little waitress' face, when Arthur solemnly ordered: "A couple of bees' knees on toast, please"!

During this period I appreciated my freedom and independence more than one can imagine, and life in London with my friends was fun and spontaneous, but I longed to see my brother Archy and for the adventure to the Far East to begin.

Voyage to The Far East

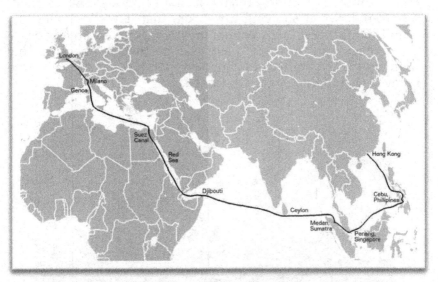

My 5 week journey from London to Hong Kong
via train, ferry and passenger ship

July 20, 1933, London. The great day finally arrived when I set off on my longed for journey to the Far East. My excitement was intense, mixed possibly with a little (very little) apprehension at going on such a very long journey into the unknown all by myself. But, on the other hand, that made it all the more exciting.

I was booked to sail from Genoa on a German vessel named the *Fulda*. So I had to leave London by train for Dover, take a cross-channel ferry, and then get a train to take me to Milano, Italy. There I changed into another train for Genoa and finally found my ship at the dockyards.

It was a long and tiring trip, and the hard benches of the second-class carriage overnight to Milano were very uncomfortable and very crowded. I must have fallen asleep eventually out of sheer exhaustion, because I awoke with a start to find myself in an empty carriage. The train had stopped in a very big station, and a man was washing down the window outside against which I was leaning! Panic! This must be Milano. I must have missed my train to Genoa. Where do I go to find it? What about my luggage?

I jumped down from the empty train with my small hand baggage and an old fur coat of my mother's, a castoff from years before. Hurrying along the platform, I wondered if I could find an information office where someone might speak English. After much running around, I saw a train marked Genoa and discovered, when showing my ticket, that it was actually the train I should take. I figured that my luggage must already be in the luggage van. Anyway, there was no time to check, as the train suddenly started moving off. On arrival I was very relieved to find the luggage in Genoa.

Leaving the docks, I was not too impressed with the *S.S. Fulda*. Watching Genoa fade into the distance as I leaned against the railing of the ship, then looking down at the blue waters of the Mediterranean slowly passing below us, I thought: "How are we ever going to reach Hong Kong at this speed?" I found out soon that the ship's speed was eleven knots!

I think there must have been about 200 passengers altogether, with probably about 100 in each class. We were not allowed to mix, and the deck space for second class was at the afterend, mostly around the hatches, except for a smaller part on the upper deck.

Everybody hired his or her own deck chair from the deck steward and kept it for the whole voyage in the same place. I quickly discovered a place where I could sit peacefully on my own without the possibility of anyone else joining me. There was a small wing of the upper deck that jutted out over the water on either side of the ship. It was just wide enough to take my deck chair, and with hardly any room to squeeze by. There I was to spend the greater part of the whole voyage, unless the sun became too unbearably hot in the middle of the day.

My cabin was tiny, and I shared it with two other women. We always had to dress one at a time and then get out of the cabin, as it was so small. One of the women was a young Dutch girl, who had just been married by proxy in Holland and was going out to join her new husband, whom she hardly knew. The other was a very buxom German woman. They were both quite nice, but as we did not speak each other's languages, apart from a very few words I had of German, we did not spend much time trying to converse.

There were many missionaries on board, also nuns and monks, all going to different places in Indonesia. The dinner conversation was naturally all in German so that I was left out of it, to my relief, although the officer at the head of the table did speak some English to me at times.

I kept to myself and did lots of reading and writing—tucked away in my little niche on the top deck jutting out over the sea. I spent hours just watching the water below me, enchanted by the patterns made by the bow waves as the ship cut through the sea, peeling the water back in an ever-widening V, and as the voyage progressed into warmer waters I saw all kinds of aquatic creatures, fish, whales, porpoises galore, turtles, snakes and the occasional shark.

Port Said, Egypt, entrance to the Suez Canal and Red Sea

At Port Said all the passengers who went ashore visited an old-fashioned store called *Simon Artz*. It made me think of all the times my mother had told us of going there on their way to and from India so many years ago. It appeared to stock an incredible variety of goods, from all kinds of leather work made in Egypt to English tweeds, Italian and Indian silks, French Lalique crystal and perfumes, Scotch Whiskey etc., etc., and "filthee pictures"!

Shopping at Simon Artz, Port Said

While looking around, one of the first-class men passengers tried to become very friendly with me, and when we got back on the ship in the evening I had a real struggle not to get pulled into his cabin. He said he had a box of "Rahat Loucoums" (the aphrodisiac known as Turkish Delight) for me! I was happy to go without it!

I found the trip through the Suez Canal fascinating and was tremendously impressed at the courage of man envisaging cutting such a passage through this hot, vast expanse of sand, and getting the water to flow through it in sufficient quantity to carry great ships from sea to sea.

As we entered the Red Sea the weather became hotter and hotter. The cabins were stiflingly hot and air-conditioning was unknown then. In our cabin the one little fan swiveled from side to side but did not reach my top bunk. I used to lie in a bath of perspiration with my nightdress so wet that I had to get up often to change it or just wring it out. Consequently I would always be up very early in the mornings just to get out on deck and feel less suffocated.

A very small swimming pool had been rigged up at the end of the lower deck for the second-class passengers. It was just a large canvas bag strung up between two derricks and could not take more than a few people, but just to be in the water was refreshing. I used to go along there whenever I woke up and was always alone at that early hour.

Then one day a notice was put up that the pool was reserved exclusively for men between the hours of 6 a.m. and 8 a.m. I knew that this was brought about by the monks and missionaries as I had seen them looking at me with disapproval quite often when they happened to arrive for a dip and I happened to be still in the pool. I was very cross and decided I would then have my swim at 5 a.m. and be finished by the time they arrived.

The heat became more unbearable each day and I could no longer stay in my deck chair on the upper deck without any shade. Sometimes the ship had to turn around and steam northwards in order to get some slight breeze through it, particularly into the engine room, which must have been like a burning oven. In fact, one stoker died, and there was a burial at sea.

One morning I was on my way to the pool as usual at 5 a.m.—when nobody was around—but this morning I saw a very tall black man coming towards me. His eyes looked wild, and his head was shaking from side to side as he stared at me, coming closer. I suddenly felt too afraid to pass him and turned quickly and ran back to the cabin. I thought afterwards how stupid I had been and also to miss my swim because of my sudden panic.

That same day, in the afternoon, the sun beat down mercilessly on the ship as she plowed steadily through a sea that looked like molten lead with the only sound the slight rumble of the propeller. A few people lay in deck chairs sweltering, trying to sleep, everyone torpid with the heat. I had stretched myself out on one of the hatch covers, shaded under the awning, and was half asleep. Suddenly a scream rent the heavy stillness of the afternoon and I felt myself seized and lifted off the hatch, and saw to my horror the black sweating face and wild eyes of the man I had seen by the pool that morning. He was clutching me in his arms, and I realized I was the one who had screamed. As I fought and screamed again, several members of the crew appeared in a flash and knocked the man unconscious. I saw them carrying him away as I became surrounded by people. I was shaking so much that I could hardly talk and didn't know myself what exactly had happened.

Later I found out that the man was a stoker who had gone berserk with the heat down in the engine room and had been locked up in a small cabin at the stern of the ship until he could be put ashore at Djibouti. He was evidently let out in the very early mornings for exercise, but how he was out in the afternoon nobody seemed to know. It was a horrid experience, but neither the Captain, nor any of the ship's officers, conveyed a word of apology or concern to me.

After that I was regarded by some of the older people and the missionaries with considerable suspicion, and anonymous letters were written to the Captain complaining of the way I dressed. I used to wear what were known in those days as Beach Pajamas when I was on deck. Although long and voluminous, they were evidently considered risqué and very modern.

As we progressed along the Red Sea towards Djibouti I was deeply impressed by the sheer ferocity of the rugged mountains to our right, along the coasts of Sudan and Eritrea—barren, burning rocks towering high in the hot blue sky and not a sign of any vegetation anywhere. Passing Aden, the mountains on the other side seemed to close in as if to prevent our passage beyond.

At night, after dinner, the stewards of the first class would become a band and provide very nice music, from the rear first-class deck, which looked down on our hatch deck so that both classes could enjoy the music. They played a lot of Viennese waltzes and we would dance on the hatch covers under the stars.

There was a rather strange, but very interesting, German amongst the few people that I became friendly with. His name was Dr. Sulzbach, but we all called him S.U. (pronounced S-O). He had spent several years in Africa, in Tanganyika, and spoke Swahili quite fluently. He used to tell us many tales of his experiences there, which were fascinating. He was now on his way to start an aquarium in Hong Kong! He also loved dancing, and when the ship was rolling a little, crossing the open Indian Ocean, we had the hatch cover to ourselves, in somewhat hazardous conditions, but I don't remember ever losing our balance enough to fall off!

Sometimes, looking out towards the horizon, we would observe strange luminous bands of light in the water, and when dolphins came to play in front of the bows or along side the ship, the trails of phosphorescence they made were beautiful.

After leaving Djibouti, the last stop in Africa, we had long periods at sea without calling at any port. The ship progressed so slowly, and we by-passed India and Ceylon (Sri Lanka). Our next stop was at Medan in Sumatra, and then on to Penang, Singapore, and then Cebu in the Philippines. I found everything so thrilling and fascinating.

S.U. and some others used to hire an open car in the various ports we came to and always invited me to go with them on lovely drives to see as much as possible of the surroundings.

In Cebu, I remember we were driving in the countryside and passed a herd of water buffaloes watched over by a very small native boy. I decided I would like to have a picture of me sitting on the back of a water buffalo and proceeded to climb up on the broad hairy back of one nearby, much to the dismay of the small boy. The others in the car thought I was crazy. Later on, when I told my brother Archy, he was horrified and told me that water buffaloes can be very dangerous. They are notorious for hating the smell of foreigners. In fact, some friends of his had run for their lives, being chased by these creatures outside of Canton. So ignorance is bliss, and I was lucky!

Hong Kong at last

September 1933. After five weeks we finally reached Hong Kong! I shall never forget my impressions of that fairy tale evening. We steamed into Hong Kong harbour on a still and beautiful night. A great full moon hung above the massive bulk of the Peak and adjoining hills that loomed over the harbour. The lights along the roads going up the hillsides appeared as sparkling diamond necklaces looped around the dark mountain. Hundreds of lights, from the houses tucked here and there, studded the steep mountainsides, while the area at the edge of the water was a blaze of lights everywhere.

Hong Kong waterfront with Victoria Peak

There were many ships in the harbour and picturesque junks sailing quietly by. Busy little sampans were being *yewloed* to and fro between ships and across the harbour to Kowloon or to Hong Kong.

Chinese junks sailing near the harbour

The *Fulda* dropped anchor in mid-harbour and waited for the agent's launch to come alongside. Suddenly, from amongst a number of launches approaching our ship, I heard a voice floating across the water, calling "Iris—Iris". Of course, I knew it must be Archy, but I was so overcome with excitement that when I tried to call back to him, no sound came out! There was a little English boy standing next to me with whom I had become friendly on the trip, and I begged him to call back for me.

Archy shouted back that he was coming on board to get me, even though the passengers were to depart in the morning. As he was in the shipping business, he had obviously used his influence with the agents of the *Fulda* to be allowed to take me off the ship then and there.

The company launch that Archy had fetched me in sped across the harbour and deposited us at the pier. I was tremendously impressed by the way all the Chinese were running about doing everything so eagerly and efficiently and that Archy could speak a few words of Chinese to them.

Evening street scene in downtown Hong Kong

Finally we drove off, up one of the steep zigzagging roads that brought us to the mid-levels of the Peak to Conduit Road. When we entered "our" flat, I could have wept with sheer joy and appreciation of what my wonderful brother had done for me in bringing me here.

The view was breathtaking. A dazzling carpet of lights spread steeply below us, stopping at the water's edge, but then carried on with all the lights from the ships and their reflections on the water. Beyond the harbour, on the mainland, the myriad lights of Kowloon twinkled, and beyond, hills appeared softly in the moonlight. It was pure magic!

Archy had filled the flat with flowers to greet me, lovely sweet smelling frangipani and tuberoses. I had never seen such flowers before or smelt such a sweet fragrance. As I tried to go to sleep that night, my eyes kept opening just to gaze again through the long French windows by my bed at that incredible view. I wondered: "Can it really be true? Will I wake up tomorrow morning and find it all gone?"

Busy streets during the working day

The next days, we then went exploring down the steep narrow streets leading from the flat into the town, and went for wonderful drives up to the Peak, Repulse Bay and around the island, and went swimming at Big Wave Bay, Repulse Bay and Deep Water Bay.

Nathan Road, Kowloon, Hong Kong

Aberdeen, Hong Kong

What an utterly different life I suddenly found myself leading. We had a cook-boy, who did the food marketing, cooking and serving; a coolie to do the housework; and a *wash-amah* to do all the laundry. So I had no household duties, except to give suggestions now and then, especially if we were entertaining someone.

I spent a lot of time just exploring the city and looking at so many fascinating Chinese handiworks in the shops.

Many weekends we would be invited to *launch picnics*, boating to different islands where there were glorious, deserted beaches, by the bosses of the largest firms who were known as the *taipans*. Archy was not very senior in Mackinnon's when I first joined him, but his friends would invite us along.

With my dear brother Archy

Anyway, we led a marvellous life, full of fun and joy. Archy was the most wonderful brother in the world, looking after me so solicitously and wanting to make up, through his loving care, for some of the miseries I had experienced with our parents. But he found at times that it was more of a responsibility than he had foreseen, trying to look after a high-spirited, but very unsophisticated young woman.

There were far more young bachelors in Hong Kong in those days than girls, so that soon I was being asked out almost every evening, though I did not want to leave Archy alone too often. He had had a number of girlfriends before I came, but after my arrival he seldom saw them on his own, saying it was more fun getting to know his sister again. It was six years since I had last seen him, when he first left Europe to take up his job with Mackinnon's in India, so we had both changed a lot during that time.

Archy was due to go on long leave and he had arranged to go with a friend who was Chief Officer on a British India ship that called frequently at Hong Kong. They had made this arrangement long before there was any idea of me coming to Hong Kong, so I was just included in the plan, which was to go by ship to the United States and then get a secondhand car and drive across the States. Whenever Denis arrived in port, he would come and dine with us, and we would discuss this plan over and over again. We were all looking forward to it greatly.

I then nearly went and spoilt everything by getting engaged. Geoffrey was a good friend of Archy's, and he told me afterwards that when Archy had shown him a photograph of me, he had said: "You must bring her out because I want to marry her"! He was stationed in Canton, but used to come to

Hong Kong frequently, and he was so persistent in asking me to marry him that in the end I agreed. The moment I said "Yes" I knew it was wrong, because I did not love him. I just felt sorry for him. He had been "let down" by another girl he had been engaged to. This, of course, made it even more difficult for me to tell him that I, too, was going to "let him down." But to begin with I thought: "Surely I will come to love him." He was very good-looking and had a nice personality and a good job.

Canton (Guangzhou)

He invited Archy and me to Shameen, which was the International Settlement on an island in Canton where all the foreigners stayed and the branches of the big foreign firms were located. There was no motor traffic at all on the island, and it was a peaceful place with great old-fashioned houses along the tree-lined avenues. There were no Chinese living on the island. Several bridges joined the island to Canton.

Shameen, Canton

We were invited to attend the Bachelor's Ball on New Year's Eve, which was *the* big social party of the whole year for all the foreigners living in Shameen and in different ports up the coast. Many people came from Hong Kong to join in the mad gaiety of that fancy dress celebration.

With Archy in Canton

It certainly was a wild party, dancing all night, and everyone was in a state of semi-collapse afterwards. But as I never drank any alcohol, I kept dancing and dancing.

Geoffrey was a great huntsman and he wanted to take me on a shooting party on a houseboat going up the Pearl River. There were some married couples on board, so I was very well chaperoned.

The houseboat was somewhat dilapidated, but spacious. As we were all prepared to rough it, nobody minded the discomfort, and we all slept up on deck under the awning. I thought it was so lovely lying there, peacefully moored by the banks of that shining river, with the soft night breeze playing over us, and listening to the myriad little sounds of nature all around us. Rice paddy fields stretched on either side of the river, and the occasional pagoda could be seen, while in the distance gentle hills appeared.

Those of us who went shooting had to get up before dawn, so as to be able to hide behind the high banks of the rice paddies. We had to lie down just over the top of the bank and keep absolutely still, waiting for the early flights of duck or geese to fly over. Eventually, as the sky brightened, there came a sound of the swishing of wings, and the birds started flying across the fields towards the river. Then the men started shooting.

I had been given a gun and very careful explanations by Geoffrey of how I should shoot. I had no wish to kill any of those poor birds, but thought I had better try to make a good impression. Thinking of all the instructions to shoot a little distance in front of the bird and to hold the gun very firmly against my shoulder, I shot. To my astonishment I saw the bird start falling! But I was falling too, right down the bank and into the muddy rice field. I had not held the gun firmly enough, and its kick had knocked me off balance. My shoulder was very sore, and I felt so sorry to have killed the poor duck.

We went for a lovely walk later in the day, exploring the Chinese countryside and climbing quite a long way up in the hills to visit some pagodas.

Back in the houseboat we were going on an evening hunt further up the river. It was so beautiful, with the setting sun reflected on the calm water flowing softly by as we crept up stream as quietly as possible in order not to disturb the birds. But when the birds took off and flew away, the men shot again, and again Geoffrey wanted me to shoot.

We were inside the houseboat then and shooting through the open windows, trying to keep out of sight as much as possible. So, remembering the instructions about following the bird, then aiming a little in front of it, I pulled the trigger. But to my consternation, I found I had shot right through the framework of the window! By then I had already decided I never wanted to shoot again!

Coming back to Hong Kong we found there were three days still to wait until our Japanese ship, the *Tatsuta Maru*, sailed for Japan, Honolulu, and Los Angeles. With such a long trip on the horizon for us, Archy had terminated his flat rental, so we were without a place to stay. Fortunately, S.U., the German from the *Fulda*, offered us to stay at his new aquarium. He said he would let me occupy his study where he sleeps, and he and Archy could sleep on camp beds downstairs amongst the fish!

S.U. handed me a flashlight, saying: "You may need it if you want to go downstairs to the bathroom in the night, and just watch out where you step, because one of the cobras has escaped"! He explained that a snake would make a slithery sound when gliding over the matting that covered the floor and advised me to remain in bed if I heard such a sound during the night. Well, neither Archy nor I slept too well during the next three nights. We spent most of the days hunting for the escaped cobra but never found him.

One day I told him about my engagement to Geoffrey. We talked for quite a while, and he was telling me some facts about marriage (being married himself), when I suddenly fell off my chair in a dead faint! When I came to, Archy was sitting beside me looking terribly worried, and I was lying on the bed. There seemed to be no explanation for my fainting—except perhaps, that the thought of marriage was too much for me at that time. I resolved that I simply had to break off my engagement. I hated to hurt poor Geoffrey all over again. But what a tremendous relief I felt to be free again!

A Trip Around The World

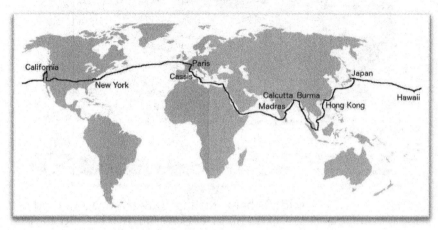

Our trip around the world in 1934
via ship, automobile and train

1933-1934. A short time after her five week voyage from France to Hong Kong, Iris, her brother Archy, and their friend Denis embark on an around the world trip for nearly a year. The circumference of the globe following the equator is nearly 25,000 miles (40,000 kilometres), but their trip was much less direct. They travelled the majority of the time by ship crossing the Pacific, Atlantic and Indian Oceans, as well as the Mediterranean, South China and Red Seas.

They also drove up and down the west coast of the United States, then across the county to New York, all on rough roads in a classic Plymouth convertible with Iris exposed to the elements in the rumble seat. In France they all went their separate ways, leaving Iris to once again travel many weeks alone back to Hong Kong.

Voyage to the States

At last we were off on our voyage to the United States. Denis had arrived the day before, and we were all full of excitement. The *Tatsuta Maru* was a very fine ship, and the second-class was very comfortable and spacious in comparison to the *Fulda*. We had a lovely voyage and enjoyed our stop overs in Japan and Honolulu on the way.

However, I couldn't help feeling rather disappointed at Honolulu. The beach at Waikiki was so narrow I could hardly believe it, after having heard so much about it, but the great waves came rolling in and the surfriders were wonderful to watch. We went out in a catamaran and came riding in on top of a wave, which was very thrilling.

When we reached Los Angeles, some reporters came on board. I think they must have come to see if there was anybody of interest to interview arriving from the Far East—as recently there had been some troubles with the Chinese and Japanese fighting in Shanghai. They interviewed Archy and Denis.

In the meantime I was wandering about the deck and thinking how thrilling to be actually arriving in the U.S.! A young man came along and started chatting to me. Then he asked me if he might take a photograph of me, to which I agreed and perched myself on the railing, and gave him a big "toothpaste" smile.

Next day, Archy and Denis bought a newspaper to see if their interview had been printed about the situation in the Far East, but all they found was a large picture of me sitting on the railing that had a notice saying "Reserved for First Class Passengers". An article below read: "Miss Hay-Edie, having just arrived from Hong Kong on the *Tatsuta Maru*, plans to buy a good used car and tour the United States with friends." They felt somewhat peeved!

Yosemite, California

After a few days in Los Angeles visiting the main sights and buying the "good used car", Archy and Denis had to take their driving tests. Then we left Los Angeles and spent a week driving around California via the Redwood Highway up to the border of Oregon; then south again to Yosemite, which was fabulous; and then to the Sequoia National Park, where we saw bears wandering around in the still snow-covered forest. Thinking they must be tame, we got out of the car to take photos, but as the bears lumbered closer and closer to us, we jumped back into the car.

Afterwards we told this to a Ranger who had stopped us on the road. He said we had been extremely foolish as the bears could easily have attacked us, looking for food.

On our way south we stopped at Pismo Beach for the night in a tiny cottage right on the edge of a cliff. Next morning, looking down on that beautiful beach far below, Archy and I decided we must go down and have a swim, but as we entered the sea our legs became paralyzed with the cold. The Pacific Ocean in April was icy cold!

On the beach I picked up a beautiful abalone shell and hid it away in the back of the car, as I was afraid Archy might stop me from carrying it with us. Many hundreds of miles, later under the hot sun, there was a horrible smell that took us ages to figure out what it was. I had to leave it on the road in Arizona.

The car was an open two-seater Plymouth with a rumble seat in which I sat, as the two men, not trusting my skill as a chauffeur, did all the driving. But that suited me, as I loved sitting at the back by myself, my face and arms covered in Nivea Oil to prevent sunburn, which also covered me with a thick layer of dust by the end of the day!

We drove to the Grand Canyon and were overwhelmed by the awesome grandeur and beauty of the scenery. Afterwards, we continued through the Painted Desert, Arizona and New Mexico, then Oklahoma and on up to Chicago, and finally, to Niagara Falls which was also tremendously impressive.

We wanted to see as much as possible, but we were limited with time and, most of all, with money. Before even starting on our trip Archy had to borrow money from Denis, who had very kindly offered to lend him what he needed. Of course, my presence nearly doubled the expenses. But again Denis obliged.

The snag came when we found that although Denis was such good company most of the time (he was jolly and had a great big laugh to go with his great big frame), there were times when he was so moody and morose we could hardly get a word out of him. We ended up having a good talk about it all, and things worked out in the end.

We were as economical as possible, and when mealtimes came we always ate in very cheap little restaurants or cafes and ordered the least expensive dishes. Our night's lodging at auto-camps (which were the equivalent of motels) generally cost one dollar each! They generally consisted of a small wooden shack with two rooms and a shelter for the car in between.

We spent four days in New York sightseeing and then embarked on the *Mauritania*. She was an enormous ship with four funnels and was very old, probably her last voyage across the Atlantic.

In the second class the vibration was so great that all the cutlery and glassware on the dining tables was constantly jiggling, and it was almost impossible to read. It was also the last stage of prohibition, and it was still impossible to buy any alcohol on board. We were absolutely amazed to see what some of the passengers resorted to in order to imbibe spirits—including drinking eau-de-cologne and mouthwash!

France

We finally reached port Le Havre where we disembarked, leaving Denis to go on to Southampton. We had just enough money to buy our third-class train tickets for Paris, plus two francs extra so that we could take the metro from the Gare du Nord to Montparnasse. I was relying on finding my friend Michael Lenson and being able to borrow some money from him, until Archy received his paycheck.

When we arrived in Paris and unloaded all our baggage onto the platform, I couldn't help feeling rather embarrassed. I had to sit on top of the pile and say to all the porters who came running to help: "*Non merci*, we don't need help!", while poor Archy was making several trips to the *consigne* and back laden with luggage. The porters made quite a few caustic remarks!

When we reached Montparnasse and walked to Michael's art studio, to our dismay he was not there, and the place was locked. We could not think of anyone else to turn to, so we left a small suitcase outside his door with a note on it asking him to meet us at Café Le Dôme as soon as possible.

We sat at the café for quite a long while, in front of two glasses of coffee, which we had no money to pay for, trying to think of some way out of our quandary. Then, to our relief, Mike appeared, and everything got straightened out, at least temporarily.

Archy and Mike liked each other right away, and we all had a wonderful time together while we were in Paris, waiting for Archy's paycheck to arrive. Unfortunately it was for only half of his usual salary, which was the rule in those days. He had eleven months leave at half-pay. At least two months would be spent travelling by ship between the Far East and Europe and the return. So we knew we simply had to be very economical and wondered where we could go that was cheap but enjoyable. The south of France of course! But we had no wish to see our parents after all that had happened, and we felt that they would not wish to see us either.

Then a stroke of luck came our way. Another American artist, a friend of Mike's whom I had met before, offered to lend us his studio in Cassis, a delightful little seaside town near Marseilles. All he wanted in return was that we should bring him back a roll of canvases that he had left there. Of course we blithely agreed, never thinking to ask how big they were.

We loved our weeks in Cassis. It was such a picturesque and simple little place. We met a few interesting people on the little sheltered beach, one being a Greek artist called Jacques Varda. He became very well known in later years for his modern style, using collages of shells and dried foliage, even funeral bouquets that he had pinched from under glass covers in a cemetery.

Of necessity we led an extremely simple life, but we enjoyed ourselves greatly. We would go for lovely walks up the rocky hills behind Cassis, and the views were spectacular and the scenery so typically Mediterranean. The sun shone most days, and we acquired wonderful suntans lying on the beach. We had so little money but so few cares also.

In the evenings we sometimes went and sat at a little café, overlooking the beach, where we could listen to French songs and dance music being played on the gramophone. We both loved it, and when the accordions were playing *Bal Musette* tunes, we would dance wildly round and round, on the tiny floor space available. Archy was a very good dancer and had mastered the rapid twirling dance steps of the *Bal Musette* as well as any Frenchman from Montmartre!

Eventually Archy's long leave came to an end, and he had to return to Hong Kong. We had been wondering how I could possibly return with him, as the cost of my passage would be so expensive. Archy had tried to get his firm's permission to convert his first-class ticket into two tourist-class tickets, but found this could not be allowed, particularly as he was travelling on one of the company's ships and he had to be seen travelling first-class.

Then Fate miraculously intervened. Lord Inchcape, who was the head of many firms, including Mackinnon's, suddenly died and left all his employees a month's salary. Naturally we could not help but be thrilled by this windfall, as Archy immediately said it must be for my return passage to Hong Kong. However, it was not sufficient to cover the whole voyage out there.

So it was decided that I would travel halfway on a B.I. vessel as far as Calcutta. There I would stay with the then Number One of the Alahabad Bank, Monty Wilson, who had known my father when he had held the same position many years previously. Archy would then be in Hong Kong, far ahead of me and immediately borrow some money to pay my passage from Calcutta to Hong Kong. Again it was a wonderful prospect for me.

Steamer via Calcutta

The faithful Jimmy came to see me off. I was tremendously excited at the thought of visiting Calcutta. I spent hours every day sitting on the prow of the ship, with one leg on either side of the flagpole. I felt quite safe up there holding on to the pole, even in quite rough weather, when the prow reared to great heights out of the water, and then plunged down again so deeply that I wondered whether I would be soaked. It was such fun, but fortunately we had smooth seas most of the time.

There was a fancy dress party before we reached Madras. I wore a grass skirt we had bought in Honolulu on our homeward voyage from Hong Kong the previous year. I also had several Leis made of paper flowers, which looked very effective. I was already quite tanned from all the hours spent on deck in the sun, but I decided I would look more the part of a real Hawaiian maiden if my skin were browner. So I rubbed myself with a solution of permanganate and water, which made quite a startling change in the colour of my skin.

I won the first prize, which was very nice, but next day I really got a shock when I saw myself in daylight. I found I could not wash off the colour! I was advised to rub myself with lemon, and eventually with endless lemons and several days later I was back to normal again.

One of the passengers was a businessman from Cawnpore who had evidently become somewhat smitten with me and tried to persuade me to marry him when we got to Calcutta. Although he was quite nice, I was not lured by the prospect of going to live in Cawnpore with him.

Madras

When we got to Madras I was met by a great friend of Archy's who was in business there. He invited me to dinner that night at the Adyar Club, which was a very fine country club set in beautiful grounds, and everybody was in evening dress, as it was a gala night. I was wearing a long white sharkskin dress, fitting closely on top, although very low cut at the back with a flared skirt. I received many compliments, which gave me a little more confidence in myself, although my mother's criticisms always remained ringing in my ears. I couldn't help wishing she could have seen me then, just to show her.

Adyar Club, Madras.

I danced all evening and had a wonderful time, but I kept asking when I should have to be back on board, as I knew the ship was due to sail that night. However, two of the men in the party were from the shipping company and assured me that there was plenty of time still, as the ship had not finished loading yet. Time for another dance!

But, when we finally got to the pier, to my utter dismay I saw that the ship had already cast off and was moving away. Panic and consternation! I leapt out of the car and raced along the pier to get as level with the bridge as possible, shouting across the rapidly widening stretch of water, "Please come back! Please come back and fetch me!"

I could see the captain peering over the side of the bridge looking surprised and furious, but he evidently decided he could not abandon me there. Amidst much churning of water, shouting and counter-shouting between the ships' officers and the crew, and cheering from the row of passengers who were lining the top deck leaning over the railings, obviously enjoying the whole show, the ship slowly drew close to the pier again. The gangway was lowered, and I sped across it, covered in confusion, but immeasurably relieved.

I knew it was not the time for me to go and make my apologies to the captain then. It was so late at night, and he would be busy getting the vessel on its way again. But the following morning I went up to the bridge and told him how very, very sorry I was to have given him so much trouble. He gave me a severe scolding and lecture, saying that it might have caused him to lose the tide up the Hooglie River to Calcutta, which would have cost the company thousands of pounds in demurrage, but actually he blamed my companions for being so irresponsible.

Calcutta

My fortnight's stay in Calcutta seemed to me as if I were living in the pages of a novel of society life in India at that time. As I was staying in the same house where my parents had lived years before, I wondered if it were the same type of life they had lived. One or two members of the staff said they remembered me there as a baby.

There were many different activities; riding on the *maidan* every day before breakfast; going to the Saturday Club and Tollygunge Club and to the races and parties galore, and always lots of dancing. Donald Bowie was stationed in Calcutta at that time and still hopefully persevered asking me to marry him.

The Garden City and Pagoda of Rangoon, Burma

Soon I was on board a fairly small passenger ship of the British India line bound for Hong Kong. We called in at Rangoon in Burma for some hours, and I was determined to go and visit the famous Shwedagon Pagoda. Of the few passengers none wanted to go ashore. The ship was anchored in midstream and quite a long way from the landing point, and there was no launch provided by the company.

There were some very small craft floating close to the ship like tiny gondolas cut in half, with a single oarsman maneuvering each trying to keep abreast of our ship, despite the strong current and waves that seemed to threaten swamping them at any moment. There was such a strong wind that I was clutching my skirt around me, and clinging on to my camera even more tightly, as I descended the gangway steps. I got into one of the cockle-shell boats, hoping that we would not be swamped and my camera ruined.

The instant we pushed off from the gangway we were swept swiftly down the river far beyond the point where I had thought we would be landing. The great Irrawaddy is a powerful river indeed! The pier was crowded with Burmese of all types, and traffic going in all directions–cars, buses, trucks and bicycles all honking or ringing bells–and everybody shouting and pushing.

It was chaotic. But despite this I managed to get on to a bus to the Pagoda.

By some miracle I did eventually reach the foot of the hill on which the Shwedagon was built and found the entrance to the path leading up to it. Some piles of shoes had been left at the gateway, so I took mine off and left them there too, continuing up the path barefooted.

The great golden pagoda, surrounded by hundreds of smaller ones all shining with a covering of pure gold leaf, was unbelievably impressive. I wandered on and on through the innumerable courtyards, feeling as though I had stepped into another world, especially as there was hardly another soul around, and certainly no foreigners or other tourists. The silence gave an atmosphere of peace conducive to inward contemplation.

It was the middle of the day and the heat became more and more unbearable, particularly for the soles of my bare feet. I tried to keep in the shadow of pagodas, but sometimes was forced to cross large, open courtyards. While running across one of these, I simply could not bear the burning ground any more and had to sit down on the ground in the middle of the courtyard and hold my feet up. I sat cross-legged in the lotus position hoping I did not look very peculiar, sitting all alone in the blazing sun. Although a few saffron-robed priests came through, none of them paid me the slightest attention. It was altogether an impressive experience.

Returning to the ship without any delays, we continued our long sea journey along the Indochina peninsula and the coast of China, finally arriving home in Hong Kong.

Soon began the most fulfilling adventure of my life.

Reidar

April, 1972. Jumping a half-century forward in time, Iris is living alone in a remote area on the island of Jamaica where she and her late-husband Reidar built their home, and where they spent the remaining years of his life together. Looking out across the Caribbean Sea, she fondly recounts her memories when she discovered that she was in love with him, and how much she enjoyed her exciting and magical life in the Far East.

Iris sitting in her garden in Jamaica overlooking the Caribbean Sea

Today I was sitting in the garden at our home, *Norse Hill*, under the big tree where my beloved Reidar sat the very day before he died, two years ago. The golden evening light brought out all the colours so beautifully; the tapestry of green on the hillsides; the glistening light on the palm leaves—as if they were wet; the soft mauves of the bougainvilleas covering the pergola tunnel below the garden; the vivid orange-red of the spathodia blossoms and the paleness of the white rambling roses; and beyond the blue of the Caribbean with great, billowing, rosy-tinted clouds drifting gently past. The whole atmosphere was laden with the perfume of jasmine.

The light faded and the stars appeared, some so brilliant, and Venus incredibly so. I always wonder, "What lies beyond? Are you there, my sweetheart? Can you look down upon me and know that I am longing for you? How many times we have sat here together in past years at this time of evening, holding hands and just feeling so, so blissfully happy, because we were together?"

It is the 8th of April 1972, and my thoughts take me back, inevitably, to this very day thirty-eight years ago. The day that Reidar and I discovered that we truly loved each other.

From that moment on, he was there always, a rock of strength for me to lean on and rely upon, knowing that I would never, never be let down. There for me to look up to and respect, more and more as the years went by; and to love, with ever greater intensity as we grew closer through trials and sickness. We also came to realize more deeply the unbelievable quality of our happiness together.

It is amazing how clearly one can still remember so many details of a day so long, long ago.

Can it really be True Love?

April 8th, 1934. It was a hot, steamy, Hong Kong, spring morning. Archy and I were living in a low, new building on the corner of the road to the Race Course, near the Monument. We had the top flat that looked out over it and used to hear the early training gallops go thundering past each morning before daylight, as many of the trainers seemed to prefer keeping the gallop times a secret.

Archy was quite surprised when I told him that I "had" to go to office that hot Sunday morning. I made some excuse about a letter that needed attending to, although my work as a so-called "secretary" was somewhat farcical. But I knew that Reidar Johannessen, the Managing Director of the Hong Kong office of the shipping firm Wallem & Company, worked seven days a week and was always in his desk next door...even on Sunday mornings!

Reidar Johannessen, 1934

The Macao Goa, Timor & Mozambique Line, where I worked, was on the waterfront in the ornate Victorian-style Prince's Building. The office had high ceilings, tall French doors and a large fan that hung in the centre to circulate the warm humid air. Reidar's offices of Wallem & Company were in the next rooms along a wide, wooden corridor, with saloon doors all along it.

The Prince's Building on the waterfront

That Sunday morning, I sat at the desk trying to look busy, but watching under the swinging doors for a certain pair of legs to approach. Yes! He arrived on time as usual and was headed my way.

My work as a secretary

He sat and we talked about the sort of life I led. Why did I go out so much? Every night I seemed to be out dancing with a different young man. Was I in love with any of them? I said absolutely not. In fact I would rather not go out at all with some of them. But it was so difficult to refuse point-blank and not be cornered into agreeing to go out some other evening.

It is important to remember that in those days one could go out with a young man, tête-à-tête, and not be expected to jump into bed with him at the end of the evening. One often went in an open, hired car for a drive and sometimes for a moonlight swim at Repulse Bay, but that was generally in a group. We went in hired cars because most of the young naval or army officers, who were stationed there briefly, did not have their own cars. The young men working in banks and shipping firms also often could not afford them. Nowadays a car is taken for granted, as one of life's necessities, but in those days it was a luxury.

So Reidar used to remonstrate with me about going out too much, saying that I would lose my looks and become known as a frivolous "social butterfly". I pointed out to him that he had been out dancing the night before, at "The Grips", where I had been, too.

While I was dancing with my partner we had come quite close to Reidar and his partner, an attractive Portuguese girl, also called Iris, strangely enough. I had tweaked Reidar's sleeve, much to her indignation, and she told him she thought I was very forward. She must have had some suspicion about how things were heading between us. One evening when I knew that Reidar was going to be taking her out dancing, I had telephoned to The Grips and had him paged. As the small bell-boy walked between the dining tables carrying the sign and ringing his little bell, Reidar said to her: "Some people must be very important to be called like this, even when they are dining out. I have always wished it would happen to me." Then, lo and behold, there was his name! I just said, "I hoped he was enjoying himself and to please note that I was spending a peaceful evening at home. I was not out gallivanting about the dance floor, even though it was a Saturday night"!

Reidar told me afterwards that Iris had gone to check up on where the telephone call had come from; she was in a position to do this as she worked as a secretary in the Hong Kong Hotel Company. She had been outraged about it and held a very poor opinion of me. She was in love with Reidar, too, and the realization that she was not going to win him must have been very hard.

We talked and talked that hot, steamy Sunday morning, with the fan purring gently overhead. I asked him why he would not invite me out dancing one evening, or take me for a drive in his car after work. He looked at me, smiling, and said: "Because I don't want to fall helplessly and hopelessly in love with you, which I know I would if I saw more of you!"

He thought I had so many boyfriends and was really a "social butterfly", loving parties and gaiety with no inclination to settle down to a peaceful, simple married life. I turned my back on him and leant over the stone balustrade, looking down into the street below, wondering how I could convince him how wrong he was.

Then somehow we were in each other's arms, and he was kissing me and kissing me. He sat down in the desk armchair, and I sat on his knee, but I can't remember any more of what we said. His arms were around me, and I felt so dizzy with happiness, quite light-headed.

Then I suddenly realized it was so late, far beyond the time I had told Archy I would be staying at the office. I was supposed to go to have my foot massaged by a Japanese masseur, having had it injured by a friend slipping on our stairs and coming down heavily on it with his heel.

My bad foot became quite useful after that, because I could use it as an excuse not to go out. I did try to curtail my 'dates' with a number of my men friends. But as I was not engaged officially, I didn't want to tell anybody yet about Reidar and me, not even Archy immediately. It was "our" secret that I had to think about.

Reidar said he loved me, quite overwhelmingly, and I knew he wanted to marry me. Nevertheless he went off on his long leave of eight months, without having definitely asked me to be his wife. He had told me that his Norwegian boss, Mr. Wallem, had emphasized to him time and again that if he became engaged while he was on leave, he would lose his job.

Haakon "Typhoon" Wallem with Reidar and other employees

Mr. Wallem was a fierce old tyrant who used to roar at people and bulldoze them into his way of thinking. He generally got what he wanted. He was known up and down the China Coast as "Typhoon Wallem", and most people quailed at getting on the wrong side of him. He was a great womanizer and, although he had a wife in Norway and two grown-up children in Europe, he had mistresses galore in Shanghai. He had lived most of his life in China and made, and lost, several fortunes. But although he himself led a very gay life, he had had a very disappointing married life.

I suppose he judged most marriages from his own experience and was against it. He also held the opinion that a man would not work so well if he had a wife at home waiting for him. So he was absolutely against Reidar getting married. No wonder my beloved was in a quandary and was going to wait and see what would happen when he got back from his leave.

In the meantime he did take me out for a few drives in his glamorous, two-seater blue sports car. We used to drive in the New Territories out to Castle Peak. It was beautiful along the coast with hardly any buildings on the way. (Now, one can hardly find any natural country left at all.)

Walking with Reidar in the New Territories, 1934

Wallem & Company owned a "matshed" (as the bathing pavilions used to be called) at Eleven Mile Beach, and we used to go there to swim on Sundays. Mr. Wallem was there the last time, just before Reidar went away, and he seemed to accept me in a friendly way. I was quite scared of him, because he really was a formidable man. I knew how badly he treated Reidar at times, if he was not constantly at his beck and call, at any hour of the day or night. He would telephone to the office sharp at 8 a.m. every morning, seven days a week, just to check up on whether Reidar was there or not. On Sundays, Reidar was expected to spend the mornings in the office and then the rest of the day with Mr. Wallem. He had no life of his own at all when Mr. Wallem was visiting Hong Kong, and everybody was thankful when he returned to Shanghai.

One day when Reidar and I were driving to Castle Peak, the car started to smoke going up a steep hill. Reidar stopped it and considered the situation for a moment, then hurried around to my side of the car, opened the door, and urged me to get out quickly. Then, he took my hand and ran up the steep slope above the road for a good distance before asking me to sit down. I was a bit perplexed what he proposed to do about the car, which seemed to be smoking more strongly as the minutes went by. But my Hero said: "We'll just sit here quietly until it explodes".

Reidar's leave

Reidar set sail on a Thoresen cargo vessel, which was to get him to Marseilles in five or six weeks. (Travelling by plane had not started by then.) Meanwhile, I used to see quite a lot of Mr. Wallem, as our offices were adjacent. He seemed to like coming in and having chats with me. It was at a very slack period for shipping and the market was very poor. The two other young men in Wallem & Company had so little to do that they used to invite me in for ice creams and conversation in mid-morning when Mr. Wallem was not there. Sometimes we used to play darts on the veranda—so different from the hectic turmoil of work in later years.

Mr. Wallem had very few friends in Hong Kong and always relied upon Reidar's company, even after office, when he loved to go to the cinema. So after Reidar had left, he used to ask me to accompany him, which I did very often, as I had my plans! He naturally used to take the most expensive seats, which were upstairs on the balcony. But I pointed out to him that the stalls downstairs were just as good, if not better, as they were a bit cooler. One could see just as well and pay half price. I added that Archy and I, and our friends, always went downstairs. This intrigued Mr. Wallem very much. In the afternoons it was never very crowded, and of course it was excellent to be economical. I scored a good mark there!

He also used to ask me to go swimming, together with the other two employees, Kjeld Knudsen and Paul Wilson, at his matshed, "Viking", at Eleven Mile Beach. He would get the Peninsula Hotel, where he was staying, to pack up an enormous and very elaborate picnic lunch, including bottles of Vouvray. Then off we would all drive in a hired car and spend the day on the beach.

Of course it was very pleasant swimming and having a lovely lunch in such beautiful surroundings. It was a nice little beach with only a few other matsheds. But after lunch, when I was feeling decidedly fuzzy-headed as I was unaccustomed to drinking, though he insisted that I do so, he used to make us play bridge. I had only the haziest notions of how to play anyway, but he was so expert and used to roar at the others when they made mistakes. I was petrified, but had to continue regardless. It cured me of ever wanting to play bridge again. But he was very kind and patient with me.

One day Mr. Wallem came into the office just as I was speaking on the telephone long distance to a "boyfriend" in Canton. He was a young naval officer, who was one of the most persistent suitors I ever had. He knew it was hopeless but continually tried to change my mind. Having been caught (temporarily, thank goodness!) by that method once before, I was not going to let it happen again and was rather impatient with him.

Mr. Wallem sat down opposite me and said, "You seem to have a great many young men friends. You are always talking on the telephone to one or another, whenever I come in here. I thought you were interested in Johannessen". So I replied, with a certain modest confusion at being so outspoken: "I am, but he has told me that he will lose his job if he gets married". Mr.

Wallem blinked, to begin with, in mock surprise, and then his eyes twinkled. With a knowing smile, he said "And if he didn't lose his job, would you marry him?" That really put me on the spot. What else could I say but, quite simply, "Yes!"

During all the years that we were married, when Reidar used to tease me about all the boyfriends I had as a girl, I would reply, with a very superior air, "If it hadn't been for me, we might not have been married at all!"

Engaged at last!

After that I really felt I was engaged. It was so thrilling, and I wrote a long letter to Reidar telling him all about how it had come to pass. He had left Hong Kong a free man, but on his arrival in Marseilles and finding my letter, he had become an engaged one! He sent me a telegram immediately saying how overjoyed he was at the wonderful news. Also he was going to order a morning coat to be made in London for our wedding.

This gave me a jolt, as I was far too nervous to contemplate a wedding in a trailing white gown. But I didn't dare send a telegram back asking him not to order the coat, as he might think I had already changed my mind. So, as letters only went by sea in those days, taking a good five weeks to London, the morning coat was made by the time my next letter arrived.

I kept my engagement a secret, however, except from Archy, of course. Somehow I didn't want people discussing it, especially as Reidar was away. But I devoted more of my time to Mr. Wallem, and we got along marvellously well together. I also wanted to consolidate my position, so to speak.

One morning he asked me to come into his office, where he handed me a letter, saying it was very important. I would be doing him a great favour taking it personally and delivering it to Sir Vandeleur Grayburn, the Chief Manager of the Hongkong and Shanghai Bank (HSBC). I should wait while he read it and then ask him if it was "all right", or if there was any answer.

Sir Vandeleur Grayburn

Sir Vandeleur was a fine, although rather forbidding, looking man, for whom Mr. Wallem had the very greatest respect and admiration. Chiefly, I think, because he was the all-powerful Bank Manager who could say Yea or Nay to any loan or scheme thought up by Mr. Wallem. He was therefore of tremendous importance to the prosperity of Wallem & Company. Also he was, after the governor, the most important man in Hong Kong, being the top financier in the Far East.

Whenever Mr. Wallem had to go and see him, for business reasons he would first go to the barber and have his hair cut, get a face massage and manicure, put on his very best suit with a flower in his buttonhole and parade in front of the mirror asking Reidar and anyone else who happened to be standing near whether they didn't think he looked very fine! Then off he would go, bent on making the very best impression! But I didn't realize all this at the time and blithely went along to the bank as I was.

I confess I was slightly awed by Sir Vandeleur, and more so by the magnificence of his vast office, where I was ushered in with ceremony. Sir Vandeleur was charming and had an amused smile on his face when I asked him earnestly whether

115

there was any answer, or whether it was "all right". He replied, "You tell Mr. Wallem I think it is very much all right."

So I returned to Mr. Wallem and solemnly gave him the answer. Whereupon he gave a great roar of laughter and said, "Do you know what I wrote in that letter?" So, feeling most perplexed, of course I said I had no idea. Then he told me: "I wrote, this is the girl that Johannessen wants to marry. What do you think of her? Do you think she's all right?" He thought it was such a tremendous joke, he kept laughing and laughing at how clever he had been!

Soon after this it became apparent that my "firm" and its owner, were in decided difficulties. A law case was coming up concerning the ship *Sagres'* opium smuggling activities and the amount of money owed to the HSBC bank.

The Spanish captain of the ship used to come into the office and have long chats with me, then go in to see the Captain in the other room. He brought the ship's log to me and asked if I could translate it into English. It was written in Spanish and I didn't understand much, but what I did understand was most interesting, and I related it all to Archy when I got home in the evening.

It appeared that the ship had been in the Persian Gulf. She arrived at a certain port, but dropped anchor outside and lay there all night, while the cargo was brought out in lighters. Then the name of the ship was painted out, and she set sail for Macao, or somewhere on the China Coast.

Archy really got worried when he heard about the case coming up in court. He and I knew that company had a lot of peculiar dealings with the Macao Government concerning opium smuggling and I don't know what else. The owner entertained many strange people lavishly and spent a lot of time in Macao. It was obvious that his affairs were going from bad to worse. Archy was afraid that I would be called to give evidence in court and decided that it would therefore be best for me to go away for a holiday at that time.

When Mr. Wallem heard this, he very kindly said I could travel on one of his coastal vessels going up to Tsingtao and Chingwantao free of charge and return by another of his ships later. This was marvellous, as it would have been difficult for me to have afforded it otherwise.

My trip to Shanghai and Peking, China

So I embarked on the *S.S. Sandviken* with Captain Jensen in command—a most charming and nice looking "big bear" of a Norwegian Captain. He had special instructions from Mr. Wallem to look after me very well, but, poor man, I must have given him a few near heart attacks at times.

I had the run of the ship, and my favourite place was sitting right up on the prow of the vessel with my legs dangling overboard on either side of the post. I spent hours every day up there, mesmerized by the deep blue sea and the motion of the waves. It was exhilarating to feel the wind through my hair and all around me. I wanted to laugh and sing with happiness.

One afternoon I climbed high up into the crow's-nest. I can still remember Captain Jensen's startled look as he emerged onto the bridge from his after-lunch siesta, and I hailed him gaily from my lofty position.

After a couple of days' stay in Shanghai at the International Settlement–very gay, with nightclubs and parties–we carried on to Tsingtao.

Tsingtao postcard

Then I disembarked at Wei-hai-Wei, the summer resort for many people from Shanghai, and also for the British Fleet in the Far East. It was a very simple and pretty little place with a lovely beach and only a couple of hotels and a few privately owned bungalows. One of the hotels was mostly for the navy wives, and the other, where we were, was more for casual visitors.

My friend, Simonne, who happened to be there, and I had a wonderful time together. She was always so vivacious, and as we already knew many of the naval officers from Hong Kong, we were asked out a great deal. But I used to go off on my own quite a lot too, walking in the pine covered hills and enjoying being alone with my happy thoughts of the future with Reidar.

Once, while walking peacefully through the pine forest, I heard an ominous buzz just beside me. I just had time to glimpse a large hornets' nest on the tree I was passing, with scores of angry hornets emerging. I took to my heels and ran faster than I can ever remember doing before. Hopping over the rocks and bushes regardless of scratches and cuts, down and down the hillside, never stopping until I reached the village. I had lost the heel off one shoe and was covered with twigs and perspiration, not to mention my "wounds". Simonne looked at me in amazement, but then she never could understand why I liked to go off on my own anyway.

After a fortnight there I went to Peking. Simonne decided to come too, bringing her young son Richard. Reidar always said afterwards that he came near to losing me in Peking, as I never wrote him a letter during all the three weeks I was there. I can't understand myself now, how I neglected him in such a way. But then I was not so much in love with him as I was after we were married. And I was absolutely enchanted with the magic of Peking. I fell completely under its spell.

Forbidden City, Peking

I felt as though I could close my eyes and find myself living in the same atmosphere and surroundings as hundreds of years ago. The great walls around the city and the gigantic pagoda-topped "Gates" of Ha Ta Men and Chien Men; the vast open squares, the Temple of Heaven, Forbidden City, Summer Palace, Pei Hei Park, and the Legation Quarter with all the legations so privately ensconced behind high walls and massive gates—it was all so impressive.

I used to go walking alone after dinner on those fabulous great walls around the Tartar city. The fantastic silhouette of Ha Ta Men loomed above me in the darkness until the moon appeared and the whole scene was even more dreamlike. The sound of mah-jong counters being shuffled about, the high-pitched voices of the Chinese, and the musical clip-clop of their wooden slippers on the streets below, the rising smell of burning wood and charcoal, all combined to add to the general exciting strangeness and the feeling of complete unreality.

There were two elderly gentlemen, friends of Noel Croucher's (Simonne's husband), who were evidently supposed to be keeping an eye on her and acting as guardians. Their efforts at putting the brakes on Simonne only served to create an atmosphere of friction and disharmony. We seemed to be constantly trying to escape from their supervision and company, without offending them.

The Great Wall

We went on expeditions to the Great Wall, far up in the hills at Kalgan, where the camel caravans were going on their long, long trek into Mongolia, just as they have been doing for hundreds of years. The sight of that fantastic Wall, so massive, high, and wide enough for two coaches to pass on top, was built with the sweat, blood, and bones of millions of Chinese, two thousand years go. I stood gazing over the great stretch of endless rugged land that was Mongolia and the Wall, winding over the mountains and down into the valleys for thousands of miles. It made a tremendous impression on me.

I met two men in Peking, both very different from each other, who did their best to persuade me to marry them. I was not in the least tempted to change my mind. But it was amusing as Simonne had not the slightest idea about one of them, and was convinced that he was a great admirer of hers. Needless to say, I never enlightened her.

One evening we had been out to dinner at some party or other and were on our way back to the hotel in our own rickshaws, that we had hired for the length of our stay. Our two old men were trailing along in their rickshaws behind us. We wanted greatly to give them the slip so that we could go for walk on the Tartar Wall in the moonlight without them. So we bribed our rickshaw coolies to run as fast as they could and got to the hotel well ahead of the others. But not wanting the night watchman to tell them he had seen us go out again, we decided on another course of action.

The coolies had been busy sweeping the big hall carpets and were in the process of rolling them up in order to clean the rest of the floor. To their stupefaction we both lay down on the carpets and bade the coolies: "Quick, quick, roll them up". A few seconds later the old men arrived and we heard them asking for us. They were told we had arrived and concluded we had gone up to our rooms. We lay there, rolled up like cocoons simply bursting with laughter, and then emerged, slightly dusty, and went for our moonlight stroll in peace.

After three unbelievable weeks, we took the train for Tsingtao, where Simonne had decided to leave Richard in a European-run school, much to his disgust and our relief.

One evening when I was dancing at a nightclub there, I saw Mr. Wallem with an attractive woman. She was obviously a white Russian and, I presumed, his current mistress. I felt very embarrassed and didn't know how to react—whether to greet him or pretend I had not seen him. In the end I did the latter, and we left the nightclub very quickly, as I didn't wish him to feel embarrassed. But far from it. When I saw him again weeks later, he asked me why I had cut him that evening!

Wallem ship the S.S. Norviken

Simonne came with me on the *S.S. Norviken* for the return voyage to Hong Kong. We picked up a few passengers from Shanghai too. It was a dreadfully rough trip and most people were seasick. I spent a lot of time nursing Simonne and another French lady who had joined the ship in Shanghai, a Madame DuPak, a famous Shanghai hostess and beauty. They were both so seasick that they just lay in their bunks for the whole trip. I trotted from one cabin to the other, holding basins and doing odd jobs, until I was overcome by sickness myself (the first time I had ever been seasick in my life). But it was the horrid atmosphere of those cabins. After I had been up on deck and breathed some good fresh air, I was able to enjoy my food as much as ever—which I regretted in a way, as I was already trying to slim!

Hong Kong with Archy

When I got back to Hong Kong at the end of September, Archy and I went to live at the Repulse Bay Hotel. It was such a lovely place, rather old-fashioned even in those far off-days.

With two stories only, it had lovely large rooms, each with its own enclosed veranda, serving as a nice sitting room, all overlooking the beach and Repulse Bay. There was a line of beautiful Flame of the Forest trees all along the road at the back of the beach and then a row of privately owned matsheds. It never seemed too crowded.

Repulse Bay Hotel from the water with Victoria Peak behind

At night the brilliant lights of the fishing sampans lit up the whole bay, and one could see them far out at sea near the Lema Islands. It looked like a big floating city with its twinkling lights on the horizon.

Lots of friends came to see us there and we had great fun with a nice "Indian type" canoe we kept on the beach under Simonne's matshed. Every evening after returning from the office, Archy and I used to paddle across the bay, into Deep Water Bay and swim from the rocks out on the point. On weekends we used to be able to get away from the other people on the beaches, taking a picnic and exploring the unknown rocky coast outside the bay.

I had many male friends, although by then I had told most of them that I was already engaged to be married, there were several who still persisted, very earnestly and vehemently, in wanting to marry me. I liked two or three of them quite a lot. One in particular was a really special friend, who was quite hard to resist, but I did not want to change my mind to marry any of them.

On the other hand, Reidar had been away so long by then, (it was eight whole months by the time he returned) that I seemed to have got out of touch with him. Not that we did not write to each other often. He did particularly, and I tried to make up for my sad neglect not writing to him while I was in Peking! But I felt I couldn't remember clearly what he looked like any more. And of course I kept asking myself whether I was truly in love with him and whether I should marry him after all.

The persuasions of my other suitors did not help matters either. Although Archy was sweet and tried to be as understanding as possible, and he liked Reidar, he knew him so very little at that time that it was difficult for him to form a real opinion. I know he felt a little disappointed that I had not chosen a Britisher. Even the very day before Reidar was due to return I remember so clearly one of these men saying to me,

"How can you possibly marry him? You've got to be firm and say "NO" tomorrow and marry me instead"!

Well, no need to say that I did not act on his advice.

Reidar returns from his leave

When the great day finally arrived for Reidar's return, I was in such a state of nerves and anxiety that I had a terrible headache. His ship, another Thoresen cargo vessel carrying 12 passengers, dropped anchor in the middle of the harbour during the afternoon.

I went out in the company's launch and climbed up the gangway steps in a state of complete jitters. I was wearing a raincoat as the weather was wet and fairly cold. I looked up as I started up the steps and saw Reidar looking over the side with a whole row of faces on either side of his, all friendly and curious.

When I got to the top and I stepped onto the deck, a man greeted me with a tremendous flourish and laid down his coat for me to walk on! Of course this threw me into more confusion than ever. Then I felt myself being grabbed into Reidar's arms and I just buried my face in his shoulder, not daring to look at anyone.

But, of course, I had to be introduced to the Captain and all Reidar's travelling companions. They knew that he was meeting his fiancée and were intrigued to see what she was like, particularly his cabin companion, who had greeted me so dramatically.

I was so thankful when we were able to leave, as I was on the verge of tears with high tension and nervous strain. When we were alone together and were able to talk freely and put our arms around each other, everything was different. I was no longer filled with doubts and fears, wondering whether I loved Reidar or not. I knew I did! It was all so wonderful and I became so filled with happiness and gratitude to have him back again, knowing that we would be married, that my headache just vanished. When we met Archy at the Peninsula Hotel for dinner a little later, I felt absolutely serene and radiant. We were truly in love!

Our first home together

From then on we were busy looking for a place to live. We used to go for drives in search of a flat a little way out of town. One day we were lucky and saw a new house going up. We were enchanted with the top flat that had a glorious view out over the sea towards Lantao Island. The building was situated on a promontory, completely on its own, about a hundred feet above the sea, with a pine forest below. Our flat had a lovely wide covered veranda running all along the front and a big flat roof, and such heavenly views on three sides.

We were thrilled about our future home, but we did think it was rather expensive. Reidar had already told me that we would have to live very carefully to begin with as his salary was not very high. He said that when shipping improved, he was sure Mr. Wallem would increase it.

The views from our new flat

In fact Mr. Wallem had promised to take him into partnership in the very near future. It was at a time when shipping was completely in the doldrums and firms were hardly able to pay their expenses, let alone make any good profits. Though it may sound uncharitable, that was surely the reason that Mr. Wallem took Reidar in as his partner in Hong Kong, on a fifty-fifty basis, and Sverre Froland in Shanghai.

Reidar was so badly off at that time that he told me, much as he would like to buy me an engagement ring, it would mean that he would not be able to pay his insurance if he did. Naturally I told him I didn't want an engagement ring. And it was true. (I had not been lucky with my first engagement ring.)

But Reidar used to make extra money quite often, from quite a different source. He used to say in a laughing way: "I have to admit that I am the best shipping man in the Far East!" Well, it was a fact, and many other people said it too. He was frequently called upon for arbitrations, where both disputing sides agreed to abide by his decision as sole arbitrator. Sometimes he acted for one side and another arbitrator, or advisor, was called by the other side. But generally he was the sole arbitrator, both sides considering that they could get nobody better. He received quite good fees for these arbitrations.

He was extremely proud when the big firms, and even the HSBC bank, appointed him to act for them. Mr. Wallem also realized how clever Reidar was and let him negotiate big deals, particularly with the HSBC. He knew that Reidar was held in such high esteem by them, although he would never admit it. If anyone praised Reidar, or told Mr. Wallem he was lucky to have such a fine shipping man in his office, Mr. Wallem would beat his chest and roar "I taught him everything he knows!" Which was largely true too.

Reidar's beginnings

Reidar Johannessen was born in 1899 in Bergen, a large seaport town surrounded by immense fjords. Fishing and merchant shipping were the primary industries there at the time. An ambitious young man, at the age of 18, he left Norway to seek his fortune in America.

Bergen, Norway, 1915

Reidar found work for four years with the Norwegian American Shipping Line in New York, from 1917 to 1921. He then was hired by Wallem & Co. in Shanghai, where he worked another four years.

Reidar, Hong Kong, 1928

In Shanghai he lived in a "mess" with several other men, who were all British. There he learned to speak the "King's English", without the broad American accent he had picked up in New York. He used to tell me of the parties and gaiety that went on in that mess. The stories they told and the bawdy songs they sang! Reidar adapted himself to it all with great aptitude and enjoyed life enormously.

Reidar in Shanghai working as a shipping clerk

He played the piano well, and was always a popular person at any party. He would sit at the piano for hours playing all the latest dance and song hits, as well as whole parts out of light operas, then very much in vogue. He also learned a lot about how to enjoy the lighter side of life from Mr. Wallem, who loved to give parties and to drink and dance and celebrate.

Shanghai 1920's

Shanghai was indeed the "Paris" or "Pearl of the Orient" in those days, with countless nightclubs and thousands of pretty White Russian women, refugees from the Russian Revolution. The majority of them claimed to have royal blood and to be princesses, countesses, or baronesses. There is no doubt that many of them were from very good families and were highly intelligent, but there were also a great many from the lower stratas of society, who became prostitutes and dance hostesses. Anyway, all this contributed to the wild nightlife of Shanghai, which was notorious throughout the world.

Reidar would celebrate New Year's Eve and other important nights with Mr. Wallem, and would both go to the office the following day, still in their white ties and tails!

Reidar, Haakon Wallem and Sverre Frøland, Shanghai, 1923

Reidar also kept a pony and used to go on hunts and paper chases, which was the thing for young bloods to do in those days. It was there that he first became greatly interested in racing and never missed a "meeting". He knew all the horses and many of the jockeys and the owners, and became very knowledgeable. But he never could afford a racehorse of his own.

In 1925, after four years in Shanghai, Wallem sent Reidar to open a new office in Hong Kong. It was a difficult time. Being the only employee was entirely different from working in a big firm with many others. Here he had to make all the decisions and start everything from scratch. To make matters more complicated, during the initial years strikes and boycotts almost paralysed shipping. In both Shanghai and Hong Kong, China's key trading ports for the West, a violent anti-British feeling created turmoil that affected trade, finance and daily life.

But Reidar was confident and enjoyed the challenge.

He also continued his interest in horses in Hong Kong and was thrilled when Mr. Moller, a well known society horse breeder, used to come down from Shanghai to the yearly big race meeting, bringing several race horses with him that won all the top races. When Mr. Moller went back to Shanghai, he asked Reidar to look after them for him. It involved going to the stables and having long talks with the trainer, watching the horses exercise and going down to the race course in the very early morning to see the training gallops. It was lots of fun, especially when the horses won and I led them in.

Finally Reidar took the great plunge and decided to buy a horse of his own. It was called *New Moon* and did win a few races.

The wedding

January 3rd, 1935. Although I loved Reidar enough to marry him, I was sceptical about lasting happiness in marriage. I had the unhappy example of my own parents to ponder upon.

Although my parents remained together, there was so much misery for us all during that time; such a lack of understanding and tolerance on my mother's part; so much unkindness and selfishness that it made our family life almost intolerable at times. And it was all so unnecessary.

There were far too many other examples amongst our friends and acquaintances, of unhappy marriages. After all, what a tremendous gamble it is to decide to live the rest of one's life, in the most intimate circumstances, with somebody who is a comparative stranger!

So on that third day of January, my wedding morning, I was in a turmoil of different feelings. But the predominant one was a nervous, but happy excitement. I was far too shy to think of having a traditional white wedding. The fact that my parents were not there and no other member of my family, except my dearest and most wonderful brother, made both Archy and me feel rather 'at sea' about the whole procedure. How did one get married?

Mr. Wallem very kindly said he would pay for our wedding luncheon at the Peninsula Hotel. Archy's head of Mackinnon's, Mr. Gordon Mackay, had offered to have the wedding at the taipan's house on the Peak, but we preferred to keep it more to ourselves. So Reidar went to Michael, the Russian manager of the hotel restaurant and a great friend of Mr. Wallem's, and ordered a fabulous luncheon.

We were first married in town at the Registry Office, with Birger Naess, the Norwegian Vice-Consul, and Kjeld Knudsen as witnesses. Kjeld was Reidar's best man. Then we drove, via the vehicular ferry, out to Tao Fung Shan in the New Territories, to a picturesque little church built like a pagoda. This was the Norwegian Mission church, up in the hills overlooking the lovely green Shatin Valley and the blue waters of Taipo Inlet, with Ma On Shan mountains on the other side.

It was the most lovely and romantic setting for a wedding. I was wearing a pale dove-gray dress and tailored jacket to match, and hat also of the same material, carrying a bouquet of flowers. There must have been about 15 or 20 in all at the little church. We had not wanted any more.

Our wedding day, 1935

The service was held by the old Norwegian Pastor, Reichelt. He looked like the God of Longevity himself, with his great domed bald head, but in a stiff white collar and flowing robe, which gave a quaint touch to the otherwise Chinese atmosphere.

At the wedding luncheon afterwards there were about thirty-five guests. Everybody said that it was a sumptuous meal. All I can remember is that Reidar and I went from table to table and talked with all our friends, and the champagne flowed. I can't remember having a wedding cake but I suppose we must have.

We managed to get away sometime during the afternoon, without too much fuss, leaving all the rest of the party to carry on celebrating. We heard later that some of them did until the evening of the following day!

We were not going away on a honeymoon as Reidar could not get away from his office. We were married on a Thursday and on the Saturday morning he was back again in his office. But we were so thrilled with our beautiful flat, right out in the country, that it almost felt like going away.

That evening in our new home, sitting on the terrace drinking more champagne, we asked ourselves whether it really, really could be true. It was all so wonderful, so beautiful, so unbelievable.

The view from our flat

Then suddenly the silence of the night was shattered by the roar of engines. Three planes swooped low over the house with deafening noise and then skimmed low over the sea below us. They had flares on their wing tips, and as they rose into the air in formation, they made a Prince of Wales Feathers design against the black velvet sky. It was most impressive and spectacular.

We realized that it must be some of my Fleet Air Force friends. We heard afterwards that it was indeed them and that they were all uproariously drunk and had tried to smuggle Archy onto one of the planes dressed up in uniform. But he had been discovered and stopped. They had evidently all driven back from the airfield at Kai Tak in a battered old open car, all along the sidewalk pavement instead of the road! It was a miracle nobody was killed. It also shows how deserted the roads were then in comparison to now.

Our married life was blissfully quiet to begin with. We hardly ever went out to parties, as we much preferred to be just the two of us at home. At weekends Archy would come and spend Sundays with us. We used to swim or go for walks along the water catchments in the late mornings.

Reidar always went to the office regardless of it being Sunday. But he came back after spending a couple of hours there, so that we had time to get out for a while. After, we would have a late lunch and siesta and then a six o'clock cinema. It was an almost unvarying routine on Sundays.

Every day of the week Reidar would be in the office before eight o'clock in the morning. He was always the first to arrive, even before any of the office boys. Throughout his life in Hong Kong, he was a tremendous worker because he was completely bound up and fascinated by his work. He loved it.

It was no hardship at all for him to spend a whole Saturday afternoon or Sunday morning in the dockyard climbing all over a ship that was being repaired, or passing survey. And of course I pattered along behind him and became very interested in ships' interiors, the propeller shafts and engines as well. It was wonderful, as long as I was with him.

Our flat, at Pokfulam, was about twenty minutes drive from the centre of town. As we only had one car (I had forgotten how to drive anyway at that time), it meant a long walk up the Dairy Farm Hill to catch a bus into town if I wanted to join Reidar, or to go shopping but thankful our cook-boy did the marketing every day, so there was no real need for me to go.

I was never bored and always found plenty to occupy myself, including exercising and learning Norwegian. Reidar gave me some books that I studied, which he corrected when he came home. I used to learn phrases and grammar etc., and got along quite well. But after the first year the Norwegian lessons stopped. I was too busy with my son!

John "JoJo" is born

December 5, 1935. We had firmly made up our minds that we would not have any children for the first three years of our married life, so that we would have time to enjoy being "just us", without any encumbrance. Also we thought we could not really afford it yet.

However despite our resolutions, John Johannessen ("JoJo"), our bouncing son and heir arrived eleven months after our wedding on December 3rd, 1935. A day of excruciating pain and finally, overwhelming joy. I felt as if I had created a miracle, as I lay in my hospital bed afterwards, surrounded by so many flowers, with my husband, my brother, and quite a large bundle in my arms (he weighed 9 lbs., 8 oz.), yelling lustily. I realized he was no beauty at that early age, and his head was a bit squashed-looking. But of course to Reidar and me, he was just the most marvellous baby ever!

December 25, 1935. I shall always remember our very first Christmas together. It was not just the twosome we had thought it would be, but a real family one. I had only returned from the hospital a few days before and was still spending quite a lot of time resting. Reidar mysteriously kept the door into the living room closed all day and would not let me go in.

It was Christmas Eve, the time Norwegians always celebrate most. When it was evening, he opened the door wide and ushered me in. I was carrying our baby son in my arms. There stood the most beautiful Christmas tree, nearly touching the ceiling, all decorated and illuminated. It looked so lovely that I just burst into tears with sheer happiness, and was so touched at all the trouble he had taken to give us this great surprise.

In all the years of my life, until then, I had only once before had a Christmas with a tree. That was when I was a little girl and was in Scotland with my Uncle and Aunt Bartholomew. My own parents had never celebrated Christmas in any special way at all. In later years, when we lived in France, they took us out occasionally to a restaurant for a special dinner.

So, to suddenly behold this beautiful symbol of Christmas, in our own home, with my husband and my darling little son, it all seemed too wonderful to be true.

JAPAN RISES

In the late 19th and early 20th centuries, western countries including Britain, Germany, France, Spain, Portugal, as well as the US and Russia, competed for influence, trade, and territory in East Asia. Japan sought to join these modern colonial powers with an imperialism of its own.

In the 1920s and 1930s, the small but highly-populated island nation of Japan needed to import raw materials such as iron, rubber, and oil for it's economic growth. Most of these resources came from the United States that had formed important economic bonds with Japan. The Japanese felt that acquiring their own resource-rich territories would establish economic self-sufficiency and independence, especially during the worldwide Great Depression of the 1930's. Japan set its sights on East Asia, specifically Manchuria with its many resources.

After the Invasion of Manchuria in 1931, which established the puppet state Manchukuo under Japanese control, tensions between the Empire of Japan and the Republic of China increased dramatically with various military clashes, or "incidents" as they were called, occurring in northern China.

Meanwhile, Iris and Reidar were at a distance from the threats, living in the British Crown Colony of Hong Kong, far away on the South China Coast. As European citizens, they and most other foreigners had little reason to be nervous, feeling the incidents were an Asian problem. Colonial custom at the time was to keep at a distance from Asian affairs, and on a personal level, most colonialists believed in segregation of the races. Asians were hardly allowed into the International Settlements, apart from the servants there.

Consequently, sentiment felt by many Japanese and other Asians was that "Asia should be ruled by Asians". Imperialist Japanese generals argued to their Emperor to replace European colonial rulers with Japanese rulers throughout Asia.

However, under Japanese control Manchuria was one of the most brutally run regions in the world, with a systematic campaign of terror and intimidation applied against the local Russian and Chinese populations. But as it was so far away from the rest of the world, it didn't capture its attention. Soon after, Manchukuo was used as a base to invade the rest of China, piece by piece.

Lake Chuzenji, Japan

Summer 1936. Before we were married, I used to say that I thought it was a good thing for a husband and wife to have a short holiday on their own, away from each other every year. Reidar, somewhat dubiously, agreed. But when it was decided that I should go to Japan for a couple of months to recuperate from a bout of malaria and to get away from the heat of Hong Kong's summer with the baby, I felt very sad going without him. He said he could not possibly leave his office as shipping was just beginning to pick up again.

Fortunately Archy was due some local leave and he gladly agreed to accompany us on the ship and for a week up in the mountains, leaving us there for several weeks longer.

In Japan we travelled from the port at Yokohama to Tokyo, then on by train up into the Japanese Alps to beautiful Lake Chuzenji. It was such lovely scenery, surrounded by high mountains, thickly wooded with all kinds of different trees. On the shoreline of the lake were only a few buildings that were hotels and some others that were owned by embassies in Tokyo whose staff used to come there for their summer vacations.

At first Archy and I stayed at the foreign-style hotel which was very old-fashioned and had a stuffy British atmosphere, which I found most depressing in such a place and setting.

We found a delightful Japanese hotel further along the shores of the lake. I moved in there with JoJo and the baby-amah after Archy had left, and it was enchanting.

It was a typical Japanese style inn, all built of wood with attractive sculpting and mouldings on the outside, and the roof turned up in pagoda-fashion. The entire front of each room consisted of sliding windows where one sat and was always able to see out. The walls inside were made of thick opaque paper and could slide. In fact, the size of the rooms were easily adjustable by either removing a whole wall or sliding in an extra one to make it smaller.

The floor was covered in *tatamis*, a special Japanese padded matting, and the size of the room is determined by the number of *tatamis* on the floor. At nights we slept on layers of *futons* (quilt-like mattresses) with several quilts to keep warm.

There was a niche called a *tokonoma* where a slim vase with a solitary flower in it was displayed and a lovely scroll hung on the wall that depicted a mountaintop emerging through swirling mists and a setting sun glowing hazy orange through the clouds below. The proprietor told me that the scrolls were changed at different times of the year so that they would be appropriate for the season.

I had to be careful about my bath-time if I wanted to have it in privacy. The usual time for the guests to take their bath was around six o'clock in the evenings, when they all had a friendly reunion sitting together in the communal bath. The system was to disrobe in the first room and proceed into the next room where there were taps on the walls and little wooden tubs on the floor for washing oneself. Then you proceeded on to the main bathroom, to take a seat in the big sunken bath in the middle of the room and exchange the day's gossip with your companions!

It was most friendly, but I preferred to be on my own. So I would go in at five-thirty and have a nice soak, though I did find the water almost unbearably hot. The bath attendant had a way of popping up through the floor where he attended the fire that was burning under the big bath.

Summer 1937. In the second year that we were there, JoJo was 18 months old. The miniature size furniture in the rooms suited JoJo perfectly. There was a low table in the middle of the room where our meals were served, and a minute dressing table with a mirror and tiny drawers, just like a doll's set. This kept him occupied for hours, pulling out the drawers, looking at himself in the mirror and striking all sorts of poses in front of it.

In the centre of the little table was a sunken charcoal fireplace. It was always full of ashes, which could be heaped on top of the glowing charcoal to keep it alight, even when it was not in use. If I wanted to make myself a tiny bowl of green tea, it was so easy to heat the little kettle after I had scraped off the ashes.

When the *nei-san* (servant) came to make our food, JoJo thought it the greatest fun. It was all prepared under his nose, at just the right height for him to lean on the table and try to put his fat little fingers into everything. All the *nei-sans* adored him and there was great competition to play with him.

The hotel owner was a most charming Japanese gentleman who adored JoJo. If he heard a bellowing, which happened all too frequently when JoJo was not allowed to have his own way, the proprietor would come rushing up to find out if anything was wrong. I think he thought that I was too severe with him, but the Japanese are notoriously fond of children and make a tremendous fuss over them.

Jojo with the Japanese hotel owner

He was so well taken care of, that I sometimes went off for the whole day, walking in the forest and up in the mountains. There were some woodcutter's paths to follow, and I hardly ever met a soul all day long. If I did, it would be a peasant wearing the traditional loose blue or black short jacket with a large Japanese character, in bright red or white, stamped on the back.

They were always so friendly and beaming, and I knew enough words to wish them good day, or tell them the time. I never felt in the least nervous, even though I was so far away from any village or people.

One day I walked three quarters of the way around the lake. I then took a track that led up through woods and into rather wild rocky countryside. I hoped it would lead me to a little hot-springs resort at Umoto, where I had heard there was a nice hotel.

As I walked up I saw so many snakes lying curled up on the narrow path ahead of me, basking in the warm afternoon sunshine. I managed to get myself a bamboo stick that I split at the end and held in front of me as I walked, tapping the ground. As I approached each curled-up snake, the noise would make it slither off into the thick undergrowth.

On my walk trying to avoid the many snakes

At one time on the path in front of me I counted eleven of the poisonous adders! I must confess that I was tempted to turn back, feeling quite frightened to proceed, but it was getting quite late in the afternoon and to return was many hours longer than to continue towards Umoto. I finally made it, but it was a horrid experience.

When I reached the hotel I was more than thankful, as I was very, very tired. I told the proprietor about my walk and he was amazed. Looking at a map, he showed me where I had been and calculated that I must have walked seventeen miles!

The hotel was really beautiful, very ornately carved both outside and in. The public rooms were enormous with very lovely coffered ceilings in fine wood. There were many beautiful Japanese screens and scrolls hanging on the walls and lovely porcelain jars with flowers and plants in them. It must have been a very fashionable place for the Japanese gentry from Tokyo to come for a cure.

I was also thankful to be told that there was a bus that left for Chuzenji in another hour, and while waiting I had a most refreshing mineral bath. The natural hot water came pouring out of the rock wall on one side of the bathing area.

Afterwards I sat on the lovely veranda overlooking the beautiful garden, eating bean curd cakes with a little bamboo knife, and watched the people below.

The colourful kimonos, never two alike, were gorgeously embroidered and woven in the finest silks, and were tied with sashes at the waist.

One night after I had gone to bed I heard the sound of drums and chanting, drifting across the lake. I got up and hung out of the window, listening and wondering what it was all about. I could detect a glow in the darkness that came from further along the shore, where the lake curved. I knew there was a large temple there, at the base of the sacred Mount Hee-ay-San.

The night was cold and dark, and the temple was quite a long way off, but I was irresistibly drawn by the beat of the drums. So I put on my clothes and went out to see what was going on.

When I reached the temple, I saw torches flaring all around the courtyard, throwing a flickering light upon hundreds of figures. They were swaying in unison, dancing in a vast circle around a high centre platform. Upon it sat the musicians, beating their drums and playing various other strange instruments. The people were chanting as they danced and it was a most stirring sight. As the rhythm got into my bones, I wanted to join the dancers, but I was afraid I might be intruding on some religious rite so I thought it was more prudent to remain in the shadows. Afterwards I discovered that it was a harvest festival and thanksgiving of sorts. The proprietor said it would have been all right for me to join in.

Another evening, which may have been a continuance of the same festival, there were thousands of little bright candles set floating upon the lake. They gradually drifted past the hotel, towards the river, flowing swiftly over a cliff in a beautiful waterfall. It was really a fairy-like scene. Later on that same night, I saw from my window tiny lights, flickering and bobbing, but this time slowly climbing in zigzags up and up the sacred mountain. I wished I was there with them.

The scenery all around Chuzenji was so very beautiful, with the lake stretching from beneath my window for several miles until it curved gently out of sight. The tree-clad mountains were taking on glorious autumn tones of gold, russet and vivid red. They entranced me and I longed to explore them all.

Sometimes the proprietor would take me out fishing on the lake before dawn. We would wrap up in warm clothes and an oilskin cloak, and set off in his long flat-bottomed punt. But he did not use a pole to move it, as the bottom of the lake was far too deep. He used a single oar at the back of the punt to *yeulow* (the Chinese and Japanese way of propelling their craft through the water by twisting the oar). When I asked if I could try it, he laughed and said, "If you please, but you will fall in the water, because it is very difficult and you will lose your balance". I tried and luckily did not fall in.

He would have several fishing rods out at the same time and at the top of each was a tiny bell that jingled if a fish was nibbling at the bait. Very practical, particularly when it was impossible to watch the rods in the darkness. He caught lovely rainbow trout, as well as other fish, and put them alive into a large wooden cage under the pier back at the hotel. There they could swim around, and were always available to be caught in a net and cooked in a most delicious batter called *tempura*. They would then be presented on the bare dining table, where we sat on the floor cross-legged, with a reverance as if it were an offering as well as a meal.

This remote area of Japan has such a wonderful feeling of spirituality and philosophical integration with nature. Simplicity and insight is the basis of their *zen buddhism*, so profound that even a foreigner like myself could become enlightened.

Shipping picks up in Hong Kong

Both times that I went to Japan with JoJo for the hot summer months of 1936 and 1937, I went without Reidar. He was far too busy to even contemplate leaving Hong Kong, even briefly.

Shipping was just beginning to pick up again after so long in the doldrums of the worldwide Great Depression and the political problems going on in China. Mr. Wallem's three *Viking* ships were partnered with Jardine Matheson's – *The Princely Hong of the Far East* – the largest British trading firm in East Asia. The *Vikings* were tramp steamers trading up and down the China coast, from Hong Kong to Kwangchowan in the south, to Swatow Fuchow, Amoy and Shanghai, and up as far as Chinwan Tao and Dairin in the north.

The captains were Norwegian, as were most of the officers, but the crew was Chinese. They carried all kinds of cargo and many hundreds of passengers. We heard that many people preferred to travel by the Wallem ships, rather than other Jardine vessels, and commercially for freight, these ships were also very popular. The Chinese shippers seemed to have extra confidence in the tough Norwegian captains, who boasted they could "smell" their way up the river to Shanghai.

Since time immemorial, there was always the danger of piracy at sea. Armed guards were carried, but all too often, this was not sufficient to thwart the pirates. Amongst the hundreds of deck passengers coming on board at one of the small coastal ports, there would be a band of pirates. Once the ship was well out at sea, at a given signal they would emerge from below decks and take possession of the bridge, after the guard had either been overpowered or bribed. Sometimes they would remove wealthy Chinese passengers to be held later for ransom, as well as the cargo.

After having robbed the whole population of the ship of whatever valuables they had, the pirates would rendezvous with their accomplices in one of the many pirate hideouts along the coast. Their great ocean-going junks were armed and could carry several hundred people. Two of the most notorious and dangerous places for pirates were very close to Hong Kong, called Mirs Bay and Bias Bay. People travelling on the coastal vessels were always glad when they were safely past those infamous bays. Many times the Wallem ships were pirated, even when the whole bridge was enclosed with bars and guards on board.

As the shipping market became revitalized, Reidar became busier than ever. He was recognized by all the main shipping firms as being a very clever shipping man, not only in the Far East and on the China Coast, but by firms in England and other countries who did business with Hong Kong. His shipping knowledge and judgment were greatly valued and sought after. He was offered good positions in other shipping firms, with better salaries than he was getting, but he remained faithful to Wallem, despite the fact that he was then being treated very badly by him.

While I was away, Mr. Wallem had come down from Shanghai and was creating difficulties all around. It was partly due, Reidar thought, to the fact that many of their Chinese clients preferred to deal with him rather than with Mr. Wallem. Reidar was always courteous and patient and understood them better, whereas Mr. Wallem was inclined to roar at them if their opinions differed from his own.

If he wanted to build a new ship, or put a proposition to the HSBC bank, which involved borrowing a large sum of money, Mr. Wallem would then generally send Reidar to lay the project before Sir Vandeleur Grayburn. Then if it were turned down, Mr. Wallem would not suffer any "loss of face". But Reidar nearly always succeeded, and was often told by Sir Vandeleur that it was only due to the confidence he had in him that he would agree to any proposals. Mr. Wallem was both pleased and annoyed at the same time, as he must have been jealous of Reidar's position with the bank.

When I returned from Japan in 1936, I found Reidar in a very exhausted state, physically from working so hard throughout the long, extremely hot, humid summer, and mentally because Mr. Wallem was being so horrible to him. They would sit opposite each other at an enormous desk at the office, and Mr. Wallem would not say a word to Reidar all day long. It was a miserable situation. When Reidar got home from work in the evenings, he was so mentally distressed that he had to go and rest for an hour or more on his bed, and relax his frayed nerves.

Everybody was more than thankful by the time Mr. Wallem took himself back to Shanghai again. He continued to be nasty by writing disagreeable letters, constantly finding fault with the Hong Kong office and accusing the office of stealing their Shanghai clients. It was true that many of the Shanghai ship owners were coming to Hong Kong and asking Reidar to look after their ships for them, but when they were former clients of the Shanghai office the Hong Kong office shared the commission with Shanghai.

Then one day, so unexpectedly, Mr. Wallem packed up his bags, emptied the company's bank accounts, and left Shanghai for Europe, never to be seen again in the Far East!

We were all stunned, and at the same time incredibly relieved. He maintained contact once in a while, having final word in major descisions, but left Reidar in control of Hong Kong and Sverre Frøland in control of Shanghai. Mr. Wallem then opened a new office in his Norwegian hometown of Bergen, which was a world away from us, so we had great plans for our future.

The Battle of Shanghai

For nearly 100 years, Shanghai had been the most important British settlement on the North Coast of China that was built in the image of England and had attracted investments from most major powers. The vast Shanghai International Settlement had swelled to more than half the size of Manhattan and now was a diverse cosmopolitan city that offered diplomatic and personal security to foreigners by having proper government, banks, office buildings, schools and hospitals, as well as elegant homes for those who had made their fortunes there.

For those living in the International Settlement, primarily Japanese, British and Americans, their sheltered lifestyle revolved around developing industries and business contacts, and enjoying a grand social scene that rivalled anywhere in the world. Maintaining "business as usual" was their primary goal no matter who controlled China.

By the summer of 1937, the Japanese military was quickly gaining ground in Northern China and was now in a fierce battle to control Shanghai. War was officially declared between the two countries. During the fierce three-month battle, Chinese and Japanese troops fought in downtown Shanghai, and overhead Japanese planes dropped their bombs, but the International Settlement was left a war-free zone that did continue its business as usual.

Western Powers were unwilling to condemn Japanese aggression into China because of their preoccupation with the unstable political situation in Europe that was closer to home, and the fear of undercutting western commercial investments in Asia. It was also thought that Japan could not sustain a war against the United States, the greatest economic power, and the United Kingdom, the greatest colonial power, so appeasement and isolationism permeated the international community.

Generalisimo Chiang Kai-shek, the Chinese nationalist supreme commander, was advised that China must be prepared to fight alone for at least two years of the war. He then had to prove that the conflict between China and Japan was a major war, not a collection of "incidents". Based on this political strategy, Chiang Kai-shek ordered his troops to fight to the death in an attempt to arouse international sympathy and cause the international community to adopt measures that would help China and to place sanctions on Japan.

In the end, Shanghai fell and China lost a significant portion of its best troops, while also failing to elicit any international intervention. The battle produced nearly 400,000 troop casualties and thousands of civilian casualties, making it one of the bloodiest battles in Asian history. After securing control of Shanghai, the Japanese army began its advance towards Nanking, the Chinese capital.

Hong Kong becomes the busiest port in Asia

On returning from my second summer in Japan, in 1937, I learned that the Japanese had taken much of Northern China, and Shanghai was now in their control. The months spent on remote Lake Chuzenji in Japan were blissful to me and I had such appreciation for the Japanese people and their culture. They had treated JoJo and me so kindly. The news of the brutal war waged by the Japanese forces against the defending Chinese troops and the civilian population in Shanghai seemed so out of character and hard for me to believe.

At this time more and more Chinese ship owners were moving permanently into Hong Kong as they felt that as a British stronghold it was a safer place for their businesses and their ships, instead of China where the Japanese navy could seize any ship under Chinese flag. These ship owners began to register their ships in the name of Wallem & Co. in Hong Kong to fly under the Norwegian flag, to avoid seizure and also have more favourable terms with the Hongkong and Shanghai Bank through Reidar's relationship with them.

Reidar was also the first shipping man in the Far East who thought of putting ships under Panama flag by opening a registered office in Panama City under a Wallem subsidiary he named Pan-Norse Steamship Company. The Panamanian law did not require the ship's officers to be British or Norwegian, as did British and Norwegian registered vessels. The Panamanian registered ships could have a foreign captain and Chinese officers. This was more economical and with a number of other reasons making the ships easier to manage and therefore more profitable to run. To begin with, other shipping firms in Hong Kong were amazed and critical, then envious when they realized the results. Finally they followed suit.

Many of these Chinese who wanted to buy a ship would come to Reidar for his advice and guidance, and then propose that he himself should take a share in the ship. This was generally because they felt that if Reidar had a share he would then obviously give preference to that particular vessel. Sometimes Reidar agreed, but only with very few owners in whom he had confidence. Mostly he did not want to get involved, as these vessels were often owned by a whole group of people who, as often as not, ended up by disagreeing with each other and causing a lot of trouble.

Reidar's main client and good friend was Hajee Mohammad Hassan Nemazee, an Iranian born in Bombay, who had many fine ships and was prominent in the tea trade, as well as in the Muslim pilgrimage to the Middle East. It was also suspected that the Nemazee family traded Iranian opium that was legal in their country with Chinese smugglers, where it was prohibited. However he made his money, he had lots of it. Soon he became a very important person in our lives.

Mr. Nemazee

Another important client of Wallem & Company in Hong Kong was Robert de la Sala, of John Manners & Company, a Portuguese for whom Reidar had the greatest respect concerning his shipping flair. The three of them purchased various ships together.

This was at the time when Reidar was beginning to make a little more money than when we started our married life. He used to say that one of the reasons Mr. Wallem was being so disagreeable to him was that he felt Reidar was now getting too much money. Because of the improvement in the shipping market, and Wallem & Company in Hong Kong beginning to show good profits, Reidar also benefited accordingly. Mr. Wallem freely stated that if he had known that things were going to develop so well, he would never have given Reidar his partnership on such advantageous terms.

Chiefly due to the war, the Shanghai office was not as profitable, and unfortunately the bitterness between the two offices became a source of real concern for Reidar.

The Great Typhoon

The Great Hong Kong Typhoon on 2 September 1937 was one of the worst typhoons in Hong Kong history killing 11,000 people with winds up to 240 km/h (149 mph) and a tidal surge of 9m (30 ft). As Hong Kong was one of the busiest ports in the world at the time, many ships in the harbour were destroyed including 18 ocean liners and other large vessels. Thousands of Chinese died in their floating "junks" and simple village homes were swept away by the heavy winds, waves and tidal surge. Many travellers and their crew died at sea on ships that perished under these extreme conditions. Iris was returning by ship from Japan at the time it hit Hong Kong.

When I returned to Hong Kong, we arrived in the wake of a horrible typhoon. We had experienced very heavy seas on the way down, but fortunately for us the typhoon had changed course and veered inland before it reached us.

Ships grounded during the Great Typhoon, 1937

When we approached Hong Kong, the scene as we entered through Lyemun Pass, was quite incredible. Several large ships, including the Japanese *Asama Maru* and the Italian *Conte Rosso*, ships of over 20,000 tons, were up on the rocks near Sheko. The B.I. ship, *Talamba*, lay on the other side of Lyemun, also up on the rocks with her back broken. It was the most amazing sight.

I was up on deck before dawn, as we passed Waglan, so excited to be coming home and to see my beloved husband again. In the semi-darkness I could not understand why there was such a blaze of lights on rocks, where I knew there should be nothing at all, being inaccessible from land. As the sky lightened, the shapes of the ships were discernible, but all a peculiar angles, the decks ablaze with lights. I was told afterwards that this was to discourage pirates.

So many ships were destroyed and people killed

In the harbour dozens of ships lay in extraordinary places where they had been blown by the fantastic force of the wind, even with their engines running full speed and their anchors down. Several ships were blown onto Stone Cutters Island and one had its prow high up on the breakwater in front of the post office. Of course innumerable junks had been sunk, even at the anchorage. A tremendous amount of damage was done to buildings all over the island, and the squatters' settlements suffered badly in Kowloon. There had been torrential rain, as always with a typhoon, which had caused enormous landslides and blocked many roads.

Reidar, who had Archy staying with him in our flat, told me what had happened to them during this dreadful night. I was forewarned not be too horrified at the state I found the flat in. When the 'Number Ten' Signal was put up and they heard on the radio that the typhoon was headed for Hong Kong, they made themselves comfortable in the sitting room with drinks and smokes, and prepared for the night's vigil. The two of them sat there listening to the wind's ever increasing fury. Bed was completely out of the question. The rain was being driven against the windows in torrents, on three sides of the sitting room. Twigs and branches from the trees nearby were hurled against the glass.

Finally the two men decided to move out of that room, as it was too exposed, to the kitchen at the back. The servants were in their own quarters and better protected. Reidar sat on the stove and Archy lay on the ironing board, both smoking endless cigarettes and quaffing numerous whiskeys, listening to the roaring rage of the elements. Then they found they had no more cigarettes!

They knew that something had happened in the sitting room, as the wind was shrieking under the kitchen door and there were ominous bangs and crashes on the other side of the wall. It would have been really dangerous to open the doors.

However, after an hour or two, the wind seemed a little calmer and they judged it to be the "eye of the typhoon". During this time the wind dies down and it becomes quite quiet, but soon the wind starts blowing again in the opposite direction and as strong as ever. Archy decided to risk it and go into the sitting room, hoping to retrieve some cigarettes that were on the table. But the wind was still blowing tremendously and he was nearly knocked over by it as he opened the door. So he was forced to drop down onto his knees and crawled into the room!

Nearly all the windows had been blown in. The whole room was a shambles and the rain was falling in torrents. Broken glass was all over the floor and the chairs and sofa were under a deluge of water. Archy, however, undauntedly pursued his perilous course, braving the flying glass and drenched to the skin. He finally managed to get hold of the cigarette box and crawl out of the room again. His main thought was whether the cigarettes were too wet to smoke or not. They were not, so the risk had been worth taking!

The Japanese "Rape of Nanking"

After the three month battle to capture Shanghai, ending in November 1937, 50,000 Japanese soldiers marched to Nanking, the Chinese capital. Unlike the elite troops at Shanghai, the Chinese soldiers at Nanking were poorly led and loosely organized and they withered under the ferocity of the Japanese attack. On December 13, 1937, after just four days of fighting, Japanese troops smashed into the city with orders to "kill all captives", and proceeded to murder at least 200,000 out of 600,000 civilians and soldiers who had surrendered.

The Japanese felt they needed to eliminate the 90,000 Chinese soldiers who had surrendered. Most were systematically transported out of the city and executed by machine-gun fire or bayoneted, while others were tied-up, soaked with gasoline and burned alive. The Japanese soldiers prided themselves with killing contests of who could execute the most prisoners with their swords, the results of this grotesque game were published in the daily newspapers.

Then the Japanese soldiers turned their attention to the women of Nanking, as they were given free rein to do as they please with the remaining Chinese population. More than 20,000 females (with some estimates as high as 80,000) were gang-raped by Japanese soldiers, then stabbed to death with bayonets or shot so they could never bear witness.

The six weeks of carnage would become known as the "Rape of Nanking" and represented one of the worst atrocities during the World War II era, in either the European or Pacific theatres of war.

However, political leaders and news sources in both America and Britain remained overwhelmingly silent, as Japan was an important trading partner and buyer of western products. America had helped to modernize the Japanese military by sending mercenary advisors to train their troops, and it sold Japan goods used in their imperial expansion, including oil, steel and arms. Japan was a large income source that benefitted those in power from acting against Japan.

China was also so large and had a weak and fractured government in a civil war against communist groups, so many international governments figured that if Japan were to control China, it would keep the country out of the hands of the Communists and present an order that would benefit relations with the West. Western businesses in Shanghai and Hong Kong seemed to agree.

World news was also focused on the situation in Europe where Adolf Hitler was rapidly re-arming Germany and expanding the borders of the Nazi Third Reich.

Unfortunately, Japan would soon grab the world's attention in a big way.

Our New Family and Home at Skyhigh

Europe revisited

April 1938. The war in mainland China was becoming more and more violent and destructive. We heard many shocking news reports of the horrific treatment the Japanese were inflicting on the civilian population in Nanking. They say that many thousands of Chinese soldier POW's were executed and thousands of women have been raped and killed by the Japanese soldiers. How could it be? Why have the Japanese lost their honour and respect for life? It is simply dreadful. Hopefully this war will come to an end soon, but it seems very unlikely.

It was decided that I should go to Europe with JoJo and visit Reidar's parents in Bergen. Although Europe was having problems with Hitler, we thought it was a good opportunity to make a visit now in case things worsened in the future.

Once again Reidar said it was impossible for him to get away from the office—there was far too much work. But as Archy was due for his long leave, I was thankful that I would be able to meet him in France and we could spend most of the time together. It would be like old times, before I was married, except that now I had my darling little son with me and his *amah*, the faithful Ah Ping.

It was awful leaving Reidar, knowing it was for such a long time. Each time I went away on my own, it became more and more of a terrible wrench to leave him. I thought what an utterly stupid idea it was of mine to spend time away from each other every year. I was doing just that, but was thoroughly miserable about it.

We were travelling on a fine new Danish ship called the *Jutlandia*. I had to change ships in Singapore and can remember how horrified I was, as we approached her by launch in the harbour and saw that she had no funnel at all, just masts. It seemed wrong for a ship not to have a funnel. It made me feel even more unhappy and insecure!

But the *Jutlandia* was very nice once aboard, and the voyage was quite a pleasant one until a few days out of Marseilles, when little JoJo became very ill. The doctor did not seem to know what was wrong and said he thought it was probably something he had eaten which had upset him.

When we arrived in Marseilles we were met by Archy with his lovely open Ford touring car. We planned to drive along the coast to the *Villa Castel Blanc* at Cap d'Ail, but as JoJo was so ill we went to a hotel and called a doctor. He assured us that it was a tummy upset and that in a few days he would be fine. So we went on to Cap d'Ail.

It was nice to be in our own home again, even though our parents were noticeably absent. They had decided to go to Paris just a few days before our arrival. Typical of our mother, and very hurtful, as naturally I was longing to show them their first grandchild. In the circumstances, however, we thought it was just as well that our mother was not there. She certainly would have been no help.

My poor little boy was so miserable and he had a constant low temperature. I was afraid to give him any solid food, even though he begged for it. And this proved just as well as when I called a British doctor from Monte Carlo, on checking him said that it was peritonitis and that he would have to be operated on immediately. My heart seemed to stop at this announcement, but we drove him straight away to the hospital in Nice.

The following two weeks I shall remember to my dying day. It was so ghastly, not knowing whether our beloved little son was going to pull through. I would sit by his bed hour after hour holding his tiny hand. I felt almost though I was holding onto his life.

My poor Reidar waited with such anxiety in Hong Kong for news, and yet I didn't know what to tell him. Nobody knew what would happen. He visited the post office looking for telegrams many times a day and even in the night, and then would dread opening them for fear of dreadful news.

Our poor little JoJo had tubes into his tummy draining his intestines and yet that doctor had a very brusque way of treating him which made me so angry. Thankfully there was a very sweet English nurse there who was a wonderful help throughout our stay.

Afterwards, when JoJo was well enough to leave, Archy and I decided we did not feel like staying on any longer at the villa at Cap d'Ail but preferred to go to England. JoJo still had to have another follow up operation to have his appendix removed. His tummy had to be completely drained of all the poison, before it was safe to remove it. We decided that we would drive north in easy stages, and the very nice English nurse agreed to come with us, which was a big relief to us.

Jojo recovering from surgery in the English countryside

We were anxious to be in the country because of JoJo and were lucky in finding a charming little antique farmhouse. It was set amongst fields, on the slope of a hill in Kent, a little way off the main road to Maidstone. It was called Hognore Farm, on Pilgrims Way. There were no animals or farming there, just a pretty rustic garden and then the surrounding fields. It was ideal for us and so attractive, with thatched roof and old oak beams. We banged our heads on these with great regularity going along the uneven passages.

Life was peaceful at Hognore Farm with good food and the lovely early summer weather. We used to spend most of the days in the pretty garden, and all of this did JoJo so much good. From looking like a frail little ghost when we arrived, he soon put on weight and got back his rosy cheeks. It was heartbreaking to think that he had to go into hospital so soon again to have another operation.

Reuniting with our brother Vean

Our other brother Vean joined us there. We had not seen him for so many years while he was working in Canada. He had always been so interested in agriculture and farming. Hoping to gain experience in this, he went to work on a very big farm in Saskatchewan.

It was a very hard life. During the long dark winters he had to be out in all kinds of weather, with temperatures reaching down to 20 or even 30 degrees below freezing. The cattle had to be fed. When he finally decided to leave, the owner refused to pay him for all the months he had worked there. There was nothing Vean could do. It was a bitter blow to him, but that made him more determined than ever to get away.

Eventually he got work on another farm, where he was treated better. When he had made sufficient money, he decided to visit our parents in France for a short while. They had been begging him to return. But when he did, they more or less held him prisoner for the next two or three years. They played upon his feelings, telling him it was his duty to stay and help them in their difficult situation. They could no longer afford to live in the style they were used to. They were both suffering from ill health and advancing years, and could not allow him to return to Canada again.

They kept him there as caretaker for the villa at Cap d'Ail, which they had been unable to sell. It was essential to have it occupied so that it could be shown to prospective buyers at any time. Also the large garden needed continuous upkeep and Vean was particularly good at that.

The hermit-like existence he was forced to lead for months on end, when they were away in their flat in Paris or Monte Carlo, was truly soul destroying for a young man of thirty with no friends.

During the hot summers he would go down the steep cliff path to the little pebble beach far below and go for long swims along the rocky coast. That was really his only pleasure, as he could never afford transportation elsewhere.

However, after two years Vean became so desperate, he made up his mind that he simply had to get away somehow. He decided to go to Marseilles and join the French Foreign Legion. But without money for the fare, the only way was to walk. It was a distance of nearly two hundred miles along the coast!

He eventually reached the outskirts of Marseilles, but was suddenly taken ill during the last two days. In great pain, he forced himself to struggle on until he could find an hospital. But before he could reach one, he collapsed and was discovered in the early hours of the morning, lying face down on the floor of a tram at the terminal. The police contacted the British Consul in Marseilles and he called our parents.

After sometime in hospital, where he was operated on for appendicitis, he was sent back to the *Villa Castel Blanc* and trapped in the same dreary life as before until he was able to join us in England in the summer of 1938.

JoJo and Vean sharing a glasss of milk

We were so thankful to have finally been able to get Vean over to England with us. But it was the finish of our relations with our parents. Archy was so incensed by our mother's behaviour that he told her on the telephone what he thought of her. I never saw either of my parents again.

In the meantime it was my turn to get involved with visiting very sophisticated London doctors in their luxuriously-furnished consulting rooms, complete with tiger skin rugs on the floor and one in particular who put his arm protectively around my shoulders, after having examined me, and said, "My dear, you have so many things wrong with you. You are like a museum!" And that was the beginning of being passed from one doctor to another. I spent three weeks in a hospital in London where I nearly died of a hemorrhage. It was very frightening.

JoJo and his amah, Ah Ping, in Europe

When I eventually was better, little JoJo had his operation. The surgeon was called Sir Lancelot Barrington-Ward! Such a fine name, but it suited his personality perfectly for he was an exceptionally fine man. He operated so smoothly on JoJo that he recovered very quickly with no more complications.

The Norwegian family

After all the miserable weeks spent in hospitals, for both JoJo and me, we had another 'ordeal' to face, but of a very different kind: our first visit to my parents-in-law in Bergen! I was rather dreading it, without Reidar. Again my wonderful brother came to my support and accompanied us there by ship along with his fine car.

As the ship drew alongside the quay, we were at the railing, scanning the sea of faces below. I was wondering whether we would be able to pick out members of Reidar's family from photographs I had seen. The whole family was there and gave us a most wonderful welcome. Archy was also accepted into the bosom of the family, and made himself very popular immediately with my mother-in-law and the four brothers.

My mother-in-law was a very large woman, with a heart to match. She and father-in-law both adored JoJo and spoilt him outrageously, despite my pleas not to do so.

With Reidar's father and mother

All the uncles and aunts and cousins, of whom there were vast numbers, wanted to meet Reidar's foreign wife and his little son. There were so many parties given with long speeches and long hours of sitting around which I found completely exhausting.

Everybody was overwhelmingly kind and my mother-in-law was particularly wonderful and loving to me, because I was Reidar's wife and she said he was her favourite son.

Hiking in Norway with Reidar's father and brothers

It was sad that Reidar could not have been with us. Before the advent of flying, it was the custom for Far Eastern firms to give their employees 'long leave' every seven years, with only a week or two of 'local' leave given each year. Reidar had returned to Norway from America, then went to Shanghai at the age of 22. He had visited them years before, but now the war prevented him going on leave and they both died before it was over. He never saw his parents again.

Back in Hong Kong

1939: As the Japanese tightened their grip on China and other parts of Asia, more and more Chinese shipowners were moving permanently to Hong Kong and asking Reidar to manage their ships. Under these circumstances, matched with his ability and determination, business was booming. Between their own vessels and all the others for which they stood as "straw-owners", Wallem was managing a total of fifty-five ships at the time of the Japanese invasion of Hong Kong in December 1941.

Back in Hong Kong again, after eight months separation, I found Reidar busier and more involved in his business than ever before. Wallem & Co. had moved into much more spacious and very fine offices in the new Hongkong and Shanghai Bank Building, the tallest and finest building at that time. But he was working so hard that we were often not able to go for our lovely Sunday walks together.

The new Hongkong and Shanghai Bank Building

Reidar worked and worked. He had to be at the office all day, seven days a week. At times I used to wonder whether he had lost the ability to relax and enjoy playing for a change. But I realized that he loved his work; it was such a challenge and it fascinated him. Also, when I sometimes begged him not to work so hard, he would say to me "You wait and see. In the end you'll be glad because I shall retire when I am fifty-five and enjoy life, when all the others will still be slaving away."

Skyhigh

We had decided that we could now afford a home of our very own, much as we liked our lovely flat at Pokfulam. Not without some trepidation we bought an enormous, old fashioned, gray and dreary-looking house on Victoria Peak.

It was built on a basement that had walls one yard thick, and these saved our lives during the war, when the bombing started. All the windows and doors that gave onto the closed-in verandas were heavily shuttered. It was dark and thoroughly depressing.

But it was in the most wonderful position perched on a little peak all of its own called Mount Gough, with the most spectacular views in all directions. It was the highest house on the island of Hong Kong. We later called it *Skyhigh*, which it was.

People thought we were mad to have bought such a dreary place. But we engaged a Belgian architect who had lots of good ideas and rebuilt it on the fortress-like foundations. In the end the result was a tremendous success.

I loved *Skyhigh*, not only for its beauty, comfort and spaciousness, but most of all, for the breath-taking views on all sides. The house was so light and bright with enormous windows all around and open verandas. There we could sit and look out over vast distances of sea, islands and far away mountains.

We had incredible views of the whole city of Hong Kong and the harbour 1600 feet below us; the Victoria Peak, then to

Kowloon and the New Territories with the mountains of China in the background; over to Lantau Island, Cheung Chau Island, the Lemmas; down on to Aberdeen and around towards Repulse Bay.

Our driveway came up sharply below the enormous retaining wall, which supported the main garden and the house. We really were perched sky high and I used to feel we were in a little world all of our own.

I never minded when the clouds came down and enveloped us, blotting out all the rest of the world. Sometimes the clouds lay like a thick fleecy eiderdown covering everything below us and we remained in brilliant sunshine. It was all so beautiful, with the ever changing moods of the elements. It was a fantastic outlook of which we never tired.

Saigon, Manila and Singapore

In September 1939, shortly after the Invasion of Poland, war was declared by the Allies against Germany, but no Western power committed to launching a significant land offensive. It was referred to as the "Phoney War" and seemed very far away for the people living in the Far East.

Reidar was taken ill one night, and the doctor announced that he had an acute attack of appendicitis that would have to be operated upon immediately.

Reidar had been working so hard, without any leave at all for the five years of our marriage. Work at the office had assumed such proportions, that he dared not stay away for even one whole day. Telegrams with offers of charters arrived at any time, day or night. Work in a shipping office never stops, so he was completely exhausted and run down.

When Reidar was able to leave the hospital, the doctor insisted that he should get away for three weeks for a complete rest and change, or the consequence may be grave.

We went off on a lovely Dutch vessel, the *Boissevain*, to Saigon and then to Manila. As it was wartime, with the *Phoney War* going on in Europe, our ship had to be "blacked out". This was quite exciting.

Much to Reidar's own surprise, he enjoyed the journey enormously. We finally had time to relax together, sitting in the sun and swimming in the pool on deck, with fresh ocean breeze and views out to the horizon. A stark contrast to his busy office! He did not worry too much about the firm managing to survive without him.

But when we disembarked in Manila and went up in the mountains to Baguio, he did not feel at all well. The height of 4,000 feet was too much for him, so we returned to Manila for a week. We then went on to Singapore where we stayed for a while, and later took a small British vessel back to Hong Kong.

Our darling little son was waiting on the pier to greet us, with his amah and some friends of ours. As we waved excitedly and shouted greetings to him, a passenger standing next to us remarked, "Is that little boy really your son? We all thought you were a honeymoon couple!" We had spent most of the journey in our cabin, and when we were on deck, I couldn't keep my hands off him!

War in Europe and the German invasion of Norway

On April 9th, 1940, Germany invaded Denmark and Norway. The invasion of Denmark lasted less than six hours, the shortest military campaign conducted by the Germans during the war.

Norway never surrendered to the Germans and participated as an Ally in the war, rather than as a conquered nation. King Haakon fled and represented "Norway in Exile". Against the might of the Germany, however, the Norwegian Army capitulated, although Norwegian armed forces continued fighting the Germans at home and abroad until the end of the war in 1945.

Much of Norway's local shipping fleet escaped capture by the Germans and took refuge in Allied ports. Norway then nationalized the entire Norwegian merchant fleet of more than 1,000 vessels and 30,000 seamen, becoming the largest shipping company in the world under the name "Nortraship". Nortraship instantly became crucial to Britain's fight against Germany.

Later during the war, Reidar would manage Nortraship's Far East operations and be knighted by King Haakon. Nortraship was credited for giving a major contribution to the Allied war effort, but it wasn't without great sacrifice. By 1945, 706 ships were lost to enemy action, along with the lives of nearly 5,000 Nortaship seamen.

It was a few weeks before Christmas of 1940 when we moved into *Skyhigh*. We had a lovely party on Christmas Eve, Norwegian style. The young men from the office and some captains who happened to be in port all came and enjoyed a "home" feeling. JoJo received far too many presents, from all the kind "uncles". I wore a black velvet dress with a wide lace collar which fell in a frill down the front and hid my pregnant condition quite effectively; it looked very pretty I was told.

Ingrid "Ingeling" is born

By January 9th, 1941, I was very tired of waiting for the arrival of my baby. I remember being in town shopping, then taking the Peak tram up to the top and getting into a sedan chair to be carried up to the house. I had been told that the bouncing motion of the chair might help things to get moving. Then I had a hot bath before going to bed. Sure enough, a little while later the pains started and we quickly drove to the hospital.

Our darling little daughter Ingrid was born just before midnight. We had both been longing for a girl this time. It was as if fate was being almost too kind to us; I was almost frightened at the overwhelming happiness we were being blessed with. I kept thinking to myself, "It is too wonderful to be true. People aren't meant to be so happy. How can it last?" It lasted for less than a year, and then the war came to Hong Kong, just 11 months later.

In that year of 1941, life in Hong Kong was very gay; parties and horse races, Chinese dinners, the usual charity dances and shows, launch picnics and swimming. Everybody seemed to be carefree, despite the growing rumblings from the war in Europe, which had passed from the *Phoney War* stage to far more serious events.

The Annual Race Meeting in Hong Kong lasted for five days. Most businesses came to an almost complete halt during that week. Everybody went to the races. The Chinese are tremendous gamblers so that the attendance, even in those days, was of many thousands.

It was very festive with all the ladies in their best dresses and the military band playing between the races. Most of the big boss *taipans* of the large firms had their own boxes, where they entertained their friends to lavish luncheons. There was a constant flow of drinks from the moment of arrival, around noon, until well past the last race at six in the evening.

Reidar at the racetracks

Reidar was in his element. He was fascinated by the whole business of racing and horses. His own horses did well, and he would visit the paddock and discuss form with the trainers and various owners.

We also did a lot of entertaining at home where we often sat on the small open veranda overlooking the harbour. The millions of lights of Hong Kong and Kowloon were spread out far below like a vast carpet of jewels, and when the moon came up over the mountains beyond Lyemun Pass, it was a sight never to be forgotten.

The glorious view from our veranda at Skyhigh

June 23rd, 1941. The news of Germany's invasion of Russia came as rather a bomb shell, in spite of all the rumours and talk that had been circulating for some time. Nobody seemed to really believe it would happen. But it was good that the Russians were fighting and so the Germans would expend a lot of their resources. But most people seemed to think that Russia would not be able to hold out very long. And now, of course, there was no Siberian route to Norway.

My father was in Paris then, my mother had died shortly after the war began. We got news of him eventually through the Society of Friends, a Quaker Society that had connections in Marseilles. We had tried to send him money through the French Consulate to begin with. Then he died just before the war ended. It was terribly sad, as he was ill and old. He must have been so dreadfully lonely in the flat they used to have, where I stayed so long on my own before I ran away from them. He and I were very close to each other then, until I realized that my mother was jealous, so perhaps it was better that I left.

At this time a group of young Norwegians arrived in Hong Kong. They had escaped from Norway and made their way across Russia, to Turkestan and then to Canada. There they joined the forces of Little Norway that were training there. These boys, who were all of prominent families, some of them sons of wealthy ship owners, certainly had made a sensational journey and were indeed courageous.

The Norwegian Consul, Wesman, told us that they arrived with hardly any clothes and in a very low state altogether. Reidar said that he would pay for any clothes they needed. Then the Norwegian community, and others, set about entertaining these young heroes in a great way. We gave a lunch party one day, then took them on an all day picnic to Castle Peak another day, and finally had a buffet supper party for them.

With five servants in the house – cook, boy, coolie, baby amah and wash-amah – plus two gardeners and, in later years a chauffeur, entertaining was a comparatively easy matter.

When we had a big party it was also very easy to get extra help. With regard to glassware, crockery, or even table silver, these could be borrowed by the staff on the spur of the moment from a nearby house with no trouble at all. Quite often a somewhat amazed lady would find herself eating off her own dinner service, while being entertained by another hostess!

On June 27th, 1941, a glorious sunny day, we were going on board the *Wing Fook* (one of Mr. Nemazee's ships) with a group of friends in the afternoon to see the result after she had been all refitted and done up.

The ship was lying out in Kowloon Bay, and as the launch approached her from the aft, I suddenly gave a shout of surprise and excitement at seeing her name. *IRIS* was painted on her in gigantic letters! It was such a thrill, as I had not the tiniest idea of such a thing happening. Everybody had known it for weeks and was bursting with laughter at my excitement. We all had tea and inspected the whole ship and afterwards celebrated with champagne.

The *Iris* traded throughout the war years around the coast of India and further afield. The Captain had his wife living on board and they were very happy. They frequently went to Calcutta and became good friends with Archy and his Norwegian wife Gerd who were now living there.

Throughout that summer we had several near misses with typhoons. I always found it rather exciting when the first signals were hoisted, but we were apprehensive at *Skyhigh* because of the large windows all around the house, and the exposed position right up on top of Mount Gough.

The gardener, *fah wong*, and the coolie would struggle with putting up wooden shutters from the outside, generally in a raging wind already. They also put all the pots of flowers, lining the driveway and entrance, in a sheltered place.

As the typhoon approached and the winds increased in force, ships would move out of the harbour to safer anchorage. With the high wind and seas, sometimes they dragged their anchors and bumped into other vessels, piers or bunds. When the 'Number Ten' signal went up everything stopped. Everybody was supposed to be battened down and under proper shelter. All the junks and sampans crowded into the junk typhoon shelters. The Peak tram stopped running, and most people tried to get to their homes before it was impossible to do so.

Generally the typhoons were accompanied by tremendous deluges of rain, causing terrible landslides. So it was dangerous to drive during these times. Reidar generally managed to get home before things got too bad and it always felt cozy having him there instead of at the office. We would celebrate with a drink before lunch and watch the rage of the elements from our spectacular position.

At times it was quite terrifying, seeing the black clouds that seemed almost solid, sweeping in through Lyemun Pass and obliterating from view everything below. The clouds would approach us on the same level as *Skyhigh*, and the wind would howl intensely.

Very soon another much more deadly threat would fall from the skies and alter the course of our lives.

The Battle of Hong Kong

General Maltby, commander of the British garrison in Hong Kong, felt that war with Japan was inevitable, yet the War Office in London was reluctant to mobilize more troops to Hong Kong since they were needed in the fight against Germany.

By December 5th, 1941, the Japanese concentrated over 60,000 battle-hardened troops eight miles from the Colony's frontier. Hong Kong had 14,000 troops in a mix of British, Canadian and Indian forces, but they lacked the Japanese combat experience of an army who had been at war with China for eight years.

The Eve of War

On Saturday, December 7th, 1941 the throngs at Happy Valley Race Course seemed as overwhelming as ever and completely concentrating on the all-important and absorbing business of placing their bets on the horse races. An outside observer would never have dreamed that a war was going on right at that very moment at Hong Kong's doorstep. The sun was shining brightly. The band was playing and all the luncheon guests, in the boxes overlooking the lively scene, drinks in hand, animatedly discussed the situation—but not with much sense of dire urgency.

Reidar was able to have an important talk with Sir Vandeleur Grayburn, as we were lunching in his box. He told Reidar that he was being kept informed of all the very latest developments of the fighting beyond the New Territories, and that there really was a strong hope of the Chinese army arriving in time to prevent the Japanese from taking Hong Kong.

There was also a plan to fly out the Governor, Grayburn, and some top Hong Kong executives. It was important they should not be captured by the Japanese, if the worse came to the worst and Hong Kong fell. He said that Reidar would be among those who would be evacuated, because of all his shipping connections and the importance of being able to keep supplies coming into Hong Kong. Reidar felt that this was slightly encouraging, if it really could be believed, as there were so many incredible rumours flying about.

We had only been living in our lovely home at *Skyhigh* for just over one year when our world changed completely.

The Japanese invasion of Hong Kong begins

On December 7th, 1941 (the 8th in Hong Kong), Japan announces that it is at war with Great Britain and the United States.

In a surprise attack, Japanese dive-bombers, torpedo planes and fighters mercilessly ravage the unsuspecting American fleet at Pearl Harbour. Seven US battleships and 200 aircraft are destroyed, and 2,403 Americans killed.

Simultaneously, the Japanese attack American-ruled Philippines, Thailand and British Malaya.

Meanwhile at the same time in Hong Kong, 36 Japanese fighters drop out of the sky over the harbour. Within minutes Hong Kong's entire air force at the Kaitak airfield – just 3 torpedo bombers and 2 amphibians - are destroyed, giving the Japanese total air supremacy over the British colony.

Six Wallem ships are immediately seized by the Japanese, while 27 of their other vessels escape to Australia and India to be managed later by Wallem's London agent, Lambert Brothers, for the duration of the war. The Norwegian staff of the Shanghai office are classified as "unfriendly neutrals" by the Japanese, but are not interned. Their business comes to a complete halt.

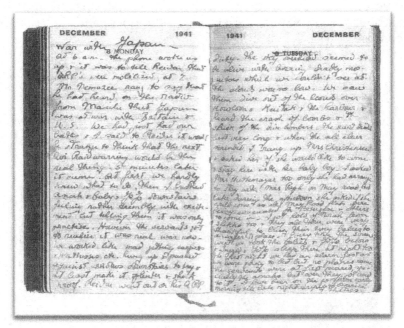

My war diary during the Battle of Hong Kong

December 8th, 1941. At 6 a.m., the phone at the head of our beds awoke us. It was to tell Reidar that all Air Raid Precaution (A.R.P.) Wardens had been mobilized. A few minutes later Mohammad Nemazee, our Iranian neighbour and great friend, rang to say that he had heard on the radio from Manila that Japan was at war with Britain and the U.S.

I had said to Reidar how strange to think that the next time we would hear the air raid warning, it would be the real thing. Five minutes later it came!

At first we hardly knew what to do. My tummy turned upside down and my heart pounded rather noticeably. Then I bustled the amah with baby Ingrid and small John downstairs into the basement playroom. I was feeling rather trembly with excitement, but told them that it was only another practice. However the servants soon got to realize that now it was real war.

We worked like mad getting carpets and mattresses downstairs, which we hung up and pushed against windows and doors, trying at least to make the playroom splinter and shock proof.

Reidar went out on his A.R.P. duty. Overhead the sky seemed to be alive with buzzing deadly mosquitoes, which we couldn't see, as the clouds were so low. But then we saw them

187

dive out into the open over Kowloon, Kaitak airfield and the harbour. We heard the shriek of dive-bombers and the crash of bombs.

Japanese bombing raid over Hong Kong

The workmen, who were building our green houses, were slowly coming up the steep drive. They gazed with vague interest at the bombers and the clouds of dust thrown up by the bursting bombs, and then lazily got down to their work.

When the "All Clear" sounded, I rang up Karin Lisbeth Christensen and Lisa Huttemayer, the young wives of Danish shipping colleagues of Reidar's living in Kowloon on the other side of the harbour, and asked if they would like to bring their two baby boys over and stay with us. She was very glad to, as her husband was in the Volunteers and she was alone in her flat. The May Road flats and others were being evacuated for the Portuguese and many other people, coming over from Kowloon.

So I drove the small car down to collect her. She only had a suitcase full of her baby's clothes and food, and no clothes for herself at all. When the bombs had started falling around her flat in Kowloon, she had run with her baby out into the foothills, together with hundreds of Chinese. There she had stayed, terrified and bewildered, until some officer had told her to go home. Her husband was also in the Volunteers.

I rang up Norah too, in Sheko. She didn't even know we were at war and had heard nothing of the bombing. She said she would prefer to stay at Sheko, but later she also joined us, with her tiny baby and Scottie. John, her husband, did not want her to be alone out there and thought the Peak would be the safest place. I got them all fixed up quite comfortably and lent Lisa Huttemayer some clothes. We were supposed to have had eleven people billetted on us, but we had not heard nor seen anything of them as yet.

Every time the siren went off we took the babies below. None of them had their baby beds with them naturally, so I fixed them up with baskets. We put them all in a row on top of the ping-pong table.

There were so many things to be organized including baby bottles, food and baths. Bed linens for everybody was quite a problem too. We were all thankful when we were able to relax for a few moments before dinner and sit in front the fire with a drink.

December 9th. *The outnumbered British forces fight desperately to hold the British-held New Territories and Kowloon on the mainland across the channel from Hong Kong Island.*

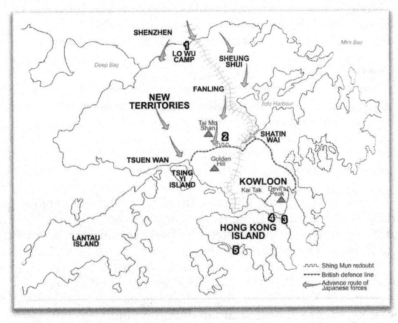

Last night we were going to bed dead beat when the siren went off. John and Ingrid were sleeping downstairs already with the amah, but we had to cart the other babies down in their little baskets. However no planes came over.

This morning while we were having breakfast in the veranda room, the sirens sounded their alarm again. We could see the planes coming in over the sea from Waglan direction. We opened all the windows, grabbed our babies and went down into the basement.

Stonecutters Island was bombed a great deal during the day because of the radio station and the gun emplacements there. Also Kaitak was still a target, although we heard that in their first raid yesterday, they had destroyed the few miserable aeroplanes we had there on the ground.

The servants were at first scared, especially the *amahs*, but they got used to it eventually. Our workmen still came, but allowed themselves to be rather more distracted from their work. I couldn't help laughing when I looked out of a window, during a raid and saw them sheltering under a minute palm tree, interestedly watching the antics of the planes overhead.

December 10th. No night raid, thankfully! We were able to get some rest although there was a lot of shelling and distant gunfire in the New Territories. We had our daily breakfast raid and finished our meal in the shelter.

Norah carries her baby around, strapped to her back in Chinese fashion. She says it is good practice and always best to be prepared. She is also going on nursing her baby for as long as possible, in case of difficulties in obtaining milk.

I tried to get down to town with Reidar. He wanted to go to the office and I needed to get some provisions. What we get is quite inadequate for such a large household. Reidar also gets a loaf of bread each day from the A.R.P.

We set off in the small car, as the other car was commandeered together with the driver elsewhere, but we were stopped by the siren. We watched the dive-bombing over Aberdeen and Mount Davis. The planes swooped low over the reservoir bombing away.

In town I was able to get tinned food, but there was another raid while I was in the shop. It was crammed with Chinese and there was no bread left. In most shops cash is the rule.

Naturally all of us mothers are most concerned about baby foods. Thank heavens we have quite a lot of vegetables in the garden and the hens are laying.

It is impossible for people to come over from Kowloon now, so these girls are lucky to be here—I hope. They have occasional phone calls from their husbands. While Lisa was talking to her husband today in Danish, a voice cut in and said that if they did not speak in English, they would be cut off.

The news about the fighting is so varied. There are all kinds of rumours and one does not know what to believe. The Japs are supposed to be advancing along the Castle Peak road and to have taken many of the outlying defenses beyond the Kowloon hills.

Surely they will be stopped in the hills. We have seen for ourselves, during our walks there, how many pill-box bunkers there are on every height and pass. But we do know that the sound of the guns draws nearer every day. It all seems so unreal still. Hong Kong at war!

December 11th. There were no air raids during the night, but constant shelling from our side. We could hear them whistling over the house and then crashing somewhere on the New Territories. I couldn't sleep because of a cold and earache, and Karin Lisbeth's baby cried most of the night.

Stonecutters Island was shelled for hours and heavily bombed too. We saw them diving over it time and time again. They seemed to score many hits, but still we can observe no real damage. Each time a salvo is dropped, the gun at the end fires back defiantly. It gives us a thrill of pride.

Then this afternoon they went for the naval yard just below us. Dozens of shells fell right into the middle of the tiny basin, where four small vessels were tied up. But in some miraculous way no damage was done. We saw one of the naval boats move out of the basin and steam slowly, oh so slowly, out into the harbour, with shells falling thick all around her. But luckily she was untouched. We wondered what the men on board felt like.

There were many air raids too and we watched the planes dive-bombing over the Standard Oil tanks and the Hong Kong

Electric. They also dropped a terrific salvo just in front of the Mathilda Hospital on the Peak.

Our anti-aircraft guns are always in action. It is so tantalizing to see the tiny puffs of smoke all around those venomous planes, but they never hit them. If only we had some fighter planes.

Our billetted guests have still not arrived, but I have been busy blacking out the dining room, to be able to use it as a bedroom. It is quite a business with all these big windows. I have also been putting away our silver things, as Mr. Nemazee says our house may perhaps be taken over by the military because of its unique position.

The news of the loss of the battleships *Prince of Wales* and the *Repulse* in Singapore shook us a lot as they were of great importance to our Eastern fleet.

December 12th. The shelling is coming nearer and nearer, all over the harbour and around the naval dockyard. The ferries have been bombed already.

All the ships anchored out in Kowloon Bay are being scuttled. It was sad to see them all keeling over or burning. I feel so fond of ships. This was to prevent them from falling into enemy hands. The junk harbours have been blocked by sinking two riverboats across the entrances.

All sorts of rumours are flying around. It appears that Kowloon is being evacuated and all troops brought over to the Island. Depressing news. Kowloon is full of rioting, looters and Fifth Columnists, militant Chinese who favour the Japanese.

There is a good deal of trouble in Hong Kong too. The police have announced that anyone showing a light at night will be fired upon. They have told all wardens to be on the lookout for Fifth Columnists, as 150 of them are reported to have been landed on the Island.

Hong Kong is surrounded

December 13th. *On the mainland, the New Territories and Kowloon are lost to the stronger Japanese forces. British, Canadian and Indian troops retreat to Hong Kong Island. The shelling and bombing of the island continues. The London Daily Mail writes: "Britain's loneliest outpost – the fortress of Hong Kong – is today fighting for its existence against the full weight of Jap military, naval and air power... The island must depend on its own recourses, with little or no hope of relief". However, a demand for surrender by the Japanese is rejected.*

Last night we heard a lot of shooting and machine gun fire down in the town, and shouting too. We saw red lights across the harbour, which sailed and bounced over the water. They must have been expecting attempts to land.

In the middle of the night there came a terrific explosion from the town. We heard today that a ship had blown up in the harbour, full of explosives, and it had broken many, many windows in the town. We spent a lot of the night on the roof, watching all these happenings, but the last part of the night was quiet and we slept thankfully.

Today has been a day of uncanny calm. There was no breakfast air raid or any shelling. Complete quietness reigned, which was rather disturbing. Thick fog enveloped us and we seemed to be living in another world. These days our Peak fog is welcomed!

All sorts of rumours, as usual, come to our ears. The Kowloon troops are all over here, and so many casualties. Friends among them. The Chinese army is coming down from Canton to fight the Japs from the rear. That seems to be the only thing that will save us as we cannot hope to get help from anywhere else.

Mr. Nemazee rings us up every few hours to give us the latest news. Now he says that a launch, with a white flag and two ladies and some Japanese officers, has come across the harbour. A dispatch rider went to Government House and returned, then the launch left again. We are all hoping desperately that there will be no armistice. We cannot stop so soon. We must go on.

We have got two of our billettees now, Mrs. Dyer and her little boy of five. They are quite comfortable in the dining-room. But I can see that she is unhappy at being without news from her husband for so long, and now he will not know where she is. She had to leave most of her belongings behind, as did the others. The small boy seems to be rather prone to being sick. Thank heavens Reidar is here so much. I feel so terribly sorry for those other girls.

December 14th. Our side was shelling a lot from the Peak, and the Japs were returning it. The top of Victoria Peak took a great battering, aiming for the radio masts there, I suppose. They were shelling a position above Magazine Gap, uncomfortably close to us.

British artillery gun battery

At noon Reidar and I went down to town, as he wanted to go to the office, and I to try and buy what I could. Our rations are hopeless. We got no meat at all today. If it wasn't for Hersehend and Palmertz, who are in the food control, bringing us some meat, butter and cheese, we would have had to fall back entirely on our tinned food supply.

Hong Kong was an extraordinary sight. All the shops were closed. All plate glass windows that were not smashed, were plastered all over with strips of paper. There was no traffic excepting military lorries laden with troops, and cars camouflaged with nets and leaves. There was a queue of literally thousands of Chinese lined up around two blocks, waiting for food. I was able to buy cigarettes and chocolates, and some things through the iron grill of the dispensary. The shopkeepers are so afraid of looters.

In the afternoon the fog lifted and the sun appeared, and raiders too. We had a very heavy bombing attack with groups of bombers diving right over the Peak. I took my movie camera up on the roof and took pictures of them without Reidar knowing I was up there. At times it looked as though they were coming straight for us. It was rather terrifying.

Many bombs fell near us, and the servants ran out on the hillside in fright. Some Sikh policemen came up and asked us to control them in future, as they would only be making themselves targets for machine gunning.

Showers of propaganda leaflets came down, mostly addressed to the Indian troops, urging them to throw off the yoke of the "tyrannous British" and join with the Japanese who were their friends.

Japanese propaganda leaflet calling for surrender

At night we saw a great fire burning down by the shore beyond Repulse Bay. It spread up the hillside like a beacon for enemy planes and ships. It must have been sabotage and it made us boil with rage.

Bomb damage on Victoria Peak

December 15th. It has been one week since the war here started. The night was wonderfully peaceful and restful again. The Japs do not seem to care for night raids, or maybe they just find them unnecessary. The poor troops must be thankful for a rest.

Our first air raid came before breakfast. It was a perfect day with brilliant sunshine. The beautiful hills and valleys stretched away below us with the sparkling sea and hazy blue islands beyond. The planes came diving right over the Peak. Evidently they meant more serious business today as there were continual alarms all day and constant shelling.

They kept shelling the gun position in front of the Canossa Hospital, half way up the Peak. From our house it was like a ringside seat. We saw the Indian soldiers there working frantically, with the greatest bravery, while the shells fell thick around them. We marvelled at how they could hold out so long. Eventually that position was evacuated, and we saw them taking away the gun. But it was unclear whether it was put out of action or not.

They bombed and shelled gun emplacements up here too, very close to us. The house shook most uncomfortably. To see the planes coming roaring down, seemingly straight for us, was distinctly alarming.

Reidar and his Chinese Wardens have to try and watch where the bombs fall; our house is certainly ideally positioned as a lookout. But they have to take shelter at times, and not expose themselves to machine gunning.

Now we are all very blasé, excepting Lisa and the *amahs*. I go about my house jobs as usual, and today I was so busy that I hardly noticed the roar so close overhead and the thundering crash of bombs.

The food problem is certainly a big one. With our rations being almost negligible, we would be in great difficulties if we had not laid in stores. Already tinned milk and sugar are very scarce. The servants too are very worried about their rice. However Reidar has managed to get a sack of it which ought to last some time. Another concern is that our water supply is being drastically rationed.

December 16th. We awoke to find that no water had been running into the tanks, consequently the toilets would not flush. It was a shock. Water is one of the most essential things of all. It made me very angry and I adopted an attitude of "Pff !! What is a little matter like that!" when the servants came moaning to me.

We got the gardener to dig a big pit up on one of the little terraces beside the house. There was a spade left there and a mound of loose earth. Each bathroom had a couple of flower pots in it and a jar of sand, taken from the masons.

The *fah-wongs* have to go down the hill to Mr. Nemazee's old property to fetch water from the well there, and the *amahs* go with them to do their washing.

The barracks on Victoria Peak were being heavily shelled. We watched them landing into the hillside below at first, throwing up clouds of earth and vegetation. Then they seemed to hit the buildings. At first when the clouds of dust cleared, the walls still seemed intact. Then suddenly great gaping holes appeared, until the whole front of the building was falling to pieces.

The British themselves have already blown up the whole block of Bank flats, just behind the barracks. We were told it was because that building was obstructing their gun aim. They did it at such short notice, that the poor inhabitants did not even have time to pack a suitcase with essential things.

Mount Davis artillery bunker

We watched the bombing of some small naval ships in Aberdeen harbour. Several of them were sunk. Also some terribly heavy bombs fell on Mount Davis. I thought of Claude Burgiss there, having been married for just five days.

Palmertz, a jolly and spirited Dane living in Manila who was caught in Hong Kong when the war started, and Herschend, a Danish businessman and long-time friend of Reidar's, both arrived late in the morning, bringing with them a tremendous leg of veal and a whole box of Kraft cheese. It was refreshing to see them. They are always laughing and joking, like a couple of merry Father Christmases, always arriving with parcels.

Mr. Christensen arrived too, quite unexpectedly, and Karin Lisbeth was so thrilled. He was dirty and hungry, and I am sure tired too, although he looked much tougher than usual in his soldier outfit. I was sorry we couldn't offer him a bath.

We had an uproarious tiffin lunch with acquavit and beer. I had opened several tins for the occasion so we had plenty of good food. I desperately want to do anything I possibly can for these chaps, who were so happy-go-lucky before, and who are now fighting grimly with their lives at stake.

When Johann, another Norwegian shipping friend, came up yesterday afternoon for a few moments, I felt a pain in my heart to see him so haggard, tired and highly strung. He told his wife Maritza that they had not had any proper sleep since this whole business started, and the food they got was very poor. All I could do was to give her a packet of biscuits and a slab of chocolate for him.

December 17th. *Churchill had given the order to hold Hong Kong at all costs. The second Japanese demand for surrender is flatly rejected, but the odds are heavily against Hong Kong without China's army coming to their aid.*

During the night there was a lot of firing across the harbour. I got such a shock yesterday when I looked at Kowloon through the binoculars and saw Japanese flags hanging out of the windows, all along Nathan Road.

This morning heavy bombing and shelling started very early all over the Peak. We stayed down in the shelter for hours. All the *amahs* and the other servants too were in the boiler room next door. We had had no breakfast. Norah was so good with the two small boys and read them endless stories.

At eleven o'clock it stopped and we saw that the naval yard had been hit. The two naval boats inside the dry dock were submerged, only showing their masts. But maybe it was done on purpose.

There was a strange silence as the Japs sent over a peace delegation. Truce reigned until four o'clock. We saw the Jap car stopped outside Government House. Later we heard the Governor had told them that next time he would not even receive them. We felt much better.

Rumours came that Macao had been taken by the Japs. The Chinese army was advancing to the border.

In the evening all the *amahs* left and Cook, who had been down at the market, never came back. Boy's brother left too. Only Ah Tse (our handsome, cheerful and faithful butler) and the two *fah-wongs* have stayed.

We had to send poor Sammy and Lila, our dogs, and Norah's Scottie too to be destroyed, because of the lack of food. It hurt. We kept Odin, because he is such a good guardian. And now the electricity is gone.

The Japanese land on the Island

December 18th. *As the demands for surrender were rejected, Japanese forces cross the harbour and land on the eastern part of Hong Kong Island. Approximately 20 gunners are executed at the Sai Wan Battery despite having surrendered. The Japanese massacre more prisoners, including the medical staff in the Salesian Mission on Chai Wan Road.*

Japanese cross border into Hong Kong

I went down the hill just after dawn to get water from the well. Lisa insisted upon coming too, although I said she wasn't strong enough. But she insisted because she felt so useless. We had an awful business pulling the buckets up the well, as they were so heavy, also carrying them up the hill. We both got cramps, but got them up somehow. The water was so necessary for drinking, washing up, etc., but above all for washing our babies' nappies. There seem to be such endless numbers of them.

We had very heavy shelling and bombing throughout the morning. We were all in the shelter and the babies all bellowed their loudest, all at the same time. At least this helped to distract our attention from the infernal noise going on outside. The raid lasted most of the morning. I was worried as I had so much to do as all the cooking and household jobs needed to be done, and we were now without servants.

The sirens have had such a busy time going on and off so rapidly, that they have got muddled, sounding the "All Clear" many times when we could see the raiders overhead. Finally they gave up, after the Peak siren had been stuck on the "All Clear" for several hours. Then they did not sound any more sirens at all.

The Asiatic Petroleum Company oil tanks, behind the Hong Kong Electric have been hit and the whole sky is covered by a pall of inky black smoke and the air is full of soot. Two bombs have hit the police station too.

It has been such a busy day and we are all dead beat.

The Japanese bomb us at Skyhigh

December 19th. Fighting continues on Hong Kong Island. The Japanese annihilate the headquarters of West Brigade, causing the death of its commander. The fighting and bombing is fierce.

I went down to our well at daybreak with the *fah-wong*. We had put a padlock on it because the water was drying up. There were other wells further away. The Dawson household used it too, as they needed it badly. The morning shelling started while we were still down there.

We spent most of the morning and early afternoon downstairs, as the shelling was heavier than ever. They were trying to get the gun positions behind us, at Mt. Gough Police Station and at Magazine Gap.

I sat under the stairs, where Ingrid slept at night, with Ingrid and JoJo, as well as Mrs. Dyer and her small John. One always hears that stairs are one of the safest places to be under. The other mothers and babies were in the playroom next door.

We could hear the shells falling closer and closer. Then Reidar, the Chinese Wardens, Ah Tse and the Boy all came down. They later all went into the boiler room. Then Reidar made us go into the playroom, where we all tried to talk quite normally through the terrific noise.

Then the first shell hit us. It came through JoJo's room and shattered all the glass in the kitchen. We did not know what other damage it did because Reidar forbade anyone to go out and look. The smell of gunpowder was very strong and there was lots of dust too.

Ah Tse came in after a while and said that most of the kitchen and outer hall had been ruined. Reidar would not allow anyone to go out and get food or anything. We had been in the kitchen just a few moments before cooking the babies' supper.

So we sat in the shelter and waited, looking at the solitary candle. Now that we had been hit, it would surely be the last time. But the shells continued falling all around us. We waited and waited, and the babies cried for food.

Finally I decided to make a bottle for Ingrid on the little spirit stove we kept there in readiness. I was kneeling beside the little table by the door when we received the next shell. It came through the hall and exploded in the storeroom. There was a terrific ear splitting crash and explosion. The door and barricade in front of it were blown into the room. The candle went out. In the darkness, we heard the crash of falling masonry and glass. The horrible choking dust and the suffocating smell of gunpowder and ammonia was ghastly.

Lisa screamed that it was gas. We called all names to find out if everybody was there and unhurt. Then we rushed to the tiny window that was open between the mattresses, and gasped for breath. Ah Tse was holding my baby all the time and was marvellously calm. The other mothers were wonderful too, but poor little Lisa was badly shaken.

We crouched there for ages and shells still came. We heard furniture and walls falling about upstairs. But I felt confident in the thick walls of our basement. Finally we moved outside into the garden, but still under the overhang, to get some air. There we waited until darkness came and the shelling subsided, each mother holding her baby. There was nowhere to sit and Ingrid was very heavy.

The poor A.R.P. Wardens and Boy had been trapped when the worst shell came. Great blocks of concrete from the floor above, had fallen across the door of the boiler room and blocked it. Through all the confusion and suffocating smell, we heard them hammering frantically at the iron bars of the window, trying to get out. Eventually they succeeded.

When it was darker and quiet, some of us took torches and crept upstairs by the garden way, into the guest room.

It was a sad sight, particularly by twilight and the dim blue rays of the torches. JoJo's room was more than half blasted away. The pantry and hall were wide open to the sky. The dining-room furniture, which was in the hall, camphor wood chests, and even the great wooden doors were all broken to matchwood. Only the sitting room, dining room and bar were intact, but covered with dust and dirt. Windows were blown open and curtains fluttered mournfully out into the night.

Bombs fall on us at Skyhigh

We decided the only thing to do was to sleep downstairs, in the part of the basement that was a little room, open on three sides to the garden, as it was the side furthest from the harbour. It wouldn't be safe to sleep upstairs. We couldn't leave the house then to go some other place, because of the curfew. Nobody was allowed on the roads after dark as they would risk being shot by being there.

So we got some mattresses and blankets and put them on the floor. We blocked up the open archways and windows as best we could, using Odin's kennel on one side. We had no food, but we got a bottle of brandy from the bar and shared it with the staff as well. I managed to get some water boiled on the little spirit lamp eventually, and made Ingrid's bottle. The other babies had nothing.

Later that night Reidar and I wandered through the house, looking at the ruins of our beautiful *Skyhigh*. Most of the stairs had been blown away, and the place where we had been sitting with the children a short while before that shell came was entirely filled with great blocks of concrete. Underneath were the remains of the seat on which we had been sitting and JoJo's bed.

In the sitting room, I had to be very strong with myself not to cry. I lit a piece of candle and stuck it on the mantelpiece where it reflected brightly in the mirror. I wanted to leave it burning, but Reidar said to put it out.

We went downstairs by the garden and lay down on part of a mattress, all huddled up with the others, trying to keep warm. It rained and the wind blew hard. Shells whistled overhead and we heard guns roaring in the distance.

In the middle of the night I heard Odin howling somewhere down the mountain. I got up and went to the edge of the garden and called and called him. I was afraid he was injured. He must have run away during the shelling of the house but finally he came up, panting, wet and shivering with fright. Then he lay down half on top of us and seemed to feel better.

Hong Kong forces wear thin

December 20th. *Hong Kong is split in two with the British Commonwealth forces still holding out around the Stanley peninsula and in the West of the island. At the same time, water supplies start to run short as the Japanese capture the island's reservoirs.*

As dawn appeared, we started off from the house, having been upstairs from 4 a.m. onwards with torches, trying to find our most necessary belongings amongst the ruins.

Both Norah and Lisa said they wanted to go to the Mathilda Hospital, where they had heard that mothers and babies would be taken in. The three of us piled the small car with as many of their things as possible.

I did the driving, but it was so dark that it was difficult to see and I was also afraid of shell and bomb craters. I first stopped at Captain Svane's house (one of Wallem's Norwegian ship captains and a good friend) and ran down with Ingrid in my arms. I had to bang on the door for ages before Mrs. Salvesen and Mrs. Bang, both wives of Wallem ship captains, arrived dressed in their nightdresses and looking somewhat alarmed. I just thrust Ingrid into their arms and dashed up to the car again, calling out that we would be coming later. I could not afford to waste a minute as it was getting lighter all the time and shelling would start any moment.

At Mathilda Hospital it was like trying to wake the dead. When finally we did arouse a nurse, she was very unpleasant and hostile. But I had to leave the two girls and their babies there on the front porch to look after themselves. I just had to get back to take more loads from *Skyhigh*.

I missed Reidar, Karin Lisbeth and Mrs. Dyer, who were walking down with JoJo and small John in Ingrid's push chair. So I found myself up at *Skyhigh* alone. I had great difficulty in turning the car, amidst shell holes and fallen masonry etc.

I quickly ran in and grabbed the babies' nappies that were hanging out to dry, some basins and anything else at hand. I couldn't help stopping for a second to look at my boxes of American seedlings, which were just coming up. I had planted them with such excitement.

Meanwhile the *fah-wong* had collected the remaining chickens, 13 in all. I dug out some more tinned food and lifted Lisa's food suitcase and some other very heavy ones onto the car by myself. Then I was off again, just as the shells were starting to whistle overhead.

When I got back again to Mathilda Hospital with the rest of their things, I found Lisa still on the doorstep as they had refused to take her in. They would keep her baby if necessary, they said, but not the mother. They took Norah because she was still feeding her baby herself.

So Lisa and her baby came back with me to Captain Svane's house. Mrs. Dyer went to another house, nearby a food depot, where they said she could stay a few days, as there was too little room in Captain Svane's house.

Japanese army advance

There was very heavy bombing and shelling all day long. We did not feel at all safe as the house seemed so lightly built and shook at each crash. Reidar, JoJo, Ingrid and I were sleeping in the dining room. Karin Lisbeth and Lisa with their two babies were in the tiny study, while upstairs there were four adults and three children. It was a lot for such a small house.

There was more shelling just after we had gone to bed, which seemed to be falling very close to us. There had been a new "Ack-Ack" anti-aircraft gun positioned near us on the hillside during the day. Everybody gathered into our room as it seemed to be the furthest away.

December 21st. Captain Svane, Reidar and I returned to *Skyhigh* at dawn and salvaged some more things, provisions and blankets chiefly. We saw that the house had sustained more hits, with great gaping holes on the harbour side, and the hall was more battered in than ever. The kitchen also was knocked in and there were shell craters all over the front courtyard.

We had torches to find our way about inside. It was so dreary and ghostly creeping about amongst the ruins, seeing things all scattered and broken. The chilly early morning air blew through the house, fluttering the torn curtains and blowing dust everywhere.

Downstairs the smell of wine and wreckage was horrible. Our store cupboard looked a sad sight. Practically every bottle was broken excepting those in cases. We managed to dig up quite a number of tins and two cases of whiskey, one of acquavit, and best of all, I found some more baby food. Fortunately the cases of provisions that had just arrived from America, were up in the drying room and we were able to get them all intact. Food was what we wanted most.

I cut my hands and feet in my frantic efforts to dig things out in a hurry. It was getting lighter every minute and Reidar was shouting for me to hurry, as the shelling had started already and our house was obviously a target.

I drove back alone with the car piled high with things, pots and pans included. Reidar had to go on duty at his post at Bellamy's house. It was not very nice for him walking to and from there four times a day, as the roads beside the War Memorial, Jardine's Corner and Peak Club, were particularly bad spots.

I was busy from dawn till night, washing nappies, cooking food, and looking after babies, all with so very little water. The children huddled under a small blackwood table whenever the bombers came too close. They never cried from fear, but rushed about laughing and shouting excitedly whenever the bombs started falling very close.

Captain Svane's house does not give one any confidence at all. There is absolutely nowhere to shelter and one feels that at the slightest provocation it could collapse on top of us. My only consolation is if it does collapse, it would not be very heavy!

People kept arriving and leaving, bringing all kinds of rumours. The Chinese Army was already at Fanling. Chinese planes, supposed to be piloted by Americans, had been seen over Kowloon.

The news about the Chinese Army, reportedly hundreds of thousands strong, is heartening, but one can not really believe it. Good news these days is so seldom true.

The new *Ack-Ack* anti-aircraft gun near us is making a colossal noise firing and it attracts their shell fire and bombing too. In spite of all this upheaval my chickens laid eight eggs today!

We have heard that the Japs have landed at Happy Valley and Repulse Bay. Now, in the evening, we can hear machine gun firing fairly close, also down at Pokfulam. It is not safe to go even across the road in darkness, because there are snipers everywhere.

December 22nd. We returned to *Skyhigh* again at dawn, although Reidar was violently opposed to it. But Anne Dyer wanted so much to get her things, as she had none of her own clothes at all, and I was determined to get the rest of the salt meat. Captain Svane agreed with me that that was very necessary.

We found the house in a worse state than ever. Our bedroom was half blown away, and all that end of the house, which we had considered safest and most protected by the great rock beside it, was hammered. We could hardly even find where JoJo's bathroom had been, nor the big cupboard at the end of the passage, where all our beautiful hand painted Limoges porcelain dinner service was stored.

It was bitterly cold and miserable. As usual we had to hurry and try to find things as quickly as possible, expecting shells to land on us at any moment. Most of the windows and shutters had gone, but otherwise the sitting room, dining room and bar were the least damaged of all. I wished we could have taken some of those things down into the playroom to try to save and protect them. But there was no time.

As usual Reidar was shouting and threatening to leave me behind. He then went to his post, and Captain Svane walked back carrying two tremendously heavy buckets of salt meat. I took Anne Dyer back to the food depot with her belongings.

Palmertz and Herschend came and stayed for tiffin. Gudrun came from the nurses' hostel, where she and about 30 or 40 other women were stationed. She was in a terrible state of nerves and looked awful. She kept saying, "I'm too old for this sort of thing!"

Their house had been hit on one corner and all the windows blown out. They all had to lie flat on their faces for ages, expecting the house to collapse on top of them.

At tiffin we had acquavit, salt meat and peas that Captain Svane had salvaged from *Skyhigh* "at the risk of his life!" It is extremely useful to have it, as it is almost impossible to buy things from the Peak store. We have not been able to get any rations or bread, but we are still able to get milk. Gudrun left later, in a very different frame of mind, after a good tiffin and plenty to drink!

When Reidar and Captain Sareusen went to try and buy some food at the store, they saw casualties being carried away from Peak Mansions which had been badly damaged by shell fire. A bomb had fallen through several top flats, killing some people and wounding many. One poor woman had her whole face and arms badly burnt.

The shells are falling thicker and faster than ever. One crashed through the front gate, leaving a large crater in the middle of the road just a few yards away. Fortunately these do not seem as large as the ones at *Skyhigh*. But I am convinced, that it is only a matter of time, before we will get hit.

December 23rd. During the night there was a banging on the door. The billeting officer was there with several refugees from Mount Cameron Road. They had been told to get out, as the soldiers were falling back to Magazine Gap, and the Japs were all over the place.

Japanese gunners on the attack

We felt we would have to be on the move again. All the soldiers were backing up to the Peak. It was obvious that this was where the last stand was to be made and where all the fighting would be concentrated.

I told the two girls to pack what they could and to be ready to leave at any moment. The refugees left by car before dawn for town. Magazine Gap was supposed to be a death trap with snipers and machine guns, so they had to make it in the dark.

We couldn't make up our minds whether to go down to Mr. Nemazee's house or not. We heard that Maritza and Sophie Rudrof, a sweet Polish girl Reidar recently met at the A.R.P. headquarters, were there, as Peak Mansions had been

209

abandoned. All civilians were supposed to evacuate the Peak. Reidar had to go to his post, so he just kissed me goodbye, not quite knowing where we would meet again.

We then decided to walk down to May Road, and set off with our babies and as much baby food as we could carry. I put everything into Ingrid's bed, tins of baby food, blankets, quilts, etc., and Ingrid on top. Everyone said I would never be able to get it down the Peak path. It was full of craters, shell holes and dead bodies. But I was determined to do it and not be left stranded without Ingrid's food and other necessities.

Some way along the road we were stopped by an officer. He looked so dead tired, and so thin and weary. He told us it was already too late to risk walking down with babies and children, exposing ourselves to bombs and machine guns, as well as to robbers or looters. He advised us to wait in a nearby A.R.P. shelter until it was night, and then we could walk down under cover of darkness.

Air Raid Precaution bomb shelter

It was a good shelter and gave me confidence, but Lisa and Karin Lisbeth stampeded. They didn't like the idea of their babies being down in that shelter all day. It was so low and claustrophobic, crowded with soldiers and people all day long. They wanted to go to the Mathilda or War Memorial Hospital.

I tried strongly to dissuade them and was very angry, as I knew they had been influenced by two women in the shelter, who took great pains telling them how bad it would be for their babies to stay there. I am sure they did not want the extra annoyance of being cooped up with yelling babies all day. However Lisa and Karin Lisbeth went off with somebody who was willing to escort them.

I stayed at the shelter with Ingrid, JoJo, Mrs. Salvesen and Mrs. Bang and their three children. Mrs. Dyer had left her small John with me. We sat right at the far end of the basement, on the floor. Fortunately we had a mattress for the children and some cushions. I had a clothes basket for Ingrid to sleep in and a candle stuck in a bottle, as it was so dark back there. Eventually Reidar turned up, as all the A.R.P. wardens had been disbanded. I was so relieved to have him safely back with us.

That was our worst day of bombardment. Shells fell thick all around, and the adjoining house was hit. Bombs fell so close, that the noise was ear-splitting. We had to cover our ears with our hands—mine over Ingrid's—as the pressure was so great.

There was only one entrance, which was protected by a pile of sandbags. The small, low windows were stuffed with sandbags too and had bars over them, which I did not like so much. Each time the planes came shrieking down, or the shells whistled uncomfortably close, the soldiers and everyone else would tumble and squeeze in, through the narrow entrance as fast as they could. We remained at the back so as not to get in their way. But the air was heavy at times, especially as a lot of people smoked.

More and more people kept coming in, including many *amahs*. Two were carrying a little fair-haired child each. The mother of one was dead and the other was doing nursing at one of the hospitals. Those *amahs* were certainly wonderfully devoted and brave, but the mother's anxiety must have been terrible.

I was feeling very unhappy myself and sat beside Ingrid's little basket all morning, singing her lullabies, as the deafening row went on. She slept a lot, and in between was very sweet. When the bombs fell, I bent over her to shield her as much as possible with my body. John and JoJo and the other children played together, but were highly-strung and excitable.

When tiffin time came, we dashed to the shelter and back with the food that we could find. It was like crossing a no-man's land, between the two houses, and on each trip we noticed new craters in the ground and damage around.

While I was up at Captain Svane's house one time, there came a particularly big explosion very near. I was knocked sideways against a wall and crouched there with my arms shielding my head, while showers of bricks, stones, glass and earth fell all over the garden.

Captain Svane had just gone up to shave and his bathroom was at the corner of the house that was hit. I was convinced something awful must have happened to him. Reidar and two soldiers came rushing up to see if we were safe. Then I heard Captain Svane's voice reassuring them, as he appeared at the top of the stairs, with one side of his face all soapy, razor in hand, as imperturbable as ever.

We waited a few minutes until, presumably, the Japs had to reload their gun. Then we made another dash for the shelter, laden with more food.

All afternoon the row continued unabated. We saw soldiers arriving, looking so tired and hollow cheeked, and army trucks, guns, lorries and supplies.

Johann appeared and told of all the ghastly carnage going on in the Repulse Bay and Magazine Gap areas. In the Tinson's house on Repulse Bay Road, about 200 men had been trapped, and only about 15 got away. It was said we could not hold out much longer.

I just sat and sang to Ingrid, watching her sleeping and JoJo playing unconcernedly. My brain didn't seem to work very well or think very far ahead.

Late in the afternoon Palmertz and Herschend came and said they could take us down to Mr. Nemazee's house at May Road in their lorry if we came immediately. So we threw all we could lay our hands on into the lorry, lifted the children up, including small John Dyer whose mother still had not put in an appearance. Ingrid and I sat on top of our belongings. I had some blankets to cover over the children in case we had to take hurried cover from aeroplanes or snipers.

We drove as fast as we could, along the road we all knew so well, but found so incredibly different now. The whole countryside looked so scarred and desolate; houses battered, fallen and deserted; great craters in the road and walls collapsed. We all gave a sigh of relief as we passed Magazine Gap corner. It was called "Hell's Corner" and it looked like it too, with innumerable cars abandoned and burnt out, and craters and shell holes everywhere.

We came to a standstill at the end of May Road. The shelling was rather intense and the children were terrified at having to run the last bit to reach the house.

Mr. Nemazee welcomed us warmly and we felt so glad to be there. But we were all stricken dumb with amazement at the sight and sound of water playing in the fountains in the hall and outside in the courtyard. It was strange how Mr. Nemazee had water at both his houses. I was sure it meant good luck.

We, the newly arrived women and children, are all to sleep in the garage, as it is considered the safest place. There are boards raised off the stone floor all around the walls on which we placed mattresses and cushions. It is really very well fixed up.

The rest of the house was full of people. Some from Kowloon who have been billetted here. Others were friends with nowhere else to go. It was nice seeing Maritza again.

December 24th. We had an awful night in the garage. Small John Dyer kept on being sick, and most of the other children were either sick or having upset tummies. As there was no bathroom out there they had to use spittoons. The big doors wouldn't shut and anyone could have walked in on us from the road. Twice I awoke simply terrified at a dim blue light inside the garage that moved right up to me and shone into my face, very close. I don't know what it was. Perhaps imagination but I was certainly very awake.

Mrs. Whitfield is marvellous, supervising the cooking for about 28 people and looking after the supplies that are almost unobtainable. She stands over the kitchen fire for hours, cooking scones and baking breads.

In honour of our arrival, Mr. Nemazee ordered the hot water boiler to be lit, in spite of the shortage and value of coal. And I was to have the first hot bath.

While I was undressing in Mr. Nemazee's bathroom the shelling increased in violence. I thought of all the glass windows and doors which surrounded me and that did not have any paper strips stuck across them. Somehow I could not concentrate on washing myself, but only on getting out of that bathroom as fast as possible.

We did not get so much bombing as we had on the Peak, but sometimes the shelling seemed very concentrated around May Road, and many of the big apartment buildings around us were hit. Throughout the day, whether there was an air raid or shells whistling through the air, the red-haired Portuguese girl strummed on the piano unceasingly.

Palmertz and Herschend, who had left on their job in the morning, came back late with many things from Captain Svane's house piled into our small car, including the cases of whiskey and acquavit that we had brought from *Skyhigh*.

Lisa rang up from the Peak and asked if she could come down to join us. She wanted somebody to go and fetch her. I do not think it would even have dawned upon her to walk down like Karin Lisbeth did, nor would she have had the physical or moral strength to do it.

I wanted to go and fetch her in our small car, but Reidar absolutely forbade me to do so. In the end Herschend went.

I did not want to sleep another night in the garage, so we three young mothers moved to the hall with our babies. Karin Lisbeth and I are sitting by the flickering light of a candle writing our diaries.

Hong Kong falls to the Japanese

December 25th, 1941. *It is clear that further resistance would be futile. British colonial officials and the Governor of Hong Kong, Sir Mark Aitchison Young, surrender at the Japanese headquarters at the Peninsula Hong Kong hotel. This was the first occasion on which a British Crown Colony had surrendered to an invading force. The garrison had held out for 17 days. This day becomes known in Hong Kong as "Black Christmas".*

Christmas Day! Twice during the night there was very heavy shelling. We sprang out of bed, confused and muddled with the crash of guns breaking into our sleep, and spent the rest of the night partly dressed with our shoes on. Reidar went out to the garage and JoJo said to Christen, "It's all right now because Daddy is here."

Last night, when the children were in bed, Mr. Nemazee went into the garage and gave each one a little present for Christmas, and each of the three babies too. He has asked Palmertz and Herschend to buy some things for the children in town, so that they could have at least something, however small, for Christmas. It certainly was not a very festive atmosphere and even saying "Happy Christmas" to each other seemed out of place.

Aeroplanes, bombs and shells whistled overhead on their way to the Peak and we spent long hours in the garage. Some hit houses on May Road. Poor Sophie Rudrof looks so sad always during these shelling and raid periods, but in the evening she sits at the piano and plays and sings. I love listening to her and to Thorne, a New Zealander. He is also in food control and goes around with Herschend and Palmertz, chiefly to act as their bodyguard.

In the afternoon came dead calm and we heard rumours of surrender. We felt horribly depressed, and yet some, I think, were almost glad as it meant an end to all the shelling and air raids. But I felt dreadful. It seemed so awful that a British Colony should surrender to the Japanese.

But if arms and ammunition had run out, it would be hopeless and, without help, futile wasting more lives. The Chinese army was evidently mythical or much too far away to be of real assistance.

Later during the afternoon we heard our guns firing from the position near here, and then planes came over again and dropped bombs. I could not help feeling a thrill to think that we were still fighting. But it did not last long. We heard of white flags flying over various places and the Union Jack being taken down from Government House.

I wanted to write in my diary in the evening while all the others were upstairs. But I just sat there in the light of the candle and could not write. When we went to bed, I was sick from sheer depression and unhappiness.

Days later we heard that this Christmas Day was when the greater part of the Volunteers were killed. So many of those poor men died just as the surrender was being made.

The Surrender

December 26th. Dead calm reigned all day. A horrible depression weighs us all down, not knowing what is going to happen next. The knowledge that Hong Kong is now Japanese—the first British possession to fall—takes a lot of philosophizing.

For the men it is really worse, as they have nothing to do all day and do not know how to occupy their time. They sit and talk, argue and discuss the 'whys' and 'wherefores' of this sad Hong Kong war. They play cards and drink from morning till night around a guttering candle, in the small upstairs hall where Palmertz, Herschend and Thorne sleep.

Those three men drink very heavily, starting in the morning with gimlets first thing before breakfast, then whiskey sodas steadily from ten o'clock onwards throughout the day. Reidar has a few, just because he feels it is not fair that they should polish off all his whisky! But they think that as they have salvaged it, they are entitled to drink it.

We heard that Hong Kong was forced to surrender through lack of arms and ammunition, also lack of water in the city, which is of vital importance. One hears so many different points of view and, of course, so much criticism. But I suppose people have to talk to relieve their tension.

Nobody went out of the house. It was quiet but we did not know what might happen, or how the Japanese soldiers would behave. The first joy of victory could so easily go to their heads, as had happened in Nanking where in the days after taking the city, they ruthlessly slaughtered tens of thousands of war prisoners and civilians, and raped as many women as possible. The city and its people were systematically destroyed with no remorse by their captors. And now they are here upon us.

What will they do with us now that we are under their authority? Will the commanders unleash their soldiers to do as they wish? Unlike when they invaded Nanking, the English and other foreigners are now enemies of Japan, so will be treated as such. It is horrible to think about.

After supper, consisting of soup and rice mixed with dill and herbs, we went into the sitting room with one candle on top of the piano. The room is so big, bare and cold and very depressing. So I suggested musical bumps, and with Thorne at the piano within two minutes everyone was laughing uproariously.

December 27th. There are 27 members of the household so far, and about forty Chinese servants and their families. Nearly 70 people under one roof to feed and maintain! The problem of food rations is a big one. There is plenty of rice in Mr.

Nemazee's store cupboard, as well as potatoes and quite a lot of tinned foods. We brought down several cases of tins from *Skyhigh*, that we had just received from America.

But we have no milk, bread, meat or fresh vegetables, excepting some carrots which I go and pull up daily for the babies. We use them also for the household but chiefly to flavour the rice, with the carrot tops chopped up as well.

When the electricity stopped the meat could not be frozen. There must be tons of it at the Dairy Farm cold storage, which has gone bad.

Most of the window panes had been smashed by a shell which landed onto the veranda, through a pillar which had stopped its force. So the windows were stuffed with cushions and curtains to keep the wind and cold out.

In Mr. Nemazee's room there are eight men. Poor Mr. Nemazee used to live a luxurious bachelor life and now he does not even have privacy in his own bedroom.

I had a proper bath this evening, for the first time in two weeks. It was not very hot and Karin Lisbeth had it after me. I was amazed at how small I seem to have become, and so bony; shoulder blades, ribs and backbone all so knobby; and as I dried myself my skin peeled off. When I appeared for dinner, I was acclaimed as the clean member of the party!

I am writing my diary by candle light before falling into my hard bed. It does not have a mattress, only a box spring and it is very cold. But I wear an old woolen shawl wound around me and a very thick, very tight white polo jersey over my black satin and lace nightgown. I have an old eiderdown to cover my bed. It is a very fine one and so big, but it has splits in many places and when I breathe the down feathers always go up my nose.

December 28th. All the women and children have their breakfast down in the dining-room everyday, while the men, by arrangement of Palmertz and Herschend, have theirs on the veranda. They have all the best coffee and potted meats, sardines, cheese etc., while we have what we can get. Generally that is tea with some tinned milk, if it has not given out already, two scones, some butter or a spot of jam. Mrs. Whitfield always sees that everybody has something before she sits down herself.

Those two men certainly make sure that they are fed properly and like to order everybody about. Lucy, Mr. Nemazee's Chinese housekeeper, just runs in circles whenever she hears Palmertz's voice shouting, "Madame Lucie", and Mrs.

(or "Ma") Whitfield does whatever they ask her to do. I can hear their voices above all others, holding forth.

But they were wonderful in helping us, bringing us food to *Skyhigh*, then to Svane's, then taking us down to Mr. Nemazee's house and salvaging our things. So I forgive them their rather overbearing ways, as I shall always be grateful to them.

Today Ah Tse came to see us and told us that our house had been looted and everything taken, silver, carpets, curtains etc. Poor *Skyhigh*! I can't help feeling rather heartbroken, although I am unspeakably thankful that we are all alive and together.

In the afternoon fifty Jap planes flew over the Island several times and demonstrated dive bombing. They also dropped leaflets concerning changing Hong Kong money into military Yen notes.

Occupied Hong Kong

December 29th. Japs came to the house several times. Sometimes it was officers and other times just soldiers, intent on getting any jewellery, blankets, liquor or anything they could lay hands on.

We heard of Mrs. Wadeson's experience this morning with Jap soldiers beating her up when she refused to lead them into her room, has made us realize how serious things really are.

We seldom go onto the veranda outside our room, as it is overlooked by the road. Whenever we see Japanese soldiers coming down the drive, we always keep in our room. I have hidden my jewels and also films, amongst Ingrid's clothes and some amongst the toilet paper.

It looks as though we might be turned out of the house, as the Jap officers asked Mr. Nemazee why he did not go and live in one of his houses on the Peak. I only wish we were allowed to return to *Skyhigh*. I would gladly live in the basement, whether the place has been looted or not. But Reidar says it is too isolated and would be dangerous.

The Japanese flag flies over the Hongkong and Shanghai Bank

The Hongkong and Shanghai Bank Building, where Reidar has his office, now has a Japanese flag waving over it and all other big buildings have been taken over in town. Everybody is wondering what is going to happen with the British and the Volunteers. Nobody seems to know anything, but we are told they are awaiting the arrival of some authorities to govern the town.

Japanese atrocities

December 30th. This is a day of sad news, hearing of husbands killed and husbands missing. We heard that Sophie's young husband is dead, killed on Christmas day during the final defense with the volunteers. It is a terrible shock and we don't know how to break the news to her. We keep just hoping that it is not true. She is so sweet, affectionate and lovely. Although she is dreadfully anxious and sometimes brakes down and cries, she keeps such a bright outlook on things.

We have heard the ghastly news of what happened at Stanley Hospital, when the first waves of Japanese shock troops swept over the peninsula. They broke into the hospital, murdering Dr. Black, who tried to bar their entrance. Then they dragged out the Chinese and English nurses, beating, raping and mutilating them. Many of them died. Some were friends of ours.

One girl in particular was so lovely, sweet and gentle. She was dragged out of the hospital, under the eyes of her husband, who was wounded in the fighting at Repulse Bay and had managed to get to the Stanley Hospital the day before. She was raped by many soldiers and left dying in the undergrowth. Later her husband managed to find her body and bury it. He was almost out of his mind with grief.

We keep hearing of innumerable horrifying experiences that have happened to people we know. It is like some awful nightmare come true. How can humans endure such indescribable agony of mind and body? They will surely carry the scars on their souls for the rest of their lives. I hardly dare think how fortunate we have been so far.

December 31st. New Year's Eve! I was busy during the day helping Mrs. Whitfield make some sort of a feast for evening. We had four chickens killed, two of mine and two of Mr. Nemazee's. I felt sad about it, but we had nothing else to serve. I made some custard for trifle pudding and put quite a lot of wine in it. (There is a pretty good supply of that.) Thirty people to feed took a lot of food.

We joined all three tables into one long one, and I produced my beautiful long red candles, bought for Christmas at *Skyhigh*. Somehow or other I had them with me. I gathered red poinsettias and Sophie arranged them.

We had *Skyhigh* acquavit, then red wine and finally champagne! Palmertz, of course, made himself "toast master". Everybody was laughing and cheerful. Afterwards we went into the sitting room, taking with us the red candles. Then Thorne played the piano and we danced. But we stopped at ten thirty, because we were afraid of making too much noise and causing the Japs to come and investigate. Each one wished the other Happy New Year, but it was a sad process.

When it came to poor little Sophie we all felt terrible. I couldn't help crying. She is so brave, but is so horribly worried all the time. The fact that we know that her husband is dead weighs dreadfully upon us all. We are just waiting for more official news of it before asking Feahly to come down and tell her. He is her closest friend and the best person to do it. We all dread that time, imagining how we would feel in her position.

Karin Lisbeth and Lisa are also feeling very sad, wondering about their husbands, although they have heard for certain that they are safe, interned at North Point. Karin Lisbeth is a trooper and knows how to philosophize. I admire her for it.

I am hardly ever able to speak to my Reidar alone and, even when I do, I can't help feeling guilty at being so fortunate, in comparison with the others, having him here.

January 3rd, 1942. It is our seventh wedding anniversary. Everybody seems to know about it and congratulate us. For tea Maritza had a cake made, and at dinner they toasted us with red wine. I was looking such a mess all day, spending most of my time with the babies, in the kitchen and looking after chickens.

In the evening I looked at myself in the mirror properly by candlelight, for the first time in ages, and was rather shocked. My face looks so thin and my eyes so tired. I hope that the gaunt look and the damage of lines is not irreparable. And yet in spite of all this, my sweetheart still tells me that I look beautiful. We love each other more than ever.

Lisa and Karin Lisbeth visited their husbands at North Point. They were taken in a car by Pagh and came home quite late in the afternoon, very excited and overwrought with emotion. They were able to talk with their husbands for nearly half an hour. Both men are well, but in need of clothes, shoes and warm things.

So we got together some things then and there, to keep up the girls' spirits. I asked Reidar and he agreed to give his heavy Norwegian shoes to Nils Christensen, also a pullover, my little razor and soap, and some chocolate. They are going to try and go again tomorrow.

Pagh also gave things for Lisa's husband. The Paghs still have their flat and all their belongings, and so have the Necklemans.

January 4th. As Mrs. Whitfield and I were standing in the kitchen the electric light suddenly came on. It was such an amazing sight that we could hardly believe our eyes. To have the Frigidaire and stoves working again was marvellous. But most amazing of all, was to come into the habitually dark and dreary dining room at night, and see the chandelier a blaze of light. But we quickly took out the surplus bulbs when we heard what the charges were going to be.

Outside at night the town seems to have come to life again. The lights showing from the windows of the buildings behind us seem to have some hope in them, after all the weeks of dead blackness.

Mr. Feahly came down from the Peak and broke the news to Sophie. She cried but seemed more dazed than grief stricken. She goes about now trying so hard to be brave and behave as usual, helping everybody, smiling, and the sitting at table for meals. But in her heart she must feel dead.

She loves Maritza and seems to be genuinely fond of Reidar and me too. We want to do all we can to help her, even adopt her, if necessary, if Feahly is unable to look after her. She is so completely alone in the world.

We heard that Johnnie Potter, a British architect friend of ours and husband to Norah, as well as Tim Mackinlay, the two Finchers and many, many others are dead.

Wallem and its ships are battered

Wallem & Co. also suffered greatly at the fall of Hong Kong, both personally and economically. As members of the Hong Kong Volunteers, Fløisand was killed in the fighting, and Ragnvald Reiertsen and Kenneth Nelson were taken as prisoners of war.

The business was forced to halt, but Reidar continues in a state of frayed nerves as he tries to protect the Wallem fleet from capture or destruction. The ships are at risk of falling into Japanese or German hands and used against the Allies, as well as them being torpedoed or scuttled (sank on purpose).

In Shanghai, the Chinese government requisitioned a large number of ships from their Chinese owners and scuttled around 200 of them in the Yangtse River in an attempt to block the Japanese navy from encroaching upon Shanghai and Nanking. No payment was made to the shipowners for the loss of their ships.

Immediately after the invasion of Hong Kong, the Japanese seized six Wallem company-controlled ships, but many others escaped to friendly waters where they would be used for delivering war supplies to the Allies or armed to fight (as seen in the picture above of Wallem's S.S. Utviken with gun turrets fore and aft).

Internment for the enemies of Japan

January 5th. As we were having breakfast, news came that all American, British and Dutch nationals were to report at Murray Parade Ground, with all their belongings that they can carry. They had to make arrangements for the protection of their own properties themselves.

We felt so dreadfully sorry for them. All they carried were the pitifully few things that they hoped to save out of all their worldly possessions, and going—they knew not where. Mothers with children and babies, sick and old people, and we were quite powerless to be of any help at all to them. At any time we could be in the same position ourselves.

Western enemies of Japan head to internment camps

Later in the morning Feahly and Railton came in on their way down from the Peak to go to the office. The first they knew of the news was the sign on our entrance post. Then they turned and went back to the Peak, to pack some things and go to give themselves up.

We tried our best to dissuade them, saying it was much better to wait and see what happened. But they did not want to take any risks for not obeying orders. One never knows with Japs.

Railton has been wonderful and earlier salvaged quite a number of things from our house. Three Tientsin carpets, our beds complete with Beautyrest mattresses, our best lace tablecloths, and many tins of various foods, even wine and champagne. There were also some photo albums.

We felt so grateful to Railton that he should have thought of us and helped us, even when he was in such trouble himself. Actually it is amazing to see how the war has revitalized him. Before he seemed so much older, rather weak and worried about his health, and the strain of the climb up to his house. Now he is full of life, energy and good spirits. He looks ten years younger at least.

When they came down again, on their way to Murray Parade Ground, we hated to see them go, but provided them with a couple of tin bowls and mugs, and bade them a very sad farewell.

It seemed inevitable that all British, American and Dutch property will now be at the mercy of Chinese and Japanese looters. So far we seem to be more or less exempt from their persecutions, but how long will that last. Mr. Nemazee has a document, given to him by the Japanese police, saying that his house only shelters third party nationals. When they come to the house, they leave us alone.

We watched as the Japanese ransacked Major Boxer's flat nearby and all his belongings, papers and fine books were taken away because he was in the Secret Service.

There is a constant stream of looters coming down from the Peak, although we have heard a lot of shooting and seen the Japanese soldiers beating them up. It makes one sick to see all the people coming down laden with other people's most treasured possessions; family silver, lovely cut crystal, valuable carpets, clothes, fur coats, blankets, lamps, plates, furniture and photograph albums. Perhaps many of our things are amongst them.

January 8th. At last I got permission from Reidar to go down to town, as I had to have a picture taken for my pass. I went with Captain Svane, Mrs. Salvesen and Sophie. We were stopped by Japanese soldiers as we came down near the Dairy Farm head office. They looked into our basket and searched Captain Svane, then Sophie and me, but not Mrs. Salvesen. I had my picture taken by Mee Cheong, where we used to get all of our race photos of us leading in ponies. What a change! Then we went to the HSBC bank to try and get forms for our passes.

Japanese troops and bomb damage in downtown Hong Kong

In town it was an incredible sight. The streets had the most desolate appearance. There was hardly any traffic excepting for an occasional lorry load of Jap soldiers or sailors, and a few cars taken over by the Japanese military. Windows were smashed everywhere, buildings were covered with bullet holes, and the street was full of craters where shells had exploded. The Bank had stood up to the cross harbour shelling surprisingly well. In the Gloucester Arcade all the great plate glass windows were broken and all the shops completely bare and vandalized. No shops at all were open.

The worst sign of desolation were the piles and piles of garbage, covered with flies that lined the streets and sides of buildings. There had been no water in town for ages, and so many people were living in their offices. There were 17 living in Larssen's office, the Spanish Consulate, with no running water! The Chinese population had greatly increased too. There was serious danger of disease and epidemics breaking out.

In the Hongkong and Shanghai Bank Building there were thousands of people milling around in that beautiful great hall. Poor, lost, woebegone people, who all seemed still half dazed at their misfortune and wondering what sorrow would next befall them. So many strange, foreign looking faces too, now that the British and Americans had been imprisoned, as if people from an underworld were now coming to light. We saw some Germans too, who had fled to Macao or Canton at the beginning of World War II.

There were a few Bank men, wandering around aimlessly, hands in their pockets, trying to put a bright face on life. People stood about in small groups whispering rumours furtively. We picked up the forms for our passes, then Captain Svane and I went to see what we could buy.

We were held up several times by street blockades. Some important Jap was due to pass that way, so nobody was allowed near. Everyone was herded along certain narrow passages, and if you stepped off the pavement into the empty street, a Jap soldier would thrust his bayonet against your tummy.

All along Queen's Road, from Ice House Street to beyond the market, the street was lined with hawkers squatting on the pavement or standing beside stalls, selling every imaginable thing, mostly looted, at exorbitant prices. The street there was so packed that progress was very slow and difficult.

I tried to get some shoes for Ingrid, as she had worn through and half eaten the pair that Sophie made for her. But I was unsuccessful. We bought some apple rings for the babies, as the few measly fresh apples we saw were terrifically expensive and not good. All tinned food was three or four times more expensive than before. We stopped at King's Dispensary and bought a few things at hopeless prices, through the iron grill.

Food is now an important question for everybody. There are so many thousands of poor people, including white people, who do not know where to get food, as they have no money and have been deprived of all means of earning it. There has been no bread for two weeks or more, no fresh milk, no fresh fish and few fresh vegetables.

We are extremely fortunate to be with Mr. Nemazee, as he has several bags of rice stored away, some lentils, flour and ghee too, which he is able to get through Indian shops. We were very lucky in being able to salvage so many tinned provisions from *Skyhigh*. They are perhaps not the most sensible or nourishing things to have in times like these, such as asparagus tips, artichoke hearts, big tins of fruits, tuna fish etc., but they relieve the monotony of rice, bean cakes and lentils. Having a case of each is very useful for such a household, also two cases each of grape nuts and corn flakes, kept exclusively for the children.

The poor people who are interned in the Chinese hotels, which many were actually brothels, have only two bowls of rice a day. They are going to be moved out to Stanley soon, which has been converted into a huge non-Chinese civilian internment camp.

Reidar saw Noel Croucher, the Canavals and some other of our friends there, but was only able to shout to them up on the verandas. They were cheerful. But it must be ghastly there, particularly for the women and children. Poor Mrs. Cook has four children and a tiny baby there that she is still nursing herself, while her husband is interned in Canton.

January 23rd. Today we have been here one month! We heard that Norway is now on the enemy list and we are most likely to be interned. We just hope it will be in some house, like the Americans were at first, or even at Stanley, where the British are, but not in a Chinese hotel down town.

The weather has been so glorious all month. The heavenly sunshine makes everything seem brighter, but I look up at the Peak and feel sore at heart. Writing now, on the veranda outside our room, everything is so quiet and peaceful in the afternoon sunlight. Someone is playing the piano very beautifully up in Albermore Court, continental airs full of life and laughter, and then the spell is broken by the sight of Japanese soldiers marching by.

The harbour looks so desolate with nothing but the masts and tops of sunken ships to be seen towards Kowloon Bay. Alongside the wharfs are Japanese transport vessels, and each morning early we hear the three hoots of the ships' sirens, as they back away from the wharf to leave. I wish we could be leaving too.

I have been trying to plan what things to take with us when we do have to go. It will probably only be what we can carry ourselves. Ingrid and John's food is what worries me most, and then our bedding is also so important. Still on a glorious afternoon, it is difficult to think of internment and all of its dreary consequences.

A Persian New Year celebration

We have been in a turmoil for days preparing for the Persian New Year here in Mr. Namazee's home. All the women of the household and the servants have been slaving from dawn until late at night, cleaning the house from top to bottom, washing, scrubbing, polishing, beating carpets, cushions, mattresses, sofas, chairs, dragging out ancient pieces of furniture, that seemed as if they had not been moved for years. Even the marble fountain in the hall was scoured, including the graceful nymph in the centre, who had been looking somewhat grubby lately.

Mrs. Bang and Mrs. Salvesen have been going around with their heads swathed in dusters, clad in long overalls, their arms full of brooms, buckets and washing cloths. They have washed the walls upstairs and, as the ceilings were so extremely high, it was quite a job. While Ah Sai (Ah Tse's handsome, strong and cheerful brother) and Ah Tse polished the floors, Maritza and Sophie polished the furniture. I was up on top of a ladder shining up the hundreds of crystal pieces of the chandelier.

In the kitchen terrific preparations went on for days before the Persian New Year. So many special traditional dishes and delicious varieties of sweets, curries and spiced cakes had to be made, and in great quantities as so many people always came to greet Mr. Namazee on this important day.

How he managed to conjure up so much food and delicacies in an enemy-occupied city is a mystery. A few days previously he arrived with some gigantic slabs of confectioner's chocolate, each one measuring about two feet wide by three feet long, and weighing many pounds. Then two Russians came and spent the entire night making the most marvellous variety of chocolates with wonderful fillings.

Mr. Nemazee and Mehdi Nemazee, his cousin who acts as the majordomo of the household, had both explained to me very carefully about all the different symbolical things that had to be laid out on the long table. The actual time that the New Year was due to start was 3 p.m., evidently according to the moon.

We had all been up since the crack of dawn, as there was so much to do with the final preparations for such a large reception. They expected between 50 and 60 people of all nationalities: Indians, Chinese, Portuguese, Russians, Scandinavians, and even some Japanese, who were old friends. All of Mr. Nemazee's British friends are interned.

I was busy arranging the table with flowers and a magnificent embroidered tablecloth. Tall silver candelabra, vases with the sprouting grain and pedestal dishes piled with fruits, formed the background. I placed a bowl of live goldfish in the middle and next to it an enormous punch bowl of cut crystal with a special kind of drink. Then raw fish and the poultry, the bowls of grains, salt and various other things, with platters full of sweetmeats, chocolates, cakes and pyramids of raw vegetables.

I must confess I was rather nervous about the final effect, as I had never arranged quite such a variety of things before for a table decoration, but it was fascinating. However it all took much longer than I had expected. I was just dashing across the hall, still dressed in my ancient slacks and looking decidedly grubby with a large fish in my arms to put the final touch to the table, when the first guests arrived at the open front entrance! I dived panic-stricken behind a nearby screen, wondering desperately how I could make my escape without being seen.

But Mr. Nemazee promptly appeared, hardly even greeting them. He looked at his watch and informed them solemnly, "You are ten minutes too early!" Whereupon the three Chinese gentlemen backed out in confusion, to wait in the garden, until it became exactly 3 p.m. I flew upstairs to change.

Then it was quite a strain spending the whole afternoon being social and making conversation with all the guests. We passed around cakes, but did not dare to take any ourselves, in case there were not enough to go around. We were also trying to keep the children out of mischief and from eating the most fancy things.

In the middle of the afternoon everybody went out into the front courtyard and stood in front of the fountain to have a photograph taken. Mr. Nemazee gave Ingrid and the other two babies a golden half sovereign piece each. I believe this was an old Persian custom to give a golden gift on their New Year's Day.

January 1942. Persian New Year at Mr. Nemazee's house

The stress of close quarters

This month was certainly a memorable one and taught us many things, particularly about living with so many people under one roof. The stress of it has brought out so many hidden flaws in peoples' characters: Mr. Nemazee's fits of bad temper between his enormous generosity; Palmertz's and Herschend's recent selfishness, laziness and generally disagreeable behaviour; little irritating mannerisms of Lisa; and Maritza's fiery temperament, mixed with sweetness. I have no doubt my own flaws are showing as well.

This house is a bizarre environment now with so many people packed in and their things scattered all about, mixed rudely with Mr. Nemazee's collections of objects that are now completely out of place. In our room alone there are trunks piled high, marble statues, an ancient Buddha, a suit of ancient Japanese armour, and numerous ornate spittoons here and there. And all of our own remaining possessions mashed in the middle of it.

Karin Lisbeth told us how abominable Herschend and Palmertz had been to her. How Herschend had taken possession of her flat, ordering her servants, telling her not to interfere, reading her husband's private correspondence and not even letting her sleep in her own bedroom that night.

They took her all over the building and showed her the other flats that had been looted and were in a terrible mess, emphasizing how wonderful they themselves had been to look after her flat, and how grateful everyone should be to them. They criticized everybody in Mr. Nemazee's house, after having taken his food and hospitality and drunk all of Reidar's liquor. They then had Karin Lisbeth's tinned food, which she could have taken to her husband at Sham Shui Po camp, and her drinks, which Herschend has already claimed.

When that is done, they will move on to better fields. It is quite unbelievable how they have changed. They are now so utterly irresponsible, unkind, unhelpful, mean and nasty, and altogether eaten up with selfishness. We will be thankful if they never return here. They have made far too much trouble already.

Small things are apt to become mountains in difficult circumstances, but our lives have so little joy, that almost everybody tries to do their best to keep cheerful and help others. So when some do behave badly it shows up all the more.

Reidar went to visit Sir Vandeleur Grayburn and his wife at the Sun Wah Hotel, where all the bankers are interned. He also walked all the way out to the Queen Mary Hospital together with Mr. Nemazee, to visit Eric who is acting as a Red Cross handy man there. The Queen Mary Hospital inmates have been moved and the building has been taken over, along with the Mathilda and War Memorial, for the Japanese wounded being brought in from other fields of battle.

Skyhigh in ruins

When Mrs. Bang and I went up to *Skyhigh* again to salvage more of our belongings, we met hundreds and hundreds of coolies and Chinese of all kinds, mostly ruffians, coming down laden with loot; suitcases full of clothes and linen; sacks bulging with tinned food, silver, plates, cut-crystal; pictures and furniture. Then on later trips they were even carrying down doors and floor boards. I suppose for firewood.

As we came to *Skyhigh*, we saw that the entrance gate had been hit by a shell. In the courtyard were innumerable craters and wreckage. There was a very large crater in the middle of the courtyard and three others that had completely smashed the chicken house and vegetable garden further down the hillside.

Inside the house, the stairs had been half blown away and there was a great hole through into the basement and a hole through the sitting room ceiling.

The guest room was entirely burnt to a cinder, everything coal black, cupboards, panelling, parquet floors and all the furniture. All that remained were the coils of the spring mattresses, neatly in rows on the charcoal floor. The iron window grills, which I had so carefully locked and taken the keys last time I was there, were lying twisted and blackened on the ground.

In the bathroom everything was so black it was unbelievable. The water that was in the bath looked like solid pitch, and the mirror over the basin had curled right over with the heat, but was unbroken. It was the result of a fire bomb, which the Japanese had started dropping on the last day of the war.

Our room was in a horrible mess. The whole wall had crashed down and we could see right out over the harbour, past where John's bathroom and bedroom had been. In the centre of our room there was a great hole through our lovely bedroom carpet.

Looters had made such a horrible mess, adding to all the other damage. Everything had been strewn all around and the warm clothes taken. What was left was torn and tumbled, buried under bricks and thick with dust and dirt.

My Leica and movie films were lying unwound all over the house. They were scattered amongst the masonry by the front door, hanging from the broken stairs and trailing along the passage over the blocks of fallen roof and walls. That was one of the things that grieved me most, to see those reminders of so many happy days and years gone by lying torn and spoilt amongst the ruins of our home.

I can't help clinging to any small thing that has been part of our home, just hoping that some day it will help to start another. I suppose it is futile anyway, because when we do get away, it will be with the minimum of our personal necessities.

So I left our beloved *Skyhigh*, bathed in the soft gold of evening sunlight, and among its ruins are buried the happy memories of our first very own home. It had been built up with so many dreams and hopes, and so much joy. Reidar and I always had thought that we were too happy and too fortunate. We were almost afraid, wondering how we would have to pay for it. So, if the payment is no heavier than this, we can take it, with gratitude, as we are all four safe and healthy.

When I think of the other girls there who have their husbands interned, and particularly of Sophie who has lost hers forever, I feel so fortunate and just wish that I could do something to help them.

On our way down we stopped at Railton's house, as we were so thirsty. Mrs. Bang and I opened a bottle of our Chablis, which had been salvaged and it tasted so good. We felt fine after that drink and were laughing and merry on the way down. Reidar was waiting for us at the corner of the Peak Road and May Road, very angry because he was so anxious about us being so late. It was nearly six o'clock and still broad daylight. He scolded me severely, but I knew it was only because of his concern for me.

When will we be interned?

We had a great scare a few days ago. Krogmo came here during the morning and told us that he had been in Andresen's flat on Conduit Road, when some Japanese officers appeared and told them to leave the flat at once, and present themselves for internment at the Japanese Consulate at one o'clock that day. So we realized that our hour would come soon, having already heard that Norway is on the enemy list.

We got busy right away and packed what we considered most necessary and what we would be able to carry ourselves. Ingrid's milk, food for the older children, warm clothes and bedding were the most important. We have heard that many poor people in Stanley were sleeping on cement floors with no bedding at all. We try to be resigned to internment, but hope so much that it will be in sanitary quarters and not in a packed and dirty Chinese hotel down in the city.

Stanley Hospital internment camp prisoners

We were expecting the Japanese to come at any moment, telling us to leave, but we were certainly not going to go until they did. That was just as well, because when we were finally packed and as prepared as possible, Sophie came rushing in, all out of breath with news that it was all nonsense. Krogmo had got the whole thing wrong. The Japs were just turning them out of their flat and taking over the building. Poor Sophie had been so upset at the thought of us all being interned, that she had not stopped until she found out the real truth of the story.

We were so relieved and all felt as though we had a new lease of life, although we still have the feeling that it is only a postponement. Anyway it was a useful dress rehearsal, and I discovered many very necessary things afterwards, which I would have forgotten.

Our chief worries now are food and money to buy it with. Money has become communal. Anyone who has any is quickly relieved of it and it is given to Ah Tse, who goes down to do the marketing every day. We are very thankful to have him, as well as Ah So (Ah Tse's very sweet wife) and Ah Sai. Ah Tse has been so good all along, and when he came to ask if we wanted him to continue working for us, we told him straight away that we could not pay him or Ah So any wages, other than some rice each day.

Rice is so difficult to get. Thousands and thousands of people queue up for it every day down in the town, after waiting hours, sometimes all day, then only getting one catty (a little over half a pound) and sometimes nothing at all. It is priced at a government rate, but on the street it is far more expensive. Fresh meat, vegetables and fish are difficult to find to begin with. Now we can get them, but at very high prices, between three to six times their normal prices.

Some of the banks are open and only Chinese and non-enemy nationals are allowed to draw money. Norwegians are not included. How we are going to exist will be a problem. We just hope that the infallible Mr. Nemazee will be able to get money somehow. Reidar also has some very good old Chinese friends, who are evidently sincere in their wish to help him.

Ingrid is such a handful and needs constant watching. The other day when Lisa and Karin Lisbeth were keeping an eye on her, she fell all the way downstairs. I collected her at the bottom, after I heard all the bumping, but she did not seem much the worse. Mr. Nemazee is so sweet to her always, spoiling her very much and letting her do just what she likes, even to making puddles on his most beautiful Persian carpets, without a word of reproach!

The new normal

February 22nd. Reidar and I went to Repulse Bay today to see the Ritchies. We had very little money and did not want to risk taking much tinned food, as we would almost certainly have it taken from us. We got into a bus at the vehicular ferry, which was packed with many fat Indian Sikhs. They were treated very amiably by the Japanese.

There was a Russian sitting next to Reidar, who very reluctantly answered Reidar's questions. He seemed to be scared to even talk to us, but he told us that the Ritchies were still in their house. At Wong Nei Chong Gap the bus stopped. We all had to get out and pass through sentries to be searched and passes examined. They were quite civil to us and did not search me. Dr. Chaun told us that he had had his watch taken from him there, when he was on his way out to his house at Stanley.

It was such a heavenly day, and yet there was such devastation all around. The hotel garage was full of bullet holes. A Japanese battalion had been in hiding there one night and had shooting matches with the British soldiers in the Repulse Bay Hotel. All the matsheds on the beach were completely flat and, of course, their contents looted and strewn all over the place. The beautiful avenue of Flame of the Forest trees looked utterly desolate.

As we approached the Lido we saw that it was a sentry post, as we had been told by the Russian. We walked up to the soldiers feeling extremely doubtful about the success of our expedition. At first they looked at our passes very suspiciously then said, "Ah, Norrrway-ah, Sodiska", and that seemed all right. We had a lot of talking and explaining to do about our visit to the Ritchies, but finally—to our amazement—they said we could go, after having looked into our paper bags of chocolate and buns.

We walked along the South Beach Road rapidly, not daring to look right or left, nor behind us, even when we heard a lot of shooting and shouting uncomfortably close. We did not know whether they were shouting at us, or whether we might get a shot in the back at any moment. We just kept on walking steadily in the middle of the road, with our legs shaking. Afterwards we were told that it was very dangerous to have done that.

I simply could not believe that we found ourselves walking up the drive and then actually knocking at the Ritchies' front door. It felt almost like old times, coming on one of our Sunday morning visits. They were the parents of our architect friend, John Ritchie, who was married to Irene, one of my best friends from before either of us were married. I half expected to see Irene skipping out to meet us. Instead everything was so quiet and still, and there was a Japanese sign on the door.

Eventually in response to our knocking, we heard Mr. Ritchie calling out that he was coming. Our mutual joy at meeting again was unbounded. I hugged them both, as if they had been my own parents, and they looked so happy to see us. We were very shocked by Mrs. Ritchie's appearance. She was so thin and had aged a lot. She had been very, very ill they told us. So ill, that they both thought she would not live. She had even told Mr. Ritchie where to bury her and to use the box in the garage as a coffin. It was pathetic, but thank Heavens, she had managed to cure herself with her own will power and the help of Dr. Selwyn-Clarke, who had been wonderful to them. (Dr. Selwyn-Clarke served as Hong Kong Director of Medical Services prior to the war and continued during Japanese occupation until 1943, when he was arrested, kept in solitary confinement for 19 months, and tortured in an attempt to get him to confess to a list of charges, including being a spy and distributing medical supplies to prisoners.)

The sitting room had all the shutters in place, so we sat down in the little den, which was so cosy and bright with the sunlight streaming in. She had been sewing, and he reading. They told us they had been reading ancient Egyptian history together and it helped to take them away from realities.

All the front windows were closed, in spite of the glorious weather. They explained, almost matter of fact that they had to keep them closed when the wind came from the south, because there were 10 bodies lying a little way along the road, below the house. They had been left there since they were shot two weeks ago, and the smell was sickening.

We went out and looked all over the garden with her. She showed me seeds and cuttings coming up, and took me up to see their tiny vegetable garden. There they had tomatoes, potatoes and even a few strawberries, that she was very thrilled about.

It was all so peaceful and beautiful, the sun shining on the sparkling bay, so much like old, happy times. Then a puff of wind came and brought grim realities back again with the smell of death, and then I noticed how empty and deserted everything was. No junks or sampans to be seen on the blue water, and looking through the Middle Island Gap we saw sunken launches and small sloops, canoes and boats drifting upside down. On Middle Beach all the matsheds were flattened and on the sands lay two bodies.

We sat in the little den and talked and talked, telling of our respective experiences. They were so pleased with the buns and chocolate, as they had not had any bread for weeks and weeks. Mr. Ritchie insisted upon opening a bottle of lovely white wine. It was one of the few remaining from John and Irene's days. It was noon when we had arrived and two-thirty when we left. We told them that we had had tiffin before leaving Hong Kong, as we knew they must have had very little food in the house, though they urged us to have "pot luck" with them the way we used to.

They told us that the boy went in to town occasionally and bought things from the market. They fortunately had rice to last them two to three months and tins of corned meat, which they had got after the surrender, when the food depot near them had been broken open. They admitted they had no more money. The last note had been given to the boy that morning. Fortunately we had some with us, which we gave them, after much protesting on their part.

Mr. Ritchie told us how he had walked into Hong Kong after the surrender, not knowing anything about it, and had unsuccessfully been to the bank. When he returned home he found that many of their things had been stolen, chiefly bedding, and also $1,000 which he had hidden in a cupboard! It was particularly upsetting, as they suspected their own servants.

Eventually we had to go and get our bus back again. I hated saying goodbye, as one never knows when the next meeting might be, or where. They looked so lonely and small standing there at the top of the drive with Wolf, their dog, waving us goodbye.

As we walked back towards the Lido we smelt the same awful smell that had wafted from the dead bodies below the Ritchies' house. But we dared not look over the side of the road, as we thought we might be being watched, and there were still the occasional sounds of shooting up in the woods.

When we came to the Lido, we passed the sentries again quite affably and walked on to get our bus at the top of the hotel garden steps. We were just remarking on the incredible luck we had had in achieving our visit, when a Jap officer appeared and stopped us. He waved us around the other lower way, on the beach road and up under the bridge, where the 'dead' smell was very strong. He then walked over to the sentry post on the bridge. We tried to ask when the bus would come, but they shouted at us and signalled us to go back.

Eventually a Sikh policeman told us that there would be no more buses that day, because the "governor" was due to arrive at the Repulse Bay Hotel at any moment. He thought we might be allowed to walk to town, but the sentry turned us back again. We did not know what to do, so we asked if we could sit down by the roadside, until the governor had passed. But everybody had to be off the road, so we returned to the Lido. There the sergeant in charge even gave Reidar a cigarette and permission to wait. The soldiers questioned us about "Norrrrway-ah", in their stumbling few words of English. When they heard that we had two children, one of them went into the villa near us and brought out some crayons for JoJo.

It was a strain sitting there for over two hours. Apart from the fatigue, we never knew what was going to happen next. Twice they told us we could go, only to be shouted at and turned back by other sentries further on. At last after five o'clock we were allowed to leave and set off as fast as we could, as it was getting dark already and would be even more dangerous at night.

All along the way we kept smelling that ghastly smell. The Shield's house and the big new Chinese house were almost in ruins. Tinson's house was riddled with holes and completely looted. We heard that Mr. Tinson had been shot from the hillside when he came out of his house.

We were stopped many times by sentries stationed at points all along the road, who called us over so insolently, and idly examined our passes. But to our relief they let us go on. We walked and walked at top speed, till our legs and backs ached, right through Wanchai and finally reached May Road at 7.30 p.m., absolutely dead beat. I was already making plans for our next visit to the Ritchies, but Reidar did not think it would be wise.

March 25th. It has been ages since I last wrote in my diary, for the simple reason that I never seem to have any time. These are months of forlorn hopes, pipe dreams, excitement over rumours, frustrations and hard work, and making plans with the everlasting "IF". The time goes by fast because of the monotony.

Maritza and Karin Lisbeth went to see their husbands in the concentration camp at Sam Shui Po, taking them parcels of food and trying to smuggle through letters. Reidar had been to see Reiertsen, a Wallem employee who was taken prisoner as a member of the Hong Kong Volunteers, and others there several times, always taking food.

Karin Lisbeth was desperately anxious to get medicines for her husband, as he had had dysentery several times already, and she dreads him getting it again in such circumstances. We heard that poor Naess is in a very bad way with his eyes. He is nearly blind from lack of vitamins and bad food.

We have been to visit the HSBC bank people quite often lately, always taking some food with us, generally a loaf, sometimes two, sometimes we take them a pie or some kind of pudding, something that is a bit different to their ordinary food

Their quarters are very uncomfortable in the dirty little Sun Wah Hotel. It used to be a brothel. Sir Vandeleur Grayburn and Mary are in one tiny cubicle, with only a bed and a tiny low cupboard with some hooks to hang their clothes on. Next door in the same space are the Edmondstons, HSBC's second in charge, and beyond them is poor Mrs. Pierce, who was married to a prominent businessman in Hong Kong who was killed together with many others of the "old brigade" while defending an electrical power station during the last days of fighting. On the other side of the Grayburn's cubicle is one that they use as their dining-room-cum-kitchen-cum-living room. It is almost too small for them all to get in to at the same time. Outside is a Chinese veranda which is large enough for them to have a table and chairs, and where they sit most of the time.

Mrs. Edmondston seems to be the most energetic one, doing the cooking and peeling vegetables, etc., but Sir Vandeleur looks very low. The Japanese are forcing him to transfer HSBC assets and money to their control, but previous to the surrender, he wisely had transferred most to the London and US offices, out of their reach. *(Unfortunately, later during the occupation, the Japanese imprisoned and tortured Sir Vandeleur to death.)*

While we were there one day their ration of bread arrived. It was for the whole building, including all the other bank people and many small children. There was not even enough for everybody to have one slice of bread each day, so some had it one day and others the next. Fortunately the Chinese are very good and bring them a lot of supplementary food. But they are shut up entirely in that sordid and gloomy place, and never allowed out in the sunshine. What a change of destiny for the two most powerful financiers in the Far East!

The poor little children suffer most of all from this and nearly all of them have come down with dysentery and have been sent to the French Hospital, which is at least a better place for them.

We are unspeakably thankful that we are still free, to at least be able to walk in the open.

One day we had tiffin with Yamasaki at the former Gloucester Hotel, now called Matsubara Hotel. He has always been a good business friend of Reidar's, and we never know when we might be in sad need of some Japanese "friend". The prices were all in Japanese military yen and very high, but the food was good. Yamasaki is no military man and, we gather, very cautiously, there is no love lost between the military, the navy and the businessmen. None of them want to accept the other's authority.

We walked up one day to visit Mr. Nemazee's properties there, particularly the one on Mt. Kellet, as we have a vague hope that if we are still in Hong Kong during the summer, we might be allowed to live there. His two houses in the Stewart Terrace Row have both received bomb hits and are completely wrecked. But the Mt. Kellet house, which has four flats in it, has very little damage and can easily be fixed up, although there is no water and no electricity.

There had been a company of Canadian soldiers stationed there, and they had left most of their equipment, stationery, orders and telegrams etc., from London Headquarters. On the doors they had written, "Returning for balance of kit later", dated the 25th of December. The flats did not seem to have been looted, I suppose due to being in full view of the Mathilda Hospital, where they have guards.

We did a little looting ourselves and would have done more, if we had not been scared of the consequences of being found out. Even Europeans have been shot for entering houses unauthorized.

The last time we went up to the Peak was last Sunday, a perfectly glorious spring day, so beautiful it almost hurt. Mr. Nemazee had the bright idea of going up the Peak for a picnic. It sounded so normal that we all felt quite incredulous and then thought, "Why not?". So in spite of most not having passes for the Peak, we got Ah Ha to make 60 bean cakes and took rice, tomato ketchup and some chocolate, and all set off.

Reidar did not come as he had an appointment downtown, with Matsushima about the office. Also, Sophie did not feel like coming, so there were Mr. Nemazee, Chakori, Palmertz, Captain Svane, Mrs. Bang and Salvesen, Karin Lisbeth, Maritza and me and the four children. I did not like being so many, but it was fun and I tried to forget all about *Skyhigh* and refused to go there. We "camped" in Mr. Nemazee's old Fungshui garden and lit a fire to make tiffin.

Later I went exploring in Dawson's house next door and found a cooking pan (very useful), some books and an ironing board. The house was all swept and clean and all the furniture pushed into one room. All the houses around were the same. We could have walked into any one of them. They were all open and deserted, but we were cautious as one wrong move might have cost a life. On our way down we all carried things, two sacks of firewood, books, baskets, even the children carried wood and a few small things they had found in Daw's house. Taking things from another person's house is considered quite normal these days, and if *you* don't somebody else will.

I found a photo of Alec Pierce on the road and picked it up to take to Mrs. Pierce when I visited Sun Wah Hotel. Poor thing was so touched. She had lost her husband, her home and all her belongings, and her two sons were interned at Sham Shui Po. I have done quite a lot of shopping for Mary Grayburn and Mrs. Edmondston, as they are not allowed out at all.

Our plan to escape Hong Kong

Reidar has been very worried by Matshushima's warning to get out of Hong Kong as quickly as possible. Our passes expire at the end of the month. We can get them extended for 15 days, but after that we wonder what will happen to us.

We have decided to go to the Portuguese city of Macao on the mainland in only two days time, and are frantically trying to get ourselves organized and packed. It is a gigantic job to sort out what to take with us of all the things that we have gradually collected. There are no boxes or trunks to pack anything in.

We had to go to town to be vaccinated at the health centre in the National City Bank. Ingrid was the center of attraction and even drew a beaming smile from the Japanese lady-controller there. Then she rode home in a chair all by herself and was very thrilled.

Reidar has been going up and down to town in the morning and afternoon, making final arrangements for office books and files, and trying to get money to pay staff salaries. We then went to say good-bye to Sir Vandeleur and company.

We are terribly nervous, but excited at the same time, at the prospect of escaping to Allied-controlled territory. Our goal is to go first to Macao via ferry on a permit, then cross hundreds of miles by land through Kweilin to the provisional Nationalist capital of Chungking, then further over the Himalayas by plane or truck to Calcutta, and on to Bombay or elsewhere. We really don't know what will be possible or how we will travel, but we believe that it is worth the high risk that we will be exposed to along the way. The doctor's warning of a 50 percent chance of survival for our little ones bears heavily upon us. And Reidar's own health is far from perfect.

But Reidar feels that staying in Hong Kong offers very little security, as we will be interned and at the mercy of the Japanese. Meanwhile, if we can make it to Bombay, where Archy and his wife Gerd are living, we can begin to rebuild our lives and Reidar can rebuild the shipping company and be of use to many people during this difficult time. He feels it is his responsibility to escape to a free base in order to safeguard Wallem's and its client's assets.

Here in Hong Kong he feels very useless and broken-hearted knowing that all he has worked for, with such dedication, seven days a week during so many years of his life, has been stripped away from him. Our wonderful home is destroyed. Friends have been killed, and most others are now or will be prisoners in the Japanese internment camps with a very uncertain future.

We must move on.

Our Escape Through China

By the middle of 1942, Japan's Empire was at its height and included Manchuria, Inner Mongolia, large parts of China, Malaysia, French Indochina, Dutch East Indies, The Philippines, Burma, a small part of India, and many Pacific Islands. United in a "Greater East Asia Co-Prosperity Sphere", pioneered by Japan's generals, along with Vietnam, Laos and Thialand, their justification for war and conquest was for a cultural and economic unity of Asians. Their intention was to create a self-sufficient "bloc of Asian nations led by the Japanese and free of Western powers", and seemed to be materializing as planned.

However, only six months after the Battle of Hong Kong, the Japanese advance slows significantly when Japan loses the critical naval Battle of Midway near Hawaii to the American fleet on June 7, 1942. Meanwhile, Germany is fighting the Allied forces in North Africa and Western Europe, as well as the Soviets in Russia.

The Japanese Empire
at its Peak 1942

Macao

April 3rd. We have been in Macao since Sunday, March 29th, and it seems as though Hong Kong is already so very, very far away. This is definitely the beginning of a new chapter. I wonder very much whether it will end in Chungking or elsewhere. We hope to go to Chungking, as it is the new Chinese capital and departure point for India and beyond, but it will require a very long land journey with many hazards along the way.

We suddenly decided to leave Hong Kong and the quicker we went, the better. The position of Norwegians certainly would not be improving. After April 15th, when the Japanese see the complete lack of response to their orders that Norwegian ships go to Japanese ports, we are sure they will make things more difficult than ever. There are certain people who make nasty remarks about us leaving, but in the end I think most wish they could go too.

The night before we left, we had to have a dinner party at the house with Mrs. Fincher, some Norwegian and Danish neighbours and their Japanese *gendarmerie* (military police) friends. It was a very good dinner and it turned out to be very useful for us, as we were promised help from an officer to see us through the customs at the pier the next morning.

After dinner we spent until midnight packing tinned food that we hoped to get through the customs somehow. We had also sewn up some little bags containing oats and sugar, which we placed in amongst our clothes. Even the children carried some, hoping that the customs would not discover them. Finally we were too exhausted to go on anymore, so we all sat down and drank a bottle of precious champagne.

What a day it was, like a chapter out of a comic novel. At quarter to nine we set off, a most strange looking cavalcade, everyone carrying something. There must have been about 50 people in all, including about 30 coolies, all shouting, cursing, sweating and laughing, as they staggered down the steep path from May Road with so many heavy loads.

Apart from Mr. Nemazee and us four, we had with us Sophie, Mrs. Salvesen and her two children, Mrs. Bang and her little girl and Captain Svane. Mehdi and Maritza came to see us off and help carry things.

Ingrid herself rode in a sedan chair all on her own and looked the sweetest little thing imaginable, so flaxen-fair, so lovely and such a baby. Her eyes were constantly wide with amazement at all she saw and her mouth in a permanent round "0". She was as good as gold and sat so calmly up on her throne, sometimes singing to herself and sometimes calling, "Allo—Allo" to passers-by. Everyone turned round to look and smile at her.

When we got to the pier there was a terrific muddle, as the custom officials went through every single piece of our baggage, making us spread it all out on the wooden pier. It was a blessing that we had the young gendarmerie officer with us to see us off, as we were able to take a fair amount of tinned milk and other things—chiefly for the children—which we would never have been allowed to do otherwise. They are very strict about the prohibition of taking any tinned foods from the Colony.

They took a bottle of aspirin from my suitcase and asked if I had anymore, so I said, "No" and it was put back again. Medicine has become so valuable, as it would be quite unobtainable later. We had heard that two syndicates were buying it all up. Aspirin, toothpaste and most things were at least four to six times more expensive than usual.

Eventually, after all our belongings had been gathered together again, the special pier coolies dumped them all on board somewhere in the bowels of the ship, and to our consternation we never saw them again, until we got to Macao.

It was a strange departure from our beautiful Hong Kong. So different from the usual baskets of flowers and friends coming on board for a farewell drink!

Hong Kong was shrouded in mists and clouds, which was just as well, because it saved us heartaches.

Macao, the Portuguese outpost in mainland China

When we finally arrived in Macao it started to rain heavily. The pandemonium on the wharf, with passengers, coolies, baggage and hundreds of other people meeting the ship, all milling around in a small soaking space, in the pelting rain, made more chaos than ever.

We shouted like mad, whenever we saw any of our 53 pieces of baggage. Finally all our belongings were dumped in a wet pile on a corner of the wharf.

At last we set off for the Riviera Hotel. To my amazement again, Mr. Nemazee had conjured up a car, Mr. Saito's, in which I drove to the hotel with Ingrid and all sorts of baskets and packages, while the others came by rickshaw.

The hotel was much as I had remembered it from 10 years ago, though rather more gloomy and dilapidated. We got four rooms. Reidar, me, JoJo and Ingrid in one, Mesdames Salvesen, Bang, Sophie and three children in another, and Mr. Nemazee and Captain Svane each alone in grand state. The family rooms immediately took on the appearance of gypsy encampments, with luggage, children, muddle and mess everywhere.

We always meet someone we know whenever we go into town or downstairs in the hotel, as they all congregate there and talk and talk. In the streets, we stand talking endlessly, or meet elsewhere and swap the latest rumours.

Macao has turned out infinitely nicer than we expected, regarding the town and residential district. There are some very attractive little doll-size houses and lovely shady avenues. They are all painted different colours, and look so bright and cheerful from the exterior. The whole place has such a different atmosphere from Hong Kong. One could easily imagine oneself in some quaint little town on the Mediterranean. Even the steep and narrow little cobbled streets and the numerous small churches are so similar, with all the signs written in Portuguese. The only thing lacking are the wayside cafés.

April 14th. We are at last installed, temporarily, in a house of our own. We feel ourselves so fortunate to have got it, after so many frustrations. It is a small bungalow in the back compound of a big Chinese house belonging to Mr. Butt. He is a Chinese friend and business associate of Mr. Nemazee's, and is also a major opium importer to China. We are hoping and waiting impatiently to move the other half of the household into the next door twin bungalow, as ours is far too small for 11 people. But there are Chinese there who are taking their time moving out.

We have a fine garden for the children to play in and the little bungalow itself has been newly colour-washed and is easy to keep clean. We hope it will be fairly cool in the hot weather.

We are so glad to have our faithful Ah Tse with us again, and his sweet little wife, Ah So. They suddenly turned up a few days ago and said they wanted to work for us. We told them we do not know whether we will be able to pay their wages or not, as we have hardly any money left. They said they would stay with us anyway, and what a blessing it is having them. Ah Tse is so versatile and only too willing to turn his hand to anything. From being our house coolie at *Skyhigh*, he is now number one boy, cook and general factotum. He is quite good at cooking too and eager to learn. His specialty for the children, when all else fails, is "Flenchy toasee".

Ah So looks after Ingrid with blind devotion and adores her. She does her best with John too and he is very fond of her. But she is scarcely taller than he is and certainly not as strong-willed, so he doesn't pay much attention to her.

In a big room below our bungalow, there is a Chinese kindergarten for the children of Mr. Butt's own relatives. It is very attractive and clean looking. The small children look so sweet, with their moon-faces and black eyes and hair, dressed in bright blue dungarees, running and tumbling about, like a lot of little dolls.

Mosquitoes are a great problem. They are so bad that we all have to have nets. They will be indispensable if we ever are able to get away on our trip to Chungking.

The way by Kwong Chai Wan is said to be the least difficult or dangerous one, but the trouble is now whether or not we will be able to get past the Japanese to get there. The news is that the Norwegians are not allowed to leave Hong Kong any longer, and that they all must report to the Bureau for Foreign Affairs on April 17th. We have been wondering what is in store for them and feel so deeply sorry that none of them, not even the seamen, have been able to get here.

April 19th. Last night we went to the Reeves' seventh wedding anniversary party and, while we were there, we heard over the radio from Saigon, that Tokyo, Nagoya, Kobe and Osaka had been bombed by American Flying Fortresses. We were all so thrilled, because this is what everyone has been longing and hoping for. The Japanese have had nothing but victories all along and no reverses. Nothing has happened to their home country, so we just hope and trust that this will have a great moral effect as well on them.

This morning at about six o'clock, we were awakened by awful shouts and groaning and thumping under our window. I saw there was a man tied up in the garden of Mr. Butt's house and the servants were beating him. He must have been a thief.

There also seems to be a terrific number of beggars in Macao and sick people, particularly with diseased feet. They sit by the roadside or on doorsteps, with their legs all swollen, black and covered with great open sores, generally suppurating and infested with flies. They are a pitiful sight and one longs to be able to help them. I was told it is from beriberi, caused by ill nourishment.

The prices are simply staggering, and going up and up each day, for clothing, imported groceries, etc., even rice, which one is supposed to get by rations, but never seems to materialize that way. The very poorest quality is 80 to 90 cents a catty, instead of 40 cents government rate and six cents pre-war price!

Two days ago Reidar received telegrams from Nortraship (the Norwegian government shipping group), saying that they were remitting the money he had asked for, to support the Norwegian sailors in Hong Kong and for their travel here to Macao. He has already arranged that they can have accommodation to live on board a hulk here. But we still don't know what is happening to the Norwegians in Hong Kong. There has been no news concerning them at all, either on the radio or in the paper. It is so sad to think that just the very day that it would have been possible for them to come here, with safety and definite means of support for the future, they have probably been interned.

The question and prospect of our trip is continuously in our minds. Now it does not look as though the Kwong Chai Wan way will be possible for us, as the Japanese are pretty sure to prevent it. The other way entails a day or more in a junk, hidden away below board and sailing through Japanese controlled waters, with the chance of getting shot and the junk set fire to, if we are discovered. But we are told it is not much of a risk and I would be willing to take it, even with JoJo and Ingrid.

I am so anxious to get away from here, as one never knows what may be in store here, whether the Japanese will take over, whether there will be a famine, sickness, or what?

If only Mr. Nemazee would come back quickly from Hong Kong, then we could get started. Each day we wait will mean worse conditions for travelling, owing to the heat and the rainy season.

Once we are safely in free China, we evidently have a "walk" of about a week or 10 days, going by chair to Kweilin. I look over to Chinese territory, across the water and along the big highway road leading out of Macao, and wish that we could just start off. But all the territory around Macao is occupied by the Japanese. They have an airfield for aerial surveillance and a navy to control all the surrounding waters, searching the junks as they pass by. So one has to be extremely careful.

I dread the thought of the summer here. The heat and mosquitoes are already affecting the children. Malaria is very prevalent and dysentery too. Mrs. Salvesen and Inger Johanna have already spent some days in hospital, as it appeared that they might have got dysentery. The spots on Ingrid are not cured yet and her vaccination still not healed, although it was done over three weeks ago. It took so badly, I am afraid that she will have a bad scar on her leg for life. Her mosquito bites have gone septic in some places and the prickly-heat is starting. I don't know how she would stand the summer here. No more lovely pink cheeks, I am sure. She is so adorable now, learning to say new words and having new little-girl ways each day. I can't help thinking she is the loveliest and sweetest baby I have seen. Although I know it is wrong to think one's own baby so perfect, I still do!

I also think that JoJo is so much nicer and better mannered than the other children here. Particularly Christen gets on our nerves, although he is an exceptionally clever boy and reads and writes like a grown up at seven years old. But his manners are dreadful and unfortunately JoJo copies all the worst.

April 23rd. Yesterday we had a marvellous surprise. Reidar went down to meet the boat as usual, hoping to find Mr. Nemazee or some Norwegians arriving, but instead discovered two boxes of tinned foods, which Mr. Nemazee somehow sent us by the Japanese Naval launch of all things.

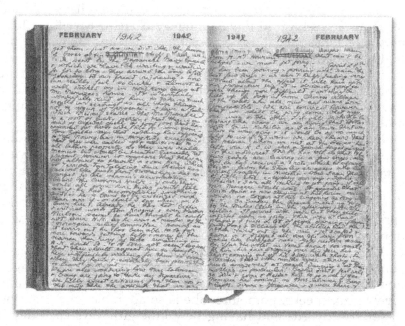

My war diary for our journey through China

It is certainly wonderfully kind of him to take so much trouble in sending us all these things, not to speak of the expense. I have a feeling, which Reidar shares, that Mr. Nemazee is a lucky person and that there is an oriental spell of good joss that has entwined our lives with his for some time.

Tony Bothello, a brash Portuguese businessman who seems to have the answers for many problems, says that nothing has happened to the Norwegians in Hong Kong. They were called up and cautioned to all behave properly, as they were really enemies and should be interned, but that they would be treated leniently at present. However, it appears that they are not allowed to travel or to come here, which is all the more bitterly disappointing, since all has now been organized for them to stay here.

If only they were able to come, then Reidar would feel as if he had really accomplished something. Reidar is bound to be criticized more than ever when we leave here. Already he has had bitter and critical words from Krogmo. Even Pastor Nilsen seems to have thought that he should not have left Hong Kong, as he was a member of the Norwegian Relief Committee. However, as it turns out, he has been able to do far more towards getting help and money for the seamen than any of those remaining in Hong Kong. We have been in Macao for one month already, and it does not seem logical that they should expect him to hang on here indefinitely, waiting for them to come, when it is evidently impossible for them to leave Hong Kong.

April 28th. My Chinese is blossoming and is extremely useful. I can argue and bargain with the shopkeepers, which they expect from their own countrymen, but not from a foreigner. They think my Chinese is a great joke and all laugh delightedly, even when I am offering them half their price! There are many exclamations of, "Aye-ah " and "no can do", but in the end we get it for considerably less than the original demand.

We have tried many new kinds of dishes, adapting ourselves to use many of the local products, as anything else is so expensive. But the two Norwegian ladies do not seem to be very adaptable in many ways, and we have had a few clashes of ideas and wishes already. To us it seems that they do not really try to cooperate in saving expenses. They insist upon having either fish or meat every day, because they are cheaper here than they were in Hong Kong, and they feel they do not get enough to eat otherwise.

The worst was when we had some porridge made of maize-meal (polenta). We thought it was good, but Mrs. Bang and Mrs. Salvesen did not like it. I suppose because they had never eaten such before, and Mrs. Bang refused to give it to the children, as she said it was not safe. All these things are really very stupid and petty, but when one lives in such cramped style they do assume an importance that is altogether disproportionate.

May 8th. So many things have happened during this week. Mr. Nemazee suddenly arrived, and we were quite stunned to hear that he had got orders to proceed to Tokyo and join the Iranian Embassy staff there for repatriation. We were so disappointed that he could not come with us, after so much planning and always counting on him being with us.

He brought authentic news of conditions in Stanley given him by Dr. Selwyn-Clarke, director of the medical department, and by Mr. Gibson, the colonial secretary. News about Sir Arthur Blackburn and Mrs. Martin (British Embassy people from Chungking), and so many others. Reidar sat at the desk and took down all that he read from his notebook. Messages to give to the British Consul here, telegrams to be sent to the foreign office and reports to be made.

Conditions in Stanley had greatly improved in the last two weeks and, at long last, parcels were being allowed through. Mr. Nemazee said he had sent about 80 sandbags full of food in the first week, including to our friends Eric, B. Whitham and Noel. Dr. Canavel had said that they were getting about 1,400 calories per day. It had previously been only 1,100 and they were requesting 2,500 to 3,000. People up to forty years old were bearing up all right, but between the ages of 40 and 50 years not so good, and over 50 were showing definite signs of deterioration. (Poor Ritchies!)

$300,000 had been paid from Japan, for the relief of internees and each internee had received $150 minus $30.00 deducted for food already received. (How long is that going to last them?)

Mr. Nemazee had all sorts of schemes afoot to try and help the internees and Volunteers. He spoke of the wonderful work being done by Dr. Selwyn-Clarke and Mr. Gibson. He also had a scheme for selling the Dutch dredger *Hankow*, which is sheltering in Macao harbour, to the Japanese for the relief of internees. Quite a lot of it was too involved for me to follow.

He is doing a tremendous amount of good in so many ways, helping people in Stanley internment camp and elsewhere, and sheltering others under his own roof. I do most sincerely hope that Reidar's predictions will come true, that some day we shall be calling him Sir Mohammed. He certainly deserves it.

Next day we were up early and went down to the docks to see Mr. Nemazee off. Before his ship left, we had a long wait in Mr. Butt's office which was very interesting and quaint in its old-fashioned Chinese style. So much heavy blackwood furniture, such hard, upright chairs and marble-bottomed stools and even blackwood opium divans, with the pipes and lamps all prepared and ready!

He manages the Government Opium Monopoly Packing Centre, and we saw hundreds of workers, downstairs busy packing the opium into tiny earthenware containers and sealing them with government stamps.

This is also where Reidar so often comes and sits talking with Mr. Butt, hour after hour in this opium laden atmosphere, drinking little bowls of tea and talking business.

How Opium controlled China

Maritime trade between Europe and China began in 1557 in the Portuguese outpost of Macau. Other European nations soon followed by establishing trade outposts in much of Asia to export products like silk, porcelain and tea to Europe. Unfortunately, China and many other Asian countries did not wish to import, or have a desire for European goods. At the time, China was largely self-sufficient and did not allow foreigners to its interior.

The problem was that Britain had an insatiable demand for tea, yet China only accepted silver as payment, which resulted in a chronic trade deficit. So European traders sought alternate foreign products to pay for their purchases.

A field of opium poppies

By 1817, the British realized they could reduce the trade deficit, as well as turn their Indian colony profitable by counter-trading China with Indian opium. The Chinese government initially tolerated opium importation because it created an indirect tax on Chinese subjects, while doubling tea exports from China to England. The Qing imperial treasury and its agents profited greatly.

The British East India Company (E.I.C.) had a legal monopoly on the British trade by selling opium grown on its plantations in India (where previously they had grown cotton) to traders in exchange for silver. The opium was then transported to the China coast by ships and sold to Chinese middlemen who retailed the drug inside China. This reverse flow of silver, along with the increasing numbers of opium addicts, began to alarm Chinese officials.

After free-trade reforms in England in 1834, private entrepreneurs joined in the lucrative trade of opium to China. American merchants then got involved and began to introduce opium from Turkey, a lesser quality, but it was cheaper to produce. The competition between British and American merchants drove down the price of opium, which increased sales and addiction in China.

In 1839, the Chinese emperor, rejecting proposals for continued legalization and taxation of opium, intended to solve the problem by abolishing the opium trade. This forced the British into the First Opium War to protect their opium business, which resulted in China's defeat and Britain's domination.

In 1842, the Treaty of Nanking granted Britain to open five treaty ports, including Shanghai, and the cession of Hong Kong Island to the British Empire. The failure of the treaty to fully satisfy British goals of improved trade and diplomatic relations led to the Second Opium War from 1856 to 1860. British victory secured the legalization of the opium trade, and gained the British Empire Kowloon across the harbour from Hong Kong as a bonus. The war is now considered in China as the beginning of modern Chinese history and marked the start of what 20th century nationalists called the "Century of Humiliation".

The production of opium has not changed since ancient times. A lanced opium poppy produces a latex sap that contains the analgesic alkaloid morphine, which is processed chemically to produce synthetic opioids for medicinal use, such as codeine, as well as for recreational drug use in opium's natural state (sometimes smoked with tobacco) and also converted into heroin which is more potent and easier to smuggle.

Opium smoking began as a privilege of the elite and remained a great luxury into the early 19th century. However, soon opium became mainstream as prices dropped and nearly every Chinese village had its opium house. By 1900, an estimated 25% of the male Chinese population were regular consumers of the drug. China's enormous population continued to be the world's largest market and a bonanza for opium production, shipping and trade.

We saw Mr. Nemazee on board and felt very tearful and depressed. I do not think he liked going either. He kissed us just as if we were members of his family and then stood waving to us until the ship was far, far away. He has been such a wonderful kind, generous friend to us. We shall never forget all that he has done for us.

I wonder so much where we shall meet again, and when? I hope in Iran, in time to taste his 99 different varieties of grapes, as we have planned!

Mrs. Salvesen, Mrs. Bang and Vera have suddenly left for Cheefo, China, to live with some friends of theirs there. It is a relief for us since they would have been difficult travellers on our dangerous journey.

May 9th. Mr. Butt most willingly agreed to lend us the Chinese dollars we would require for our trip, and he laughingly said to Reidar why had he not asked for such help long ago. He is now going to arrange that Reidar has drafts on a certain bank in various places that we stop at on our way through China. He is indeed a kind, helpful, and trusting person. What a tremendous relief to know that we shall be able to get money like this.

We have now planned to leave in another fortnight, because of the political situation with France. Since the British landed on Madagascar, France may declare war on Britain. Then it would be very awkward for us if we were stuck in Kwang Chai Wan, which is the French port of Fort Bayard.

Also the Japanese are reported to be on their way up the Burma Road from Rangoon, with many planes to back them up and there is not much use getting into Chungking if we cannot get out again. The Japs are advancing all over the place it seems. Very depressing! The fighting in Burma is practically over and now they are bombing Chittagong, and Ackiab has fallen. We wonder more and more anxiously whether we shall be able to eventually reach Calcutta. If not there then where to?

Everyone says that the food situation here is becoming increasingly serious. The rice problem has already assumed terrifying proportions, which one realizes forcibly, when one sees the hundreds and thousands of poor people, waiting in queues and crowds all day long for a meagre ration. Soon they may not be able to get it at all.

All the rice and most of the other food and vegetable supplies have to be imported into the colony. So it depends almost entirely upon Japanese goodwill. However at present it seems to suit them to keep Macao as a neutral port. We are lucky.

We have been extremely fortunate in having Mr. Vasconcellos give us 6 loaves of bread each day and a good ration of rice. It is funny now that the best present one can give a person is food or drink, some soap or other such thing. A loaf of bread is greatly welcomed, and a packet of Bastos cigarettes or Golden Buddahs loudly acclaimed. I am still on my two packets of Craven A cigarettes that Reidar gave me some time before we left Hong Kong!

Today we went for a lovely walk along the waterfront and around the reservoir. It is wonderful to be able to stroll along freely. No sentries, or soldiers pointing bayonets at one, or passes, and yet, just across the water, beyond the mountains of Lantau Island, lies our dear Hong Kong with all our friends kept as prisoners.

May 11th. This morning I was standing in the kitchen with Ah Chee when suddenly we saw a towel, that was lying on the window sill, start sliding along mysteriously and the next minute it had vanished out of the window!

The window gives onto the steps leading up from the road below to our compound but is quite high up. Ah Chee gave a shout of, "Aye-ah" and dashed out of the kitchen in hot pursuit of the thief. As he got to the bottom of the steps, he kicked off his shoes in order to give faster chase to the thief, who was disappearing up the road. But alas, the thief got away, and when the panting Ah Chee got back to put his shoes on, he found that they had been stolen too!

May 12th. It sounds strange, but it is quite true what "our Sophie" said, that Macao is an exciting place to live in. Most people have always thought of it as a little 'one-eyed' village, tucked away in a forgotten corner of the world. Yet now it certainly has acquired a mysterious glamour.

People arrive from various places, some having escaped from internment by the Japs, others coming from free China, to organize underground movements, and help more to escape.

British, Americans and Dutch rub shoulders with Japanese here and yet they are safe, and then in few days they mysteriously vanish. Nobody asks questions, as they have a pretty good idea what has happened. Later, news filters through the "bamboo wireless" that the travellers have got to their destinations of Chungking, India and even the United States. It is so tantalizing to hear of all these others managing to get off and yet here we are still. But of course it is different having children to take.

Anyway, I am sure that if we do get off soon, I shall always think with affection of Macao and our little bungalow in the Chinese garden.

I love the quaint view from our little living room into the garden, with the bamboo summerhouse at the end, in the shade of a beautiful Flame of the Forest tree. We have another Flame tree just outside our bedroom, which comes pressing its lovely feathery boughs right up against the window, looking so fresh and green. Soon they will be in flower and will surely look wonderful covered with flame-coloured blossoms, as if they were on fire. But we shall not be here to see them, I hope.

May 12th. Both Ingrid and JoJo are looking quite well, in spite of the heat and mosquitoes and different food, so we are hoping they will stand up to the trip fairly well. We cannot help remembering Dr. Selwyn-Clarke's warning that we only stood a 50 percent chance of getting through China with both of our children alive. We refuse to consider such a pessimistic outlook, but staying healthy in China isn't easy especially if you are unaccustomed to the food and environment, with innumerable diseases such as cholera, typhoid, polio, smallpox, mumps, diphtheria, measles, dysentery and so many others abound, even more in a country ravaged by war.

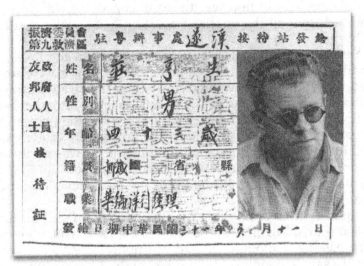

Reidar looks marvellous. So slim, boyish and brown. He looks years younger. I seem to be falling in love with him more deeply than ever. I think I am looking better too, although my face still looks rather tired and drawn. My figure is about the best it has ever been, I think, as my legs and hips are so slim, but Reidar says I am too thin.

May 13th. Oh the poverty and bleak misery one sees is ghastly. Today we came upon a dead man leaning in a sitting position against a wall. Flies and blue-bottles crawled all over him, in and out of his nose and clustered over his eyes. It was horrible. Small children were playing nearby and people walking all around paying no attention to him at all. The only consolation I could find was to thank heaven he was dead, and removed from all the misery, starvation and squalor that made up his life.

Yesterday, on our way back from a walk in the lovely old-world gardens, where the famous Portuguese poet Camoens used to sit long ago, writing and getting inspiration from the glorious view out over the sea and islands and the beauty around him, we passed some coolies carrying long boxes slung on bamboo poles between them. The boxes were crudely made of ill fitting wooden planks and on one the lid was partly open. Inside I could see a corpse with staring eyes and the fingers of one hand were caught in the lid of the box, preventing it from closing properly.

I quickly tried to divert JoJo's attention and made him turn to look at something on the other side of the road while the coolies were passing. I thought he had not noticed them, but when I went to say, "Goodnight" to him last night, I found him lying in bed in a most peculiar way with his eyes rolled upwards and his hand hanging limp over the side. I got quite a fright and called out to him, "JoJo, what is the matter?" Then he said to me without moving, "This is the way that dead man was lying in the box this afternoon. Did you see? He tried to push the top of the box off, because he didn't want to die."

My poor little JoJo, he has been through so much these last few months. I only hope he will forget all the bad parts as he grows older.

May 24th. We heard that Paul Hubbs, Reddon and the two cadets have at long last got off, hidden in a Chinese junk. Today, when we saw all the hundreds of junks sailing out over the horizon, I could not help wondering which one they were on and wishing them good luck.

May 25th. Mr. Lin came to see Reidar today. He is a business friend of Reidar's and the firm looks after his ships. He is a real old-fashioned type of Chinese gentleman and looks it, to the tips of his long-nailed fingers. He wears a long silk Chinese gown and a small, somewhat battered Panama hat perched on top of his bald head. His straggly, grey moustache hangs, walrus-fashion, over his protruding teeth and a few, much prized, long hairs grow out of a large mole on the side of his face.

He is a very charming old man, and we were quite overcome when he told us that he had decided to come with us all the way to Chungking to look after us and interpret for us on our way through China. It is true that we would probably come up against a great many difficulties because of the language problem. There are so many different dialects spoken in the various districts we shall be going through, and my meagre knowledge of Cantonese will not be any use at all. It certainly is wonderfully kind of him.

June 3rd. We have been in Macao for over two months now. While we were dining at the Reeves' yesterday, we heard on the radio the news of the terrific air raids over Germany. First 1,500 planes over Cologne and then 1,000 over Zessen, two nights running. Churchill announced that this is the beginning of future raids, in the same numbers, every night over different cities of Germany. I cannot help feeling sorry for the people who are living there, as we know the horrors of bombing first-hand.

But we were all so thrilled about this news that we shouted and whooped for joy, and John Reeves opened the windows on the side opposite the Japanese Consulate, so that they could hear us celebrating! The Japanese Consulate is so close to the British one, that they could easily hear every word we were saying, particularly the way we said it. But after a while we thought it might perhaps be better not to go on goading them, in case they take it out on us later on and prevent us getting away.

June 6th. Now Reidar is getting trouble over the ship *Masbate*. The Japanese want her. They want him to sign a bill of sale and he will not do it. This may develop into some troublesome business and prevent us from sailing at all.

Also more news of air raids in Kweilin and the bombing season over Chungking has started. Everybody here is against us going and very pessimistic about the outcome of our travels. But we are determined to go.

In the evenings I go up on the roof and love looking over the house tops, to the Pearl River, winding away inland, towards the setting sun, in the direction that we shall be travelling. It is typical up-river scenery: flat sweeps of paddy fields, sudden uprising of hills, so abrupt, and then the flatness again; and far away in the distance, the mountains and vast stretches of land, that go on and on for thousands of miles, across the most uninhabited part of the world with the densest forests, the most desolate plateaus, the highest mountains, and the hottest plains, until one comes to Europe.

This feeling of immensity always holds such a fascination for me. I long to explore so many places in this world and to go wandering into the unknown lands that lie beyond the golden sunset.

Farewell Macao

June 10th. At long last we are on our way! We left Macao yesterday by ship onward to Fort Bayard, the French port at Kwangchow Wan. In spite of our resolutions to carry the minimum of baggage, we found we had 28 pieces! However, we have to be prepared for any eventuality. We may be stuck for months, or even years in China or some remote place.

The parting from the servants was very sad. Poor little Ah So wept and wept, she was so heartbroken at seeing her baby Ingrid go. John wept too, as he did not want to leave either of them behind. Ah Chee and Ah So have certainly been faithful friends and servants, following and helping us through all kinds of adversities and even lending us their hard-earned savings in time of need. We wished we could have taken them with us.

The decks were crammed with passengers, lying all over the place with all their goods and chattels around them, spitting and coughing in good old Chinese fashion.

There were a number of Sikhs and their women too, dressed in flowing dirty tunics. The men had such long, long black hair coiled under their turbans and their beards also so long, because they must never be trimmed, just divided and drawn back on either side of their face and tucked under their turbans too.

Our cabin looked out onto this deck and apart from the thin partition between us, it seemed almost as if we were travelling as deck passengers ourselves. The smell was strong everywhere, what with all the hot, unwashed bodies, the stillness of the air and the fact that the ship always carries buffaloes from Indochina to Macao and the decks are seldom washed properly.

The officers were extremely kind to us. Ingrid straight away took possession of the bridge and captivated the captain and chief officer, who played with her for ages and allowed her to do whatever she wanted. They pressed us to come up whenever we wished to. It was a blessing to be able to be there, as it was a fine big bridge, clean and comparatively peaceful. But of course we still thought of torpedoes during the voyage. (*The Wing Wah was actually struck by a torpedo in June 1943.*)

Reidar and I stood up in the bow of the ship and gazed over the beautiful calm sea ahead, and down into the crystal clear depths. We watched the flying fish start up from the bows, as the ship cut through the sea, and go skimming over the water, glinting a beautiful silvery-blue in the sunlight. Enormous red jellyfish drifted along in the depths below, beautiful also in a rather repulsive way, as they opened and shut, like coloured parasols. We even saw a shark, which made us wonder about our chances of survival if the ship was torpedoed.

The sun was baking hot and the breeze came up off the sea, as we leant over the side feeling so happy and full of excitement at really being on our way.

There were a lot of Chinese crowded up there all around us. We could not help laughing at one man, who was sleeping peacefully in the hot sunshine, balanced on a rope stretched between some machinery and the mast. How it was possible to balance on it at all was amazing enough, let alone go to sleep!

We saw the Southern Cross in the sky before we went to bed hanging low over the horizon and gleaming like a beautiful symbol ahead of us. How exciting it was to finally be on our way.

Our walk through China begins

June 11, 1942. As we approached Kwangchow Wan on the *Wing Wah*, the low coastline came into view, with long stretches of hot yellow sands and brown dried-up dunes behind. Then it became green with mangrove swamps, and rivers branched off in different directions, as we steamed up the main tributary very slowly.

Fort Bayard did not impress us at first glimpse. It appeared like a small village, with its twin spired church as the most prominent building.

Fort Bayard, Kwangchow Wan, China

We anchored in the stream and were immediately surrounded by hundreds of sampans and junks. People swarmed on board, climbing up ropes and squeezing in crowds up the gangway, while others tried to squeeze themselves down it to get off the ship. The muddle and noise, together with the smell, dirt and heat, were quite overwhelming.

We were met by Mr. Hoi's two sons, who eventually managed to struggle onboard to greet us. Mr. Hoi is a business friend of Reidar's and Reidar looks after his ships.

Finally we all found ourselves tumbled on board a junk, including Albert Eger, a young Swiss who used to work in the Government Stores Department, and his fiancée, a pleasant, somewhat buxom young Portuguese girl. They are going to get married at once and have asked whether they can join our caravan on our journey to Kweilin.

We landed at the long, unfinished pier and walked along the 'bund' to Mr. Hoi's office. Mr. Hoi was on the doorstep to meet us, a truly venerable looking Chinese gentleman, dressed in a long gown of beautiful pale grey silk.

We were led upstairs to a very comfortable, cool sitting room, where we had to sit and pass the time of day for two hours, until we could get our passports back from the police.

Mr. Hoi's two sons, Gordon and Stephen, both spoke English very well, but Mr. Hoi himself could not speak a word. However, many fine speeches were made, with Mr. Lin, Tony or Doctor Tso to interpret. It turned out that there was absolutely no accommodation to be had in any hotel in Kwangchow Wan, and as we would have been very uncomfortable elsewhere, Mr. Hoi invited the whole party to stay in his own home. We were so grateful to him.

After two more hours of waiting, we were more than thankful to be able to climb into a car and be whisked away through beautiful green countryside, looking very European in style, until we reached Tche Kam, ten miles away, and arrived at Mr. Hoi's palatial residence. It was like a big apartment building turned into one house. Newly built, fine and modern, the style half Chinese, half European. Lovely tiled bathrooms and electric fittings everywhere, but no electric light, as Tche Kam has electricity in one half of the town on some days, and in the other half on other days.

The hospitality of Mr. Hoi Ow Chow is quite overwhelming. Nothing is too much trouble or too good for us in the way of food or comforts. His family members are all so kind and helpful. When we think that they have also taken in all the others in our party, whom they only know through Reidar, we feel more overwhelmed than ever and will never be able to thank them adequately.

Sophie and I and the two children have a fine room on the third floor, which now the newlywed Mrs. Eger shares with us. That first evening we arrived in a state of exhaustion. When I saw the fine four-poster bed, hung with embroidered white curtains and covered with a beautiful embroidered counterpane, looking so dazzlingly clean and inviting, I could not resist sinking down on it to rest my weary bones. But I got quite a startle when I came down with a bump, onto hard wooden boards just covered with a mat, no mattress at all! I had forgotten that Chinese always sleep like that. The mats are so much cooler than mattresses. Still, I can not help almost envying Sophie her camp bed!

Reidar and Captain Svane have a room downstairs, while Tony, Mr. Lin and Mr. Fung, and now also Albert Eger, have camp beds in the great entrance hall. It seems that each floor is a complete unit for each one of Mr. Hoi's wives.

There have been big parties for dinner and one given by the owner of the *Masbule*. We have never eaten such marvellous Chinese chow, or such great quantities of it.

Last night there was a wonderful party in Mr. Hoi's hotel garden. We all sat around the traditional Chinese round tables for 10 people, under the trees with lanterns hanging from them. It was such a pretty night and there were *sing-song girls* to entertain and look after the company.

The food was superlative. Birds nest soup with pigeons eggs floating in it, our favourite shark's fin soup, raw fish, cooked fish with ginger sauce, mushroom soup, melon soup, of course sweet-sour pork, pigeons in wine, roasted duck skin on tiny slices of unleavened bread, then the meat of the duck, fried chicken, delicious vegetables, sea slugs (which we are not quite so enthusiastic about), and many other dishes followed, including roasted whole suckling pig, which I never can bear to look at, as it looks so alive and reproachful. We ended up with an exquisite sweet almond soup and quaint little Chinese cakes. The Chinese certainly are artists in cooking. The only trouble is that we eat far too much and we are afraid to refuse in case we may cause offense.

We are busy getting everything organized for our departure tomorrow. Mr. Lin, hurries all over the place, followed closely by Mr. Fung, his aid and accountant, getting all the chair-coolies and baggage-coolies rounded up and fixing what they are to be paid.

The Hois have given us so many things for our journey, including thermos flasks and tins of condensed milk, both of which will be invaluable to us. They also gave us sun toupees to wear. We have been advised to wear dark, inconspicuous clothes in case of Japanese planes coming over. If they see foreign looking people they are likely to fly low and strafe them with machine guns.

The road to Kweilin

June 13th. The day of our moving-on arrived and we were up by dawn putting the last few things away. We were supposed to leave by six in the morning to get to the customs on the Chinese border by seven. But the ever-hospitable Hois insisted upon giving us a colossal breakfast. By the time that was finished and everyone rounded up, all the farewells said and our deeply felt gratitude for all their thousand and one kindnesses, and by the time the baggage-coolies were loaded and the chair-coolies satisfied with their load, it was a good deal later.

Sophie rode through town in a chair with JoJo, and I had Ingrid. Reidar was going to take chair turns with Captain Svane. Mr. Lin and Mr. Fond had a chair each, and Tony was going to share one with Dr. Tso. The newly wedded Egers were determined to walk to try and save money. Poor Sophie felt very uncomfortable with John sitting heavily upon her and their three chair-coolies complained bitterly of the weight.

We had previously had a good laugh when the chair coolies came to look everyone over before leaving. When they saw Sophie and John, they immediately said they must have an extra coolie to help. Poor Sophie is always getting teased about her weight, but she takes it marvellously and is relying on this trip to help reduce her unwanted 15 lbs.

It was past 7.30 a.m. when we started off and already boiling hot. Sophie, Captain Svane and Tony set off walking from the Chinese customs station but soon they realized that it was really hard work, as the coolies go at a great speed. Reidar and I walked for the next two hours and it was indeed strenuous going, and we were a bit anxious over Reidar's heart.

The countryside was rather uninteresting, immense, flat, dusty plains with earth roads stretching across them, small stubby plants and great clumps of bamboos. It got hotter and hotter and our shadows were practically under our feet. So we were only too thankful when we took our chairs again. This time I went with John and Sophie with Ingrid.

John in a sedan chair and Reidar walking ahead

When we got to Suichi, a tiny village of straggling little Chinese houses, the coolies dumped us down and refused to go on any more. They said it was too late to reach the next station, 20 miles more, where we had to pass a customs post again before 6 p.m.

We were set down under the blazing sun in a narrow cobbled street in front of an "hotel", which looked more like a shed, and was crowded with coolies drinking tea.

The rooms were just wooden board partitions, opening on to a small courtyard in the centre. The floors were of rough stone and the ceiling just roof tiles resting on wooden beams thickly covered with cobwebs. The walls bore the marks of numerous flies, mosquitoes and other questionable insects having been squashed upon them.

As soon as we had got our various, most necessary pieces of baggage sorted out, and Sophie was looking after Ingrid, I went in search of the kitchen. It was not difficult to find. I just followed the smell of charcoal smoke and frying peanut oil.

The cook and his assistants, all naked to the waist and their bodies glistening with sweat, were busy preparing the evening meal. There were great shallow iron pans full of steaming rice and others frying with chopped up meat and vegetables. The ceiling was black with years of smoke and dirt. Various weird looking bits of dried fish, chickens' claws and what looked like seaweed hung from the walls and rafters. And over everything swarmed a million flies.

Though my Chinese provoked considerable merriment and many exclamations of "Aye-ah!", I made them understand that I wanted to do some cooking myself. So a chatty and charcoal were produced and I boiled water for the thermos, which we always have in order to make Ingrid's milk, cooked semolina and porridge for the children's breakfast, before our early morning departure. By the time I had finished I was soaked with perspiration.

After we had finished our own meal, a somewhat different Chinese chow to Mr. Hoi's fare, we took Ingrid and John for a walk in the cool of the evening and the whole village turned out to goggle at them in amazement. They simply could not understand their flaxen hair.

That night, as we lay on our wooden board beds, poor Sophie, who was experiencing it for the first time, kept groaning and grunting, as she turned from side to side desperately trying to find a less uncomfortable position.

Finally I advised her to lie on her tummy and that seemed to work much better. Ingrid and John adapted themselves apparently better than we did to their new type of bed and managed to get some sleep. I found it so hot and stifling under the thick Chinese mosquito nets, without a breath of air in our little cubicle. I rather envied Tony and our Chinese friends, who were sleeping in the courtyard with a number of others.

June 14th. This morning we were up shortly after four, trying to get all our belongings collected and packed and the children dressed by the dim light of a tiny oil lamp. As we started off at 5 a.m., the sun rose and the countryside looked fresh and lovely. Sometimes it seemed as though we were in England, crossing wide moors, covered with bracken—but without rabbits or gorse bushes. Then it seemed to be the south of France with dry pine woods and lovely pine-scented air.

Later came the real China. Vast expanses of vivid green paddy fields and towering groves of bamboos, waving their feathery tops against the clouds. As we approached some low mountains, we started very gradually climbing, winding our way through the foothills, as the sun grew hotter and ever hotter.

Our path through the paddy fields with mountains in the distance

The coolies stop at little thatched-roof shelters, dotted at regular intervals, about every hour all along our way. There they rest for a few minutes and drink tea. We are always so hot and thirsty ourselves that we are thankful for a bowl of tea too, but we always insist upon seeing the water actually boiling, then rinse out the bowls in it before drinking. We have been warned so often that it is absolutely essential to take every precaution possible against disease, and water seems to be the most important.

One of the many small villages we stay in on the way to Kweilin

Reidar and I walked the first stretch of two hours and we must have done nine to ten miles, fast going. At times we had to run a little to catch up with the coolies. But I find it very tiring sitting in the chair, swaying up and down with John on my lap for hours and he talks non-stop all the way!

Our caravan consists of eight chairs and 42 coolies and Albert Eger walking. His wife, Joe, had to take a chair today as she was so exhausted after yesterday's walk.

One time our chair got left rather a long way behind all the others. We were going through extremely desolate country then, amongst the foothills and had seen no sign of life for a long time. We passed by clumps of stunted trees and through narrow ravines. I could not help thinking of the stories we had heard of travellers being held up by bandits along this same road, and robbed of all their possessions or held for ransom. So I felt a bit nervous until we caught up with the rest of the caravan at the next stop.

We arrived at our last stop around four o'clock in the afternoon. It is more of a town than Suichi and the hotel slightly grander, but dirty as ever.

Mr. Lin is so kind and has such gentle, charming manners. He tries to look after everybody to the best of his ability and I just don't know how we should manage without him. He takes a lot of trouble too over ordering the food that we eat each evening, trying to choose what he considers is suitable for our needs.

This evening he explained that the melon soup we had was especially good to have in great heat, as it cools the blood. He also takes charge of all our bowls and chopsticks, which he produces ceremoniously from a spotless white towel before each meal and then sees them washed, dipped in boiling water and wrapped up carefully again, when we have finished.

Later Reidar and I took Ingrid and John for a walk after the heat of the day. The peasants were finishing their day's work, some driving home their water buffalo and others watering the vegetable patches. They went slowly along the lines of *pak choy* with big bamboo poles across their shoulders, hanging with cans of disgusting looking, and smelling, water. Their conical coolie hats were sometimes lacquered a wonderful colour of orange-red.

We suddenly heard a strange sort of whirring, humming sound and looking up saw in the distance a queer-looking kite, with all kinds of ribbons and other objects floating behind it. It was an enormous affair. As we got nearer, we found a group of men around a wooden trestle, supporting a big spoked wheel, which they unwound gradually to let the kite gain height. The rope was tremendously thick and we could see that the kite must be extremely heavy, as it needed two men to hold the wheel. As it got higher it produced lovely musical tones from the many little pipes that were attached to its tail.

Further away we saw another one rising into the sky and it turned out that they were having some sort of a competition. Of course the children were fascinated and we were too.

As we returned to the town, we passed some big ponds with water lilies and ducks floating upon them. They looked so attractive, with tall water rushes growing at the edges and the little grey Chinese houses, with curled up roof tiles, in the background. But when we came near, the effect was spoilt by the smell and the condition of the water. Then we noticed that there were W.C.s built out over every pond.

Tonight Ingrid and I have a large opium divan to sleep on, made of blackwood, where I am now sitting cross legged to write this diary entry. It looks quite fine but, how hard this blackwood is! I still have not got used to the hardness of our wooden beds and feel aching and somewhat bruised all over. The candle is burning out.

June 15th. We were off again by dawn. This time we had a long day, as we had to do 36 miles. The countryside changed as we progressed and climbed gradually. We passed by small lakes up in the hills, which looked so inviting, and crossed many more vast expanses of paddy fields, all in different stages of growth.

Baggage being carried by Chinese coolies

As we hurried along the narrow mud paths between the paddy fields, we saw peasants in their blue jackets and coolie hats, which serve as sunshade or umbrella equally well. Their trousers were rolled up high, as they tilled the earth behind the patient water buffaloes that dragged the age-old wooden ploughs. Others were planting out new rice, plant by plant, in the water-covered fields.

In another place, we had seen them threshing the rice, beating it into high baskets, with openings on one side and taller than themselves. Small nursery patches are dotted all over the place, where the new rice is sewn and allowed to grow, until it is big enough to be transplanted into the big fields. These patches are of the most vivid glorious green imaginable. I have always wanted to have a dress of paddy-field green!

At one time there had been a road from Kwangchow Wan to Chungking, but three years ago, when the Japanese were near, it had been demolished. Now we travel on it at times, but there are great pits and trenches dug right across it and all the bridges have been destroyed, so the chair-coolies have a hard time making detours.

It was burning hot and I felt so sorry for poor Albert Eger, walking all the way. We stopped more frequently, as the day drew on, always at the little thatched sheds by the side of the road. There the coolies have chow or tea and rest on benches, and we get out and stretch our legs thankfully. It is generally pleasantly cool in these little shady places and smells wonderfully of pines from the branches that cover the roofs.

We arrived at our night stop, after 12 hours of travel, at about 5 p.m. Before we stopped we had to pass through another customs post. Mr. Lin introduced Reidar to the customs official and told him that Reidar had been invited to come to Chungking by the government. The official was so impressed that he passed all our baggage, without opening anything, unlike previous experiences.

The hotel we came to was the most attractive so far, standing on a little hill overlooking a fairly broad river. It was quite new and still being built, with broad open windows and in a style and setting that reminded me of Norway.

But then we discovered that the beds were simply infested with bugs, and cockroaches and spiders were everywhere. We soon heard other travellers discovering them too and banging out their bedding. We sprayed all over the beds with Flit, then I poured boiling water over the joints in the wood and shook Keatings powder all around. Thank goodness we had been warned long ago and have provisions of such items.

At sundown we went for a walk down to the lovely river. It was so cool and beautiful there, but too many mosquitoes. On our way back to the hotel we passed amongst a few straggling huts and were able to buy some plums. We took them back with much joy and stewed them with the local brown sugar and they tasted delicious. A lovely change! But alas, we had nothing in which to carry those that were left over, so in the end we boiled Ingrid's po-po toilet and put them in there!

June 16th. It was raining but we set off just the same, shut into our bouncing chairs with painted canvas pulled up over the window openings. It shut out the view, as well as any fresh air. The coolies wore their usual raincoats made entirely of palm leaves and all the baggage was wrapped in palm leaves too, keeping it dry.

John has got a chair of his own now, as the coolies refused to carry him with us any more. He is very good throughout these long, tiring days although they must seem boring to him. Poor little chap started crying this morning, saying he had a pain. So I gave him some brandy and he felt fine again very soon.

Ingrid also behaves wonderfully well most of the time. She sits on either Sophie's or my knees for hour after hour, gurgling and humming to herself. The only trouble is trying to keep her still, as the coolies grumble and get very upset if she moves from side to side. Even that can upset their balance. However they are always talking to her and playing with her and seem quite proud to carry her.

Ingrid enjoying the ride in a sedan chair

This evening after we arrived and got through the usual chores, we went out with the children to get some fresh air. A crowd of children were gathering around and following us. Then the mothers and fathers joined them and *amahs*, coolies, peasants, shopkeepers and any passer-by gradually congregated around us, staring and exclaiming at Ingrid and John's flaxen hair. The crowds pressed around us so closely that it became quite impossible to move in any direction. Some of them put out their hands just to touch Ingrid's hair. They laughed and shouted to each other in delight and amazement and the commotion kept attracting more people. The crowd around us became positively enormous and completely blocked the whole road, so that such traffic as there was, also came to a standstill,

All our efforts of persuasion and the rickshaw coolie's shouts of protestation had no effect upon the crowd. They merely laughed merrily at my Chinese and pushed and jostled each other all the closer. Everyone seemed to be having a great deal of fun and, strangely enough, Ingrid and John did not seem to mind at all being the centre of attraction. But Reidar and I felt that the situation was getting rather out of hand and were thankful when some policemen came to our rescue, dispersing the crowd and escorting us back to our hotel.

June 19th. I haven't written in my diary for three days, as I have just been too tired each evening. Whenever we arrive Sophie and I just march straight into the kitchen and ask if we may use a chatty. We realize that it is essential for us to actually see for ourselves that the water is boiling and cook everything ourselves. We have been warned by so many people about the danger of cholera, particularly from drinking unboiled water. We feel we cannot be too careful, with all the dirt and flies around.

Last night Albert Eger made us some Swiss fondue. He had been given a piece of cheese before he left Hong Kong and had been carrying it with him all this time, in all this heat! Finally he decided it had better be finished otherwise it might escape him altogether! So he got a bottle of Chinese wine and simmered it together with the cheese and invited us to share it with them in their cubicle.

Sophie, Captain Svane, Tony, Reidar and I all crowded into the tiny space, most of us sitting on the bed, and dipped spoons into the fondue, as there was no bread available. The others drank sips of Chinese wine, but it was far too strong for me, and of course, Uncle Svane never drank any. It was suffocatingly hot and stuffy in that cubicle and the fondue made us even hotter. I think the combination of high cheese and Chinese wine made it somewhat more powerful than the usual Swiss recipe. But it was extremely good and everybody enjoyed the change greatly, in spite of one or two of us feeling decidedly sick afterwards.

It rained most of the day and the coolies padded along slipping, sliding and swearing. We came to many small rivers, which we had to wade through ourselves. Sometimes the current was very swift and the water came up so high it wet my shorts, even though I had hitched them up to the limit.

The west river we were following was really beautiful. It was so wide and smooth, with massive bamboos growing along the banks. There were water wheels too, some small and some very big, made ingeniously of hollow bamboo sections, tied all around the outside of the big wheel. They were slanted in such a fashion, that as they dip into the river, they fill with water, which was tipped out into the adjoining field, as the wheel went around on the downward journey.

We crossed many bridges, very rickety and long, made of single planks or logs stretched end to end across the river and resting on none too solid-looking pillars.

Albert hired a bicycle and got along fine the first day with it, but when the rain started, he found it practically impossible to negotiate the narrow mud paths between the paddy fields. So he has ended up taking a chair.

The next hotel we stayed in was so horribly dirty. We had never seen anything like it. It swarmed with cockroaches and spiders and our room was like a filthy barn. Dirt and cobwebs festooned the rafters and the windows were barred like a prison.

The kitchen was so revoltingly dirty, I hardly dared go into it. As well as the usual grease and mess, with cockroaches running over the tables and the food, the flies were swarming in thick black blankets over everything. I felt quite sick! The sight of large bowls full of great green and yellow caterpillars floating in water ready for cooking, just about finished me off.

We went for a walk in the evening and somehow found ourselves in the garden of a very big Chinese house. There were high walls all around and it was quite deserted. There were lovely cool, green, leafy trees and a profusion of flowering shrubs and sweet-smelling jasmine, all growing rather wild and untended. It seemed like a forgotten corner of the world.

We wandered through a moon-gate and over a quaint little humped bridge that crossed one end of a large pond full of lovely lotus flowers. The peace and beauty of the spot made such a vivid contrast to our hotel. I wanted to stay on and on, just dreaming.

It is no wonder that the Chinese consider the lotus flower with such reverence, for it is not only a symbol of beauty and purity, but it is so useful as well. The stems can be eaten as a vegetable or dried and made into a powdered food like arrowroot (I make it for Ingrid sometimes). The leaves are dried and used for wrapping food. The young leaves can be eaten and the flower seeds too, while the hard seed-base is dried and ground up for medicines.

One thing we really miss is coffee for breakfast. I often think how much I would enjoy a piece of toast, instead of the usual bowl of congee or noodles. In one little town we bought some steamed bread, which was a great delicacy for us. We felt slightly apprehensive about it, as we couldn't boil it before eating it, as we do with almost everything else. But the little steamed buns were in a glass cupboard and we peeled the outer skin off them very carefully before eating them. They tasted very good, slightly sweet and were stuffed with bean curd.

Our last day's travel by chair was the most lovely of all. We passed through rich cultivated farming districts and saw such an abundance of vegetables, fruit, tobacco and many, many other things. There were laichee trees of such size and grandeur, so laden with luscious ruby fruit. Small forests of pumelo, papaya and grapefruit trees clustered nearby each little farming village.

The villages themselves seem pervaded by an atmosphere of peace, hard work and contentment. During the day everyone is out in the fields working. Mothers with babies tied to their backs plant rice or tend the vegetable patches, men plough the fields, and small boys look after the flocks of ducks or guard the water buffaloes.

In the evenings the women go home to make the food, and the small children play in the dust around the doorstep, amongst the chickens, puppies and sway-backed pigs with tummies so fat that they scrape the ground. The old men smoke their pipes, just like they do in Europe, only the pipes are long pieces of bamboo with holes in them, and they squat comfortably on their haunches, instead of sitting.

The old women sit and gossip, at the tops of their high-pitched voices, or they may be dressing the younger women's hair. This involves oiling it and smoothing it, until every hair is stuck fast in its place, then plucking out hairs on the forehead, so that a perfectly smooth, symmetrical line is obtained.

After traversing the flat farming districts, we started climbing gradually through lovely pine-covered hills. The smell of the pines was so fragrant. The weather became cooler and after some heavy showers, we sometimes felt quite cold.

We finally came to the end of our chair journey on the 19th, having covered about 230 miles by chair and walking. We were very thankful to be done with that part of the journey.

June 20. As Watlam is quite a town, the hotel was fairly full of travellers and they made considerable noise over their meals and playing mah-jong afterwards, late into the night.

During the night we hardly slept at all, the rats made such a noise. They ran over everything and rummaged amongst things on the table and boxes. They fought madly for some steamed buns in the middle of the floor, squealing and scuffing about and knocking things over. It was horrible to feel them running over our mosquito nets, but we were so thankful the nets prevented them actually coming onto our beds. Reidar shone his torch upon them and counted eight of them on top of his net.

Reidar and the infallible Mr. Lin together managed to hire a private bus, to take us to a place two days away, where we hope to be able to get a train to Kweilin. It is a dreadfully expensive bus, but we were told it was a very special one, as it runs on diesel oil instead of charcoal. There were five Chinese students, who wanted to come with us in the bus, and Mr. Lin insisted that they make some small contribution to the cost.

When we set off this morning, we were prepared for something pretty grim, but not quite as bad as it actually is. Like a large wooden box on wheels, its tiny windows on either side are barred across the middle, so that one cannot even put one's head outside. As the whole of the back of the bus is piled high with everybody's luggage, held in place by two enormous planks, the only entrance is by squeezing past the driver's seat, through a narrow opening, into the part where we all sit.

When I first saw what we were going to travel in, I insisted that we should try and get an axe to take with us, in case we find ourselves trapped inside. But although we searched throughout Watlam, an axe was quite unobtainable and we were forced to set off just hoping for the best.

How Captain Svane has survived so far, swathed in woollen underwear, I just cannot imagine! But he would never dream of taking it off, even during all his walking. He says it is the best thing to wear and prevents him from getting prickly heat, which the rest of us suffer from so badly.

The driver goes at breakneck speed along the narrow dirt roads, full of bumps and furrows. Sometimes the road runs right at the edge of deep gullies and along the banks of rivers, that look so crumbly, and across the most flimsy-looking bridges. But the driver dashes on undaunted.

At times the scenery resembled a lovely Chinese scroll come to life. The wide, smooth river, with great clumps of bamboos and clusters of tall beautiful trees growing along its banks.

Picturesque pagodas, some of them with nine tiers, as nine is a lucky number.

Ingrid and John were very good in spite of the heat and dust and the exhausting jolting and swaying of the bus. Albert Eger played his mouth organ for her and sang Swiss yodelling songs, which thrilled her and entertained all of us. We all sung at times; Sophie and I went in for French songs—"Parlez moi d'amour" and "Auprès de ma blonde"—etc. Then everybody, excepting the Chinese students, sang, "Ai Ai Ai Ai Ai I love you very much", at the top of our voices, trying to drown the creaking and groaning of the old bus. The students, perched on their bench, with their heads resting on their drawn up knees, slept through it all, swaying perilously in all directions.

We have been wearing the same clothes all along, occasionally washing a shirt overnight but our shorts are the same. Tonight at supper we were discussing the clothing situation and Sophie announced that she will wear her same shorts throughout our whole trip, in spite of their dirtiness. Joe Eger suggested that she could wash them overnight. So when I inquired whether she had said "watch" them overnight, it caused considerable merriment!

June 21st. The roads were as bad as ever and we were jolted and thrown about all day long. But the scenery was very beautiful. We drove over great flat green plains, that were hardly cultivated at all and then approached the jagged range of mountains we had seen so blue in the distance before.

From there we entered the strangest land I have seen in my life. A country of weird-shaped giants it seemed. "Stone Mountains" the Chinese here call them, and such they are. Great masses of rock rising sheer from the flat, grassy plains, towering to anything between 1,000 to 2,000 feet in such strange distorted shapes. Sometimes they are grouped closely together, with rivers of land winding in between them, and at times a solitary "giant" stands alone on a vast flat plain. It was as though we were travelling through an unreal, fairytale land.

Even Mr. Lin and Mr. Fong find it difficult to understand the people here, or to make themselves understood, as the dialect spoken here is quite different to our Cantonese, or to Mandarin. In fact it seems that in each district they have quite a different language.

We came to more and more villages, some of them walled and nearly all had clusters of beautiful, tall, shade trees nearby and cement squares, where rice and other grains were spread out to dry.

We had to cross three big rivers. We were ferried across the river by means of men with long poles pushing on the bottom of the river and walking the length of the raft. On one river the current was very strong and we had to be towed upstream by men from the riverside pulling us with a long rope, attached to the top of the mast.

It was terribly hot. Even driving in the bus we got no fresh air at all, as there was a following wind and it was like sitting in an oven. We had to keep fanning Ingrid constantly. Her pricklyheat worries her considerably and has gone septic in a few places.

At one point we came to a bridge that had partially collapsed and the bus could not go across fully laden. Either we had to unload all the baggage, carry it across and then reload it, or try to drive across the riverbed, as it was quite shallow. There was a group of coolies waiting there expectantly to cash in on the unloading business, so the "bus manager" decided to drive across.

Our bus stuck in the river by a broken bridge

We all got out of the bus and studied the terrain and hoped for the best. The driver however, picked his route badly and the bus got stuck midway across the stream with water splashing through the engine. It was amazing that the engine could still keep running. But the bus was stuck fast and all the driver's efforts to move it forward or backward, only succeeded in sinking it deeper into the mud of the riverbed.

The coolies crowded around delightedly and watched us desperately trying to push the great vehicle onwards. They refused to help us unless they received cash in advance.

Our Chinese student passengers merely stood around aimlessly gaping, making no effort whatsoever to help. I got so mad I dashed into the water and started trying to wedge large stones under the wheels to stop them sinking further in. Albert Egar was full of enthusiasm and energy too, and carried enormous flat stones. Both of us ended up soaking wet up to our waists.

Eventually the wheels gripped and the driver revved the engine so that the steam arose all around it. He was just starting to back the bus up the slope a little, when the coolies, seeing their chance had practically gone, decided to help for a third of the price. They threw all their weight on it, but the consequence was almost disastrous as, with tremendous creaking and cracking, the great clumsy structure lurched right over and was within a fraction of capsizing. Everybody, excepting the students who were still just gaping, was shouting madly and we had visions of all our miserable belongings being scattered and soaked, and ourselves stranded indefinitely.

However our luck held, and at last the bus did manage to struggle across the river bed safely. By that time all of us were dripping with perspiration and water, and our shoes were squelching with mud.

When, at long last we finally arrived at Liuchow and the famous Canada Hotel, that Mr. Lin had cracked up so much beforehand, we were sadly disappointed. We have such cramped, tiny rooms and so much baggage, with so little space to put it in. The others do not even have an outside cubicle. But it was slightly less dirty than usual. A welcome change.

Tomorrow we are actually going to take a TRAIN to Kweilin and we do not have to get up before dawn!

We spent the next day at Liuchow and in the evening found ourselves waiting at the station for the famous train. There seemed to be hundreds of other refugees awaiting it too, sitting around or on top of their worldly belongings, in the middle of a great empty plain beside the railway tracks. The only thing to denote a station was a tiny ramshackle building, with a dim light burning outside.

We waited and waited in the darkness, wondering if we would ever be able to get onto the train and what sort of a night we would spend on it.

When it eventually came roaring at us out of the blackness, all the hundreds of Chinese travellers hurled themselves at it and started climbing through windows and doors, long before it had come to a standstill. They even clambered over the engine itself.

Somehow, miraculously, we got on board and there we found, still more miraculously, a sleeping compartment, of such beauty, luxury and cleanliness, we were completely stunned by such magnificence and comfort!

Kweilin (Guilin)

June 23. Next morning at six o'clock we arrived in Kweilin. We had sent two telegrams to our friend "Tootles", whose real name is Cunningham Tweedie and is the personification of a dapper English officer with a clipped mustache and perfectly tailored clothes, announcing our expected arrival. Mr. Lin had also sent word to his friends, so we had hoped to find somebody at the station to meet us. But not a soul.

So we got into rickshaws and trundled and bumped our way to the city, which was some way off, to Mr. Lin's friends' office. They were very kind and hospitable to us there and let us dump all our baggage all over the floor, until we could find some place to go to.

Reidar, Mr. Lin and I went to see Tootles at his office. He seemed much the same as ever, trim and dapper, even in such heat, managing to look as if he had stepped out of a men's fashion magazine. But we were disappointed at his inability to help us over accommodation as we had hoped. His *Salt Gabelle* house had been temporarily loaned to the governor of the province and Tootles himself was living in a tiny bungalow.

In the end a car materialized, belonging to Mr. Lee, Mr. Lin's friend. So Reidar, Mr. Lin and I drove around town visiting all the hotels looking for rooms, which are well nigh impossible to get, as Kweilin is so full of refugees. Finally we managed to get some depressingly dirty rooms all together for us four, Sophie and Captain Svane in a very dilapidated Chinese style hotel called The Lake Side. The Egers, Tony and our Chinese friends scattered and found themselves accommodation in other places.

June 27th. We have been in Kweilin for five days now and, at the end of each day, I have been so dead tired that I have gone to sleep over writing my diary. Sophie, the children and I are now staying in a missionary house, through the good efforts of Tootles. Reidar and Captain Svane are staying at the Lo Tse Seu

Hotel, which is infinitely better than the Lake Side and is considered the best hotel in town. They come over during the day, bringing us all the latest news and rumours gathered from the various Europeans, Chinese and Americans staying at their hotel.

This house is incredibly bare, broken down, gloomy and dirty, but in spite of this we are most thankful to be here. To live in a more or less European-style house, with an English family and eat English food for a change, gives us a feeling of homeliness, in spite of the dirt.

The missionaries have two small boys of three and four years old and a baby of two months. No baby-amah. They have a cook-amah and a "boy", if he can be termed as such. He is so hopeless. Also there is an ancient man, who carries water from the river—the only supply.

Our room is downstairs and next to it is a little storeroom, lined with shelves containing the missionaries' tracts and religious literature, and on the walls hang religious pictures and inscriptions. In this little room is a small basin where we wash ourselves and...a thunder-box (substitute for a W.C.)!

The missionaries are leaving in a few days for their summer holidays up in the hills. We hope we shall be on our way too by then. Reidar and Mr. Lin have been making endless inquiries and efforts to get passages on a plane to Chungking, or Kung Ming, although we would rather not go to the latter, as we have heard that there is plague there.

Now we have to stay packed and all ready to leave within an hour. So we have repacked in order to take the minimum of baggage with us. We are allowed 15 kilos each, but not Ingrid. Mr. Lee, from the Bank of Communications, has promised us that the rest of our things will follow us to Chungking by truck.

It appears that we have a number of influential people working for us, so we may hope to get a plane soon. But others have to wait for months, so I am not too optimistic. However, today there came a telegram from Yu Yat Ching, in reply to the one Reidar had sent from Kwangchow Wan, saying he had cabled the minister of communications in Chungking to give us priority in the plane queue. It somehow seems unbelievable to think that, perhaps, within ten days or so we may be in Calcutta.

I must confess that I feel a bit worried about the plane trip, because of Reidar's heart. I have the needle and injection all ready in case he should need it on the flight and we have managed to get some of the medicine that Dr. Tso recommended for his heart. It is fantastic that one can buy almost any kind of American or British medicines on the black market here, but of course at astronomical prices.

June 29th. This afternoon we went to have tea with Tootles in his minute pine-wood bungalow. We had a lovely tea, with toast, jam, little buns and real fresh milk in our tea! I can't remember when we last had such things. We all enjoyed it so much.

But Tootles is really an old fuss-pot, and he is so narrow-minded and pig-headed in his views and in his attitude towards the Chinese and this type of life. Anything that is not one hundred percent British just doesn't seem any good at all in his opinion. But I can understand that he has reason to be bitter with the way the *Salt Gabelle* are treating their staff.

I still tease him unmercifully, just as I used to do so many years ago. I also pushed a lot of our dirty clothes on to him for his amah to wash! He has a sweet little bungalow, so clean and bright compared to our abode, and he lives like a hermit.

Kweilin, China. The Li River with its wonderful mountains

There is a glorious view right across the broad, smooth river, of lovely, meadow-like expanses dotted with trees, and beyond "the giants", their weird shapes and formations make them a truly extraordinary sight, from some other world. Their jagged peaks float in the soft evening sky above the mist, and reflect in the river below. As we were leaving, a full moon appeared for a few moments, from behind a lofty cloud to greet us.

I soon descended from my dreams, with John and Ingrid filthy as usual. They had been playing around outside the bungalow, under the supervision of Tootles' amah and had particularly enjoyed themselves rolling about in a heap of very dirty sand. But what a relief it was for us, the respite from chasing perpetually after Ingrid, and once more having an amah to do it instead!

July 9th. Here we are still in Kweilin. Still in this dreary, dirty, dilapidated and horribly depressing mission-house. The missionaries have left for their holidays, so Reidar and Captain Svane have now been able to move in with us. It is unbelievable that white people, looking after the souls of others, guiding them along the right path, can stand to live in such dirt. They are nice enough and I know they are dreadfully badly off financially, but that cannot excuse the filthy condition of this house.

Bombs have twice fallen in the garden and shaken the house to bits. There is hardly a whole pane of glass in any of the windows. It is fantastically expensive to replace, so most of the windows have just paper or plain boards nailed over the frames. The floors, walls and ceiling are patched and nailed together, and look as if they might collapse at any time.

The house has been screened against the mosquitoes, which swarm by thousands day and night. Sophie and I find that as we lie on our beds scratching our mosquito and flea bites, (Reidar of course never scratches his, he is so strong minded as he enjoys pointing out to us frequently), we can roll the dirt off our skin in little pellets, from the moisture and the heat. It is quite useful, when one is unable to wash!

Yesterday when the ancient water-carrier arrived with his two wooden pails, slung at either end of his bamboo pole, we asked him to empty some water into the bath upstairs, hoping to have a good scrub. But when we saw the water we felt we just could not get into it. It was pale green and slimy!

Obviously he had taken it from a stagnant pond nearby, instead of the river, as he is supposed to do. We were horrified, as this is the water that we use for our cooking and drinking, as well as washing. He generally pours it straight into a large, deep earthenware tub in the kitchen, which is a dark colour and the kitchen is so gloomy, that we used it without realizing how dirty is was.

I am now sitting on the upper veranda enjoying the beauty of the sky and the stillness of the very early morning, gazing across the squalid surroundings, over the river to those incredible peaks. It seems they are called "Kwangsi Luen San" Mountains, which means "The Disorderly Mountains of Kwangsi".

When we all talk now, it is of what we shall do, when we get back to "civilization", and of what each one of us most looks forward to. For Reidar it is an ice-cold whiskey and water, with pieces of ice tinkling in the glass. For both Sophie and me, it is being able to turn a tap and find hot, clean water pouring out.

Unfortunately, the air transportation has been completely discontinued for passengers, because the government has chartered nearly all passenger planes, due to the American Volunteer Guards taking over. People are told that they will probably have to wait for months for air passages, unless they have very strong "pull". Yesterday at the China National Airway Corporation office Reidar was told that women and children just did not count these days, so that it is quite likely we will be refused passages indefinitely.

We had been relying on Mr. Lin's friends to get us priority, as they had promised, expecting all this time to be off at any moment, ready to leave within an hour's notice. Now it appears that they have done practically nothing at all to help us, and that these dreary two weeks here have been entirely wasted.

After the missionaries left, we had no servants as they had gone with them to the hills. Then a few days later Tootles' boy brought us an old one-eyed amah, and the day after that a very nice young cook, so now we feel very well fixed in that respect.

Reidar and Captain Svane go to the market for our food, and considering they cannot speak a word of the local language, they do remarkably well. Reidar says he just points and gestures, then hands out a handful of money for the storekeeper to help himself. All transactions are done with much laughter and friendliness. I don't suppose they often get such trusting customers, with no ability to bargain!

I quite enjoy walking in the town. The streets are always teeming with people, it seems, no matter what hour of the day or night, and the shops and little stalls remain open until very late.

We went into many grocery shops, trying to get arrowroot for Ingrid's stomachache and also into several medicine shops. They were full of the most weird-looking assortment of dried snakes, animals' feet and insides. There were also a variety of beetles and an impressive display of big glass jars, containing pickled snakes, lizards, frogs and other questionable things.

We were eventually able to explain to one of these medicinemen what the arrowroot was for, and he told us that the Chinese use the powdered roots of lotus flowers for such tummy disorders. So now we have been giving Ingrid lilly-root gruel and it appears to have done her some good.

We often think that one of the most attractive traits of the Chinese is their readiness to laugh, particularly over their own misfortunes or mishaps. We have seen coolies struggling under the most crushing loads and nearly collapsing with laughter. But when it comes to hearing them announce the death of a wife, father or other close relative with a broad grin, we have found ourselves somewhat at a loss.

There are many Chinese refugees here from Hong Kong, Canton and other parts of south China. We have met some of our own friends from Hong Kong and they all want to get to Chungking, or at least away from Kweilin as soon as possible. They fear it is only a matter of how soon the Japanese will take Kweilin, not whether they can take it.

There is a Dutch man here, who puts out a news-sheet each day, typed in English, which is passed around among the English-speaking community. The news makes very dismal reading. It seems to be nothing but one defeat after another all along the many fronts, and the Japanese navy sinking so many British and American vessels.

During the last week we have experienced many air-raid alarms. The first went during the middle of the night, and I must admit that to be awakened by that piercing wail of sirens, sent my heart into my mouth, and in good old Hong Kong style,

I expected to hear the explosion of bombs dropping almost immediately.

We hurriedly dressed in darkness, although some houses had their lights shining brightly. All the time a high-pitched nasal voice was announcing things over the loud speakers in Chinese, which seemed to carry all over the city, but of course we couldn't understand a thing.

From outside, throughout all the darkened streets, came the hum of thousands of voices and the tramp and shuffle of feet, mixed with the clinking of wooden slippers on the roads. Everyone was on their way to the caves.

We took two cushions, a rug, some buns and water, not knowing how long we would be there. I also took such jewellery as I have, wrapped up in an old nappy of Ingrid's. It is safer than leaving it here. We didn't know exactly where to go. Tootles had told us before, somewhat vaguely, about the caves, but we expected to find him at his bungalow and go with him.

So we went out into the street and were swept along with the crowds in the direction of the caves. We were impressed by the comparative calm of the people. Nobody seemed to worry or hurry, accepting the circumstances stoically, just plodding along, carrying babies on their backs and bundles under their arms. The darkness and our shared troubles made us all the same. And as we passed by Tootles' bungalow, I shouted for him, but got no reply, so concluded he had already gone.

We were swept on, and eventually found ourselves pushed and squeezed, amongst hundreds and hundreds of Chinese of all classes, even soldiers, into a gigantic cavern in the cliff. It was dimly lit, and so crowded that we could hardly move.

But I discovered a little niche, fairly high up in the rock, and managed to climb up, over people's heads, and crouch there. It was very cramped and uncomfortable on the wet rock, with Ingrid on my lap. Sophie had to hold me up there, as my balance was so precarious. Poor John had to sit on the wet ground, amongst everybody's legs and feet, while Sophie, Reidar and Captain Svane stood wedged, hardly able to move in the crush.

The great blessing was that there was an opening at either end of the cave and, as the 'ceiling' was so high, we had lots of fresh air. We thought that if a bomb fell at either entrance we should not be in so much danger of being killed by air pressure.

The warning lasted from 2 until 3.30 a.m., when we wended our way home again. But Ingrid would not go to sleep any more.

During that day we had three more alarms and went over to the caves each time, although the last time we were tempted to stay here, but we felt we couldn't jeopardize the children's lives. After the first daylight alarm, the second more urgent warning sounded while we were still some way from the cave. Some people started running and shouting to us to hurry. There were hardly any other people left on the road, and we, not quite knowing what they were shouting, ran too. Poor Reidar, carrying Ingrid, was feeling his heart badly. We found the same niche up in the rock wall, but this time I let Ingrid sit there by herself, while I supported her, standing in a muddy pool. We had all got very hot and wet running to the cave and we soon started to feel cold standing in that damp, chilly atmosphere. Again a false alarm.

On our way back we stopped at Tootles' bungalow and he said that for the next raid he would take us to the private small cave, half way up the cliff face, used by the Governor of Kweilin and his family. Tootles was allowed to go there because the Governor had taken over the number one house of the *Salt Gabelle*, where Tootles should be living now. So we went there with him for the other raids.

It is not too far from his bungalow. We climbed up long steps cut out of the cliff face and came to quite a narrow cave with a few holes in the rock, like windows, overlooking the whole city. There were quite a few people there, all Chinese, chiefly women and children with some amahs. They were very friendly and offered us chairs. But I preferred to look out of one of the holes to see what was going on. Nothing happened. Tootles told us that three bombs had fallen in the garden of our house exactly a year ago and the missionaries were convinced that they would fall again, but next time, on the house.

July 10th. I am sitting on the veranda again while the others are still asleep. It is so quiet and the soft light after dawn makes everything seem beautiful. The peacefulness seems full of hope at the beginning of a new day.

I have been trying to give John lessons, so that he will not entirely forget the little he has learnt at school already, and also to give him something to do. Naturally he gets very bored and restless with no other children to play with. I try to be so patient and explain how to write the letters and read the words, but our lessons so often end up with crying and screaming. He makes such a noise and of course wakes up Ingrid, who Sophie has been fanning and patting to get to sleep. One has to try to keep calm and patient!

I got such a surprise yesterday when I suddenly heard the strains of the little harmonium emerging from the room that the missionaries use for their religious meetings. When I looked in, I found Reidar sitting at the harmonium with Ingrid on his lap playing Handel's Largo. I was most impressed, because it is the first time I have ever heard him play since I have known him. Ingrid was also quite enchanted and wouldn't let him stop. She kept saying, "Daddy do ding dong, Daddy do ding dong," whenever he paused. He said it was quite a business concentrating on the notes and also having to push the pedals at the same time. I thought it sounded lovely and was so relieved to have Ingrid so well entertained.

In the afternoon it began to rain quite heavily, so we rushed to put out a tub to catch the rainwater. Then Sophie and I had a brilliant idea. We told the men to remain indoors, facing the other way, while we went into the garden minus our clothes, but with a cake of soap, and stood where the rain from the roof came pouring down in a wonderful shower. We got ourselves covered with a marvellous lather of soap and were starting to really feel clean, when suddenly the rain stopped. It stopped so abruptly we just stood there, soapy all over, not knowing what to do.

Finally we had to go further out in the garden and try to rinse ourselves off in some puddles that had collected. When we went around to the other side of the house to find our tub of precious rainwater, in which we wanted to wash our hair, we found Ingrid had put all the puppies into it. She wanted to give them a bath. Fortunately none of them were drowned, but we didn't get our hair washed!

Every evening after supper Captain Svane makes us all take a dose of quinine powder against malaria. It is horrible in this form, so bitter, it really needs quite a lot of will power to swallow it. We certainly don't want to risk getting malaria to add to our problems and I would not like to have to call in one of the local doctors here. Judging by the way the dentists advertise themselves, with rows and rows of extracted teeth hanging up outside their offices, the medics don't inspire much confidence.

We have been discussing the possibility of going by truck to Chungking or Kung Ming, as it looks as though we may never get a plane out of here. The Dutch people are planning to go that way. The trouble is that it would mean many days of very hard going, over terrible roads and more danger of disease and sickness. We shall wait a bit longer and hope something will happen.

July 14th. Still in Kweilin and still hoping for a plane. In the meantime Tony has now reached Calcutta! When we heard that all of us felt like exploding. Fate certainly is rubbing in the irony of the situation. If we had not waited for Tony in Macao and so missed the *Wing Wah* sailing, then having to wait another three weeks for the next sailing, we would have been in Calcutta long ago. We received a telegram from Archy saying that he is anxiously awaiting our arrival.

We then went to Tootles and begged him to help us. He, of course, said, "I told you so" about the Chinese and their promises and said that he probably could have done things much faster for us. Well, three days ago he came marching into the house, just as I had pictured to myself and hoped for for so long, shouting, "How soon can you be ready?"

I must say that even in the excitement of the moment, I couldn't help laughing at the way he was dressed. Stepping from the drab and dirty streets of a town in the middle of China, in the midsummer heat, into our dilapidated abode, he looked like a perfect English gentlemen. Spotless tussore-silk suit with knife-creased trousers, dazzlingly white suede shoes and smart Panama hat set at a cocky angle, admirably suiting his small clipped moustache and suntan. The whole effect was rounded off by a pair of immaculate pigskin gloves and a cane!

I bounced down the stairs, in my brief and grubby shorts and said, "One hour, sure!", though he and Captain Svane looked doubtful. So Uncle Svane and I worked like mad, he taking down and packing up all the mosquito nets, bedding etc., and I packed food and clothes, and got John and Ingrid organized. Reidar and Sophie came home top speed on meeting Tootles in town. And we were ready exactly when I had said we would be.

Mr. Lin turned up in Mr. Lee's car, with Mr. Fong to take care of the baggage we had to leave behind, to be sent on to Chungking by truck. Finally, after waiting three quarters of an hour, Tootles arrived and we all got into the cars and drove to the Lok Tchin Su Hotel. There we were to transfer into another car for the hour's drive out to the airfield.

I was dressed in a light grey flannel suit with a red flannel shirt, as the trip from Chungking to India over "The Hump" of the Himalayas is very cold. The others were also warmly dressed, but it was a blazing day and we were all dripping with perspiration.

When we got to the Lok Tchin Su, Mr. Eardly was out for tiffin and there was no sign of any car. We sat anxious and impatient, in the stifling heat of the car, waiting.

After a little while he came strolling along and told us that we were too late, the plane had gone. Tootles started telephoning frantically to the airport, which took twenty minutes to get through, and eventually heard that it was quite true. We had missed the plane by about an hour!

Our feelings were indescribable as we returned to our depressing home. We found that the servants had eaten all our tiffin, but fortunately they were still there, and Reidar just managed to stop the coolies going off with our other baggage.

As we stood there in the gloomy passage contemplating all the unpacking and reinstalling beds, mosquito nets and everything, an ancient missionary woman appeared and started sermonizing us in such a lengthy and garbled fashion. Ingrid was bellowing and John was being so petulant, that we had great difficulty in retaining our patience and good manners with her. We certainly had to philosophize then and reason ourselves out of the deepest depression we had yet been in.

Now we are ready to leave within half an hour, with most of our things packed and ready in the hall. But it is depressing and demoralizing to be just waiting and waiting, day after day and hour after hour, for something to happen, not even able to leave the house, excepting to Tootles', in case we are called.

July 19th. We have been nearly one month in Kweilin. Once more frustration has overwhelmed us. Today, just before lunch, Tootles came dashing in again to tell us to get to the airfield as quickly as possible. He said a plane was due to arrive within the next hour bringing some A.V.G. men and would be able to take us on their return trip to Chungking. He then rushed off again to try and get hold of a car while we packed frantically.

Within half an hour we were all six tightly squeezed into a car, together with our meagre baggage, on our way to the airfield. When we arrived, after a long, hot and dusty drive, we found that the plane had not arrived yet. So the driver helped us to put our things in the shade of a small shed and went back to Kweilin.

Daffy Davis was there. He seems to be in charge of the airfield. Rather different from being a jockey in Hong Kong! He told us to just wait there as the plane should be arriving fairly soon, but said that quite a few military people had turned up to go by the same plane and there might not be room for us after all.

It was so hot and there was nowhere to sit except on the ground. The only buildings around were one or two miserable-looking sheds beside the airstrip. Hardly a soul was to be seen. It looked so deserted, I wondered how on earth it could be a real airfield, in constant use, fully manned and maintained with all the air force pilots and everybody that he spoke of.

It all looked so empty, except for the row of planes all lined up on the other side of the tarmac quite a long way off. These small planes all had their noses painted red with big eyes on either side, sharks' teeth and broad stripes over their bodies in black and white, creating a most weird effect. They were, I realized with a thrill, General Chennault's famous Flying Tigers, who have made themselves so celebrated over the heavy losses they have inflicted on the Japanese Air Force recently.

The painted shark's head on the aircraft increased the psychological threat against the Japanese as the Flying Tigers fought to keep open "The Hump" over the Himalayas, the Burma Road, and other routes in and out of China. Kweilin was the headquarters of the 23d Fighter Group, the "Flying Tigers", and also its command unit, the 68th Composite Wing. The unit flew P-40 Warhawk and later P-51 Mustang fighter bombers from the airport, attacking Japanese targets and supporting Chinese army units. The Kweilin Airfield was also used by the United States Army Air Forces Fourteenth Air Force as part of the China Defensive Campaign (1942–1945). Flying Tiger pilots received $600 per month, plus $500 for each Japanese plane destroyed. In 30 weeks of air warfare they downed 100 Japanese planes, losing 14 of their own.

Our spirits began to sink as time went by and we saw more and more men arrive with their kit, obviously waiting for "our" plane. Eventually it came swooping down, disgorged about a dozen people, and took in those men who had been waiting.

By that time there was, sure enough, no more room for us. The door was closed in our faces and we were left there to watch it take off, feeling almost in despair. It started to rain and there was nowhere to take shelter or to put our baggage. Finally we managed to find a dirty bit of canvas to put over it.

Daffy Davis appeared from out of the face of the cliffs that were a little way behind us. It was quite peculiar, because we could not even see any entrance to a cave. He just emerged from behind a large boulder and came down the stony scree slope at the foot of the cliffs. He commiserated with us about the plane and said that maybe we would have another chance tomorrow or the day after.

I asked if we could leave our baggage at the airfield, if he thought it would be safe, because I thought that if it was there, constantly in view and possibly getting in the way, we would not be forgotten. He rather grudgingly said we could leave it if we wanted. He then went to telephone to try and get some transport back to Kweilin for us.

Before he reached the cliff, the air raid siren suddenly cut stridently into our dismal thoughts. It shrieked and wailed so close to us, we were quite at a loss to know what to do.

Then we saw dozens of young men emerging from the cliff and tearing down the slope, across the tarmac, frantically adjusting their uniforms as they ran. Each one leapt into a plane and they all took off, one after another, in a matter of seconds. Within a few minutes of the scream of the siren, the airfield was completely empty. We were most impressed as it was so spectacular. It was more like watching a thrilling film come to life, instead of the real thing.

We realized that the airfield was the obvious place for raiders to come and drop their bombs. We were wondering where to go, when Daffy Davis came back and said we had better follow him. I felt intrigued to see what lay behind the boulder.

We followed him up the rough steps in the scree and then all got the surprise of our lives. Behind the boulder was a small entrance into a most fantastically gigantic cavern. The part we came into was divided off with wooden partitions into several rooms. The electric lighting showed up dimly the damp rocky walls nearest to us, and picked out a few jagged promontories in the lofty roof of the cave so far above. The rest was lost in darkness.

In the room we came into there were easy chairs all over the place and scattered magazines. The pilots had obviously been just lounging around resting. It seemed comfortable and quite cosy, in spite of the black void above, and we felt most thankful to be there. But Ingrid by that time was thoroughly overtired and exhausted, and she cried and cried.

On the other side of the partition was the radio station and we could hear messages coming in, over the crackling atmosphere, announcing the numbers of the raiders and their direction and various other things. The radio officers put little flags on the enormous map of China that hung on the wall. It seemed there were quite a number following up the river headed our way. I thought of those young pilots in their Flying Tigers on their way to meet them.

In spite of all my efforts to quieten her down, Ingrid yelled louder and louder. I knew it must be terribly upsetting for the men listening to the radio. So in desperation I tried to get her as far away from them as possible. I went into the back of the cave, beyond all the friendly partitions, and walked up and down with her in my arms, trying to get her to sleep. I paced up and down, up and down with her, singing softly, staying as much as possible within the orbit of dim light reflected off the walls of the cave. Further back it was so dark, I couldn't see where I was putting my feet. The great cavern seemed to go on and on into endless blackness and bats skimmed low over my head and all around me.

Eventually the 'all clear' sounded. The Flying Tigers had evidently managed to head off the raiders.

By the time we got back to the house it was quite late. The servants had well and truly gone this time and the house was locked. We didn't know who would have the key and Tootles was out. Finally Captain Svane managed to open the tiny window into the "religious" cupboard downstairs and push John through it, so he opened the door for us.

Later we went and sat on Tootles' doorstep. He looked quite amazed and thoroughly horrified to see us again, and I don't blame him!

We have decided to go out to the airfield in any case tomorrow and just wait there hopefully, all day.

Flight to Chungking

July 26th. Chungking at last! The capital of China. This great crowded, dirty, bomb-shattered city, straggles over the hills and right down the steep slopes to the famous Yangtse River and to another great river, the Kialing. They join together here and divide the town into sections with their muddy, swiftly flowing waters.

The town is an incredible jumble of tightly packed buildings of all descriptions, tumbling over each other down to the water's edge. There, there is a solid mass of sampans, ferry boats, *walla-wallas* and all kinds of small craft tied up along the waterfront, bobbing and scraping together with the movement of the water.

Large areas of the town have been burnt to the ground and hundreds of buildings are in ruins. The narrow, dusty streets wind in and out amongst piles of rubble, zigzagging up the steep hillsides, between the closely packed houses.

We have been told that many factories have literally gone underground to survive, and the hills are honeycombed with miles of tunnels, where most of the population takes refuge during air raids.

The whole city is teeming with refugees, Chinese soldiers and generals, foreign missions and diplomats, and servicemen of many nationalities.

We have been here some days already, I have almost lost count, as it is too hot to think much. The temperature in our room this morning at nine o'clock was 109 degrees!

During WWII in Asia (also known as the Second Sino-Japanese War from 1937-1945) Chungking was Generalissimo Chiang Kai-shek's provisional capital for his Kuomintang government. He shared power with U.S. General Joseph Stilwell over the Allied army of China, Vietnam, Thailand, Burma and Malaysia. Chungking was base in China to more than 50 embassies. Today, renamed Chongqing, it has a municipal population of nearly 30,000,000 people and is one of China's largest industrial centres.

Our actual air trip here was wonderful, although I was worried about Reidar's reaction to the height. The plane was a military one with metal seats along either side and all the baggage and military kit was piled up along the middle of the centre passage.

There were tiny frames in the centre of the windows, which could be opened for fresh air, and JoJo was kept busy and amused for a long time, seeing whether his hand would be blown off if he stuck it out far enough.

The other passengers were nearly all military. JoJo was allowed to go up to the pilot's cockpit and after showing him and me all the wondrous gadgets and buttons, the captain let him "pilot" the plane, much to his excitement and our alarm!

I kept looking out of the window down at the beautiful, wild country that we were flying over so fast, instead of creeping across by truck, as we had contemplated having to do. The mountains below were thickly wooded and looked absolutely desolate. No sign of towns, villages, or any life.

When I was in the pilot's cockpit, I saw that we were at 12,500 feet and was very thankful that Reidar seemed to be feeling all right. I didn't want him to know how high we were, so when Captain Svane came along and gleefully told him that we were travelling at nearly 13,000 feet I could have brained him!

After several hours flight, we arrived at Chungking military airport, which is about 35 miles from the city. It was burning hot and we were all very tired and thirsty and wondered how to get from there into the city. We seemed to have been dumped in the middle of nowhere.

Then an extremely bronzed and tough-looking individual came over to us, whom we soon recognized to be the renowned General Chennault, the driving spirit and organizer of the American Volunteer Group, the *Flying Tigers*. His appearance is so rugged, he certainly looks his part! He was most kind and asked if we had any transport into Chungking. His secretary, a very sweet girl whom we had met in Hong Kong and who is Daffy Davis's fiancée, was very helpful.

Quite a number of the A.V.G. came over and talked with us. They were obviously all very taken with our Sophie, and when we were waiting in a small bus that was to take us into town some of them actually produced, from their mess nearby, some iced drinks and creamy cakes, of all things! We were amazed and full of appreciation, as we had had no food all day and were feeling pretty exhausted by that time.

General Chennault, Generalissimo Chiang Kai-shek and his wife, the politically influential Soong May-ling.

It was nearly dark by the time we started, which was a pity as I wanted so much to see the scenery. We took two hours on the way and by the time we were deposited on the road in front of Chialing House, it was well after 9 p.m.

Then came an awful shock that there was absolutely no accommodation whatsoever for us there. Standing in the middle of the dusty road with our belongings around us, on the outskirts of a strange Chinese city at night, with no means of transport as our bus had gone off, Ingrid wailing from sheer exhaustion and Reidar, I could see, very close to collapse. We just did not know where to go or whom to appeal to.

As we stood there in the darkness, abandoned and feeling fairly desperate, trying to formulate some plan of action, an Englishman came out of the house next door and asked what had happened. When he heard our plight, he very kindly offered us shelter for the night. He said he had only two spare rooms and only one had a bed in it, but at least we would have a roof over our heads that night. We were more than thankful to him and gratefully followed him in.

We had just brought our belongings into the house when Reidar collapsed on the floor. His face was ashen and he hardly seemed to be breathing. We got him into the little bare room, that he and Captain Svane were to share, and propped him up on the floor, with some cushions and sponged his brow. There was nothing else we could do, and it seemed to be chiefly exhaustion that he was suffering from.

Then Mr. Gould, our Good Samaritan, produced a cup of hot coffee, a miracle we had not seen for months, and that helped Reidar somewhat. Rest was what he needed most, even on a hard floor.

Next day Reidar was able to contact his Chinese friends, who came hotfoot to meet him at Chialing House. There were profuse apologies, with explanations that they had not known exactly when we were arriving, which was understandable enough, as we had not known ourselves.

They managed to provide some rooms for us at the Chialing House and a few days later we were even given the private apartment of Mr. Kung, the finance minister, who is not using it at present. We are indeed very lucky.

The hotel is full of foreign correspondents and writers of all kinds and nationalities. Typewriters clatter ceaselessly. This hotel, the only European-style one in Chungking, evidently used to be very fine and comfortable, but now, due to the constant bombing of this poor city for so many years, it is extremely dilapidated. There are huge cracks in the walls, paint and plaster falling off everywhere and the whole roof has been replaced by thick straw matting. Most of the glass has disappeared from the windows and is replaced by paper glued to the framework. We always keep them open and we have to let down the bamboo blinds the moment the sun rises, as the heat is so terrific. The lack of running water in the bathrooms is something we are so used to by now, that it seems quite normal.

We have been able to hire an electric fan for our room and it makes a great difference, particularly when I am trying to get Ingrid to sleep. Poor little thing, she is simply covered with prickly heat, but I have to be extremely careful to wrap a towel around her tummy, when she is sleeping near the fan, so she doesn't catch cold. With the trouble she is having, I am sure she has dysentery. I don't know what doctor to call here and only hope that we can get to Calcutta soon.

Reidar, in spite of being in such a weak state and suffering so badly from lumbago as well, is out each day seeing Chinese and other people in the city. Many of his Chinese ship-owner friends and business associates have fled here from Shanghai and Hong Kong. Sometimes they send a car for him, amazing in such a place as this, but most appreciated as he finds it very tiring and painful sitting in a chair for long, swaying up and down, when his back is in such a bad state. He has lost about 30 lbs since December 8th.

We don't see very much of Sophie these days. She has so many admirers and goes out a great deal. I am so very glad that she does. It is the best thing for her, to have some enjoyment for a change.

She went for a picnic yesterday with some of the British Embassy people, out in the hills beyond the city. I couldn't help feeling a bit envious, as I should love to see what lies beyond the hills, on the other side of the river, that I gaze at from our window every day. And to see the fantastic Yangtse Gorges. But I cannot leave my little Ingeling.

One of Sophie's most ardent admirers, an Australian correspondent who has a room at the end of the passage, asked us in for a drink one evening. What impressed us most about him is the fact that he has a small refrigerator in his room, which actually produces ice! Oh what a difference a really cold drink makes!

A Japanese bombing run over Chungking, China

One day we had an air raid and were all hustled into a tunnel in the hillside a little way behind this building. It was so long, narrow and low-ceilinged I felt like a rabbit in a burrow. I was none too happy when I thought of what had happened in Chungking in 1941, when a bomb fell at an entrance of a tunnel with only one opening. There was panic and a stampede to get out. Thousands of people lost their lives when the entrance was blocked by people trampling on top of each other. Those inside died of suffocation. All the authorities could do afterwards was to wall up the tunnel, with all the corpses inside.

We were asked to dine at the British Embassy one evening. The ambassador, Sir Horace Seymour, is very nice. He has promised to put a word in for us about getting transport to Calcutta as soon as possible, especially as we have a sick baby. It is dreadfully difficult to get seats on any plane now, particularly for unwanted women and children.

Reidar has heard from the Norwegian Government in London that they want him to be their shipping representative, with the Ministry of War Transport, for India and Ceylon. So he is more anxious than ever now to get to India and get started on doing what he can to help.

The ambassador was very interested, apart from hearing about our trip, in hearing that we had a certain amount of household linen and clothes left in Kweilin. When we left Macao

301

we had decided to take as much as we could with us, as we did not know whether we might be stuck in some remote part of China for the duration of the war. And it is an unwritten law in Chungking, that anyone who is leaving the city should leave most of their clothes and useful things behind them. Some people sell things at fantastic prices, as almost all clothes and foreign things are quite impossible to get here, particularly woollen clothes.

When we had described practically everything we had in our left-behind baggage, Sir Horace was very excited to hear there were some fine linen sheets, blankets and eiderdowns too. He said such things were unknown in Chungking and they must certainly be brought from Kweilin in the next truck convoy available.

He and Berkeley Gage discussed the clothes that would also be available. The ambassador said he wanted Reidar's navy blue shorts and sports shirts, and Berkeley was enchanted at the prospect of getting his suits. They are very much the same build. Reidar said he didn't care what we got for these things. We are only so thankful to be here, out of Hong Kong and still all together. It is strange to think that our dear Hong Kong is nearly two thousand miles away, and yet we still we have such a long way to go.

I feel so sorry for JoJo with no other child to play with and not knowing what to do with himself all day long. I try to make him read and carry on with some lessons, but it is such a struggle, particularly in this heat. The day after we got here I missed him during the morning and hunted frantically all over the place, and then I looked out of the window and saw him, far below, down by the water's edge exploring, followed by a bunch of Chinese children. The burning sun didn't seem to worry him at all, but I thought he might get sunstroke.

Poor little Ingeling looks so pale and fragile, as if a puff of wind would blow her away, and she cries and cries. I walk up and down the passage with her, trying to keep her amused and quiet. Sometimes we walk along the road outside, when the sun has lost some of its fierceness. How tiring and demanding small children can be, especially sick ones.

I look out of our window, through the chinks in the bamboo blinds, down over the jumbled roof-tops, descending steeply to the great swiftly-flowing river some hundreds of feet below, and watch the teeming life along the water front.

The ferry boats, busily plying to and from the other shores, fill me with amazement and alarm. How they ever achieve their journeys safely seems a miracle, as they appear to be so top-heavy and grossly over-crowded with pushing and shoving humanity. The currents are so powerful and treacherous, that it seems as though the struggling little crafts must surely capsize. And yet they make it, almost always.

On the other side of the river live the Generalissimo Chiang Kai-Shek and Madame. Also Madame Sun Yat Sen. We hear so many different things about them.

The famous "Soong Sisters" (pictured with Chiang Kai-Shek in Chungking) each played a major role in influencing their powerful husbands, along with their own positions of power, ultimately changed the course of Chinese history.

Their father, Charlie Soong, was an American-educated Methodist minister who made a fortune in banking and printing. Their three brothers were all high-ranking officials in the Republic of China government. All three sisters attended Wesleyan College in the United States.

Soong Ai-ling married H.H. Kung, the richest man in China. Soong May-ling married Chiang Kai-shek, the leader of the Kuomintang nationalists and later President of the Republic of China. Soong Ching-ling married Sun Yat-sen, Father of Modern China and the first President of the Republic of China. Contrary to her other sisters, she supported the Communists, later became the joint President of the People's Republic of China.

Their marriages and motivations have been summarised in the Maoist saying "One loved money, one loved power, one loved her country".

Over China and The Hump

July 29th. Our plane passages over "The Hump" of the Himalayas to India suddenly came through. We went down to the airstrip early in the morning, carrying only tiny Hong Kong baskets and a few odds and ends. Our baggage allowance was 15 kilos each for the adults, half that for John and nothing for Ingrid. So we wore as much as we could, several jerseys each and a couple of jackets on top. I had no coat, but Sophie and Reidar had thick ones. However it was not too overwhelmingly hot as we started so early.

The runway was built on a narrow strip of land emerging from the middle of the river. I was too excited to worry too much about how the big plane would manage to take off from such a spot.

I have never been in such a big plane before. A real passenger plane with about 20 seats. Reidar and one other passenger, an American journalist, had strange looking cylinders lying in the passage beside their seats, containing oxygen.

We skimmed off the runway and over the great muddy river, between the steep banks, a straight and narrow path indeed. The country we flew over was again very wild and mountainous, but at one time it levelled out into a desolate grassy plateau. Endless wilderness with no sign of life. I believe we were skirting the "roof of the world", where the vast tablelands of Tibet begin and form so much of central Asia. It seemed indeed a very lonely place and is higher than even the highest mountains of Europe.

Then we turned southwards again and eventually came down in Kunming, which is also on a very high plateau. It had been raining heavily there and was much cooler than Chungking.

Soon we were in the air again, me with my nose pressed to the window, whenever Ingrid would let me have a little peace. I was trying to imprint on my memory forever all the wonderful things and the beautiful country we have seen.

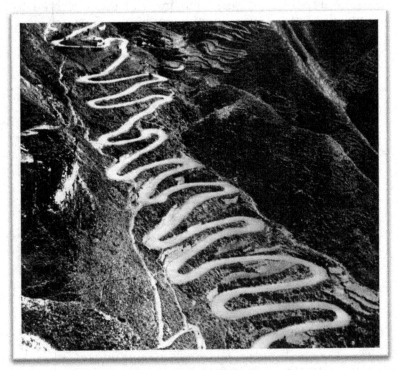

The torturous Burma Road seen from above

Suddenly, after so many hundreds of miles of mountains and valleys and dense forests, without a sign of civilization, I saw a road winding its tortuous way along. I felt a tremendous thrill when I realized that it was the infamous Burma Road! We have heard so much about its hazards and perils. The thousands of trucks and vehicles that have met with violent ends and, only too often, their reckless drivers as well.

We have had friends who have driven on this road and we might well have found ourselves driving on it too, if we had not been so fortunate in being able to travel by plane.

Then we started to climb and climb. The great Himalayas rose in tumultuous waves higher and higher ahead of us. I kept an anxious eye on Reidar. He was lying back in his seat quietly and taking big pulls at the oxygen through the rubber tube. The American correspondent was doing the same. Both of them looked horribly pale.

We had all been told by the captain of the plane before starting, that we should keep as still as possible and try to go to sleep. Any exertion would be harmful. I knew we had to fly at somewhere near 20,000 feet to clear the mountains. Everybody was motionless in their seats and most of them seemed to be sleeping. But I didn't want to miss anything of the view.

Flying over The Hump of the Himalayas

The mountains were incredible and terrifying in their ruthless, savage beauty. The very magnitude of their lofty, unassailable peaks; their fantastic precipices dropping sheer, for thousands of feet, into deep and fearsome gorges; their absolute isolation from the world of human beings seemed to exercise a hypnotic fascination over me.

Then Ingrid started crying and struggling. She wanted to go over to Reidar, but I held her fast in my arms, trying to persuade her to be quiet and go to sleep. This seemed only to infuriate her more as she bellowed and struggled frantically. I was feeling somewhat faint and peculiar myself. It was an effort to hold her firmly. Poor little thing, she became quite hysterical and her lips were blue. Then, I think, both of us must have passed out for a while, because I can't remember what happened after that.

When I started to take notice again, we were flying over dense jungle towards Assam. I looked down and thought of the wild Naga tribes that inhabit this region, and wondered what would be our fate, if we had to go down there. Soon we did descend to a little place called Dinshan. It was very hot!

Off again, and after some hours we flew over the vast, swampy plains and rice fields of the east of India. Over the mighty Bramaputra River, which has its source so many hundreds of miles away in the fabulous Himalayas. Then over the amazing delta country, a colossal network of waterways, dividing and subdividing countless times, interspersed with flat mud islands. It was like looking down on an enormous map.

It had been raining, and there were little cotton-wool puffs of clouds floating above it all, while the sunlight filtered through, shooting lovely sunbeams down onto the watery scene below. It was a very pretty effect.

Calcutta

Then we were landing at DumDum Airfield and the heat hit us again. We were all exhausted, but so happy to have actually arrived in Calcutta at last. And I was so excited at the prospect of seeing Archy again.

But there was no sign of him at the airport. We realized of course that he could not know exactly when we were arriving. It was quite late in the afternoon by then, but still blazing hot and we were all simply melting in all our thick clothing.

We took the bus into town with all our bits and pieces. Then after being dumped at the terminal, we set out to look for a taxi to take us to Archy's house. As we walked along the crowded street, we were feeling slightly dazed at seeing Indians now instead of Chinese, and trying to keep clear of the sacred cows wandering along the pavement. Suddenly a figure in uniform confronted me and flung his arms around me, kissing and hugging me, overjoyed. It was Archy. He had been waiting most of the day for us at the airport and could not get any news of our arrival. Finally he had to leave to go on duty in the firemen's unit.

He brought us here, to this lovely cool, clean house, and Reidar had his first whiskey and soda for months, with pieces of ice tinkling in the glass! Sophie and I turned on the bath taps and found hot, clean water in which to soak ourselves luxuriously!

July 30, 1942. We have heard that Mr. Nemazee beat us to Teheran by just one day! Unfortunately, as I am writing this, Reidar is in hospital. His heart is troubling him rather a lot, but the doctor says it is probably due to the fact that he is so badly run down and completely exhausted. JoJo also has been in bed for some days with fever and the doctor does not seem to know what it is.

Ingrid is being treated for her dysentery and I am so thankful that she seems to be responding to the medicines, but she looks so tiny and transparent. And it appears now that I have dysentery too, so we are a fine family! But we have nothing to complain of. We are only overwhelmingly grateful that we are all alive and that we were able to come through it all together.

India, Kashmir and Beyond

British India in 1940

Nortraship

August 1942. Calcutta was dreadfully hot in summer. We were already exhausted from our long trip through China and the various ailments we had contracted on the way. It was decided that the sooner we could get away to the mountains of Kashmir, where Archy's wife Gerd was staying in a rented bungalow with their daughter Anno and her ayah, the better it would be for us all. The area around Gulmarg in the lower Himalayan plains of Kashmir was a popular place for British civil servants and their wives to escape the scorching heat of the Indian summers.

But Reidar decided that he would not be able to accompany us, as he had to get to Bombay as quickly as possible. That made me very worried, as he had just come out of hospital, suffering from a strained heart and general debilitation. However, having been appointed the representative for India and Ceylon of Nortraship, the shipping department of the Norwegian Government in exile and at this moment the world's largest shipping company, he was anxious to get to Bombay and set up his office there.

There was an enormous amount of Norwegian shipping plying around the world, especially between the U.S., Europe and the East. The Norwegian tankers carried vast quantities of oil, and their container ships enormous amounts of supplies for the war effort. So Bombay was a vital location for one of Nortraship's main branches, and the heads of the Norwegian Government in London recognized that Reidar, with his wide shipping experience, was an ideal person to represent them. It was a considerable challenge to him, and his eagerness to get started gave him strength.

A train to Rawalpindi

From my point of view it was of great importance to find a really good ayah for Ingrid. With the help of Archy's staff we finally got a very sweet and efficient young Nepalese woman, called Jetti-ayah, but for Ingrid she was always Ayhie. We also engaged a most pleasant Nepalese bearer, named Chombee.

We had to get a certain amount of clothes for all of us, as we had practically nothing on arrival and would need some warm things up in the mountains. There were also such things as blankets and bedding for our train journey (which should have taken three nights and four days, from Calcutta to Rawalpindi). We would need all the food and drink for the entire journey, as there was no restaurant car attached to the train. Food or drinks bought at any of the stations on the way were considered unsafe. Also, now there was so much political unrest in India, with Ghandi creating so many problems encouraging the people to passive resistance against the British, but unfortunately the resistance was far from passive.

Due to rioting and widespread violence, our train was forced to stop many times between Calcutta and Delhi and did not travel at all during the nights. We passed through some stations that were crowded with angry mobs, shouting and throwing stones and bottles at the train. On such occasions we had been warned to stay out of sight. In fact the best thing to do was to lie on the floor, since there was no real protection over the windows, only thick hessian blinds. These were hosed down with water at the stations at which we stopped, in order to get some cooler air into the compartments when it moved again. There was no such thing as air-conditioning then and the temperature was 130 degrees outside.

At one of the stations that looked peaceful, we got out to see if there was any possibility of getting some drinking water as we were running low, due to all the delays. Then we found that in the next compartment there were some British army officers, who were very helpful and gave us some of their supply, while advising us not to trust any source at that station.

That evening at nightfall we drew into a very big station teeming with people, and to our utter dismay and horror, an Indian official came and told us that we had to get out of our carriage and change trains. This one was being commandeered by the army to transport troops.

Despite all my arguments it seemed there was nothing for it but to get out, with ailing children, and all our baggage and paraphernalia, to spend the night waiting with hundreds of people. We could see crowds in the waiting rooms, and lying all over the platforms. There was no certainty of another train arriving, and when and IF it did arrive, we had no reserved accommodation on it, and then there would be another change in Delhi. The prospect was too awful to contemplate and I decided to go to the stationmaster to see if anything could be done.

In desperation I decided to ask the help of one of the British officers in the next compartment. They were all very sympathetic and indignant on our behalf at our treatment. They themselves had not been asked to leave. The most senior officer said he would accompany me to see the stationmaster, which was a great relief, not having to struggle on my own through all the milling masses.

Fortunately we were eventually able to find him. The officer started explaining about our miserable situation, when the stationmaster suddenly sprang to attention, saluted my officer friend smartly and greeted him by his name! It turned out that years ago they had both served in the same regiment and my new friend had been the stationmaster's commanding officer!!

It really seemed like a miracle because from then on the stationmaster simply could not do enough for us. We were assured that we need not leave our carriage at all. He was going to arrange for that particular wagon we were in to be unhooked from our present train and hooked on to the next train that was going to Rawalpindi. There would be no changing in Delhi either! It was a tremendous relief for us. After more delays due to a goods train in front of us being derailed and large sections of the line ahead having been torn up, we eventually reached Rawalpindi after six days of travel, instead of the three we had expected.

Upward to Kashmir

I remembered Mummy's stories of travelling up to Kashmir by bullock cart from Rawalpindi, around 1903, up narrow, winding, dusty, mountain roads, where there was a tremendous drop on one side, and on the other side, cliffs rising sheer for hundreds of feet above. The bullocks walked slower and slower, until the driver would suddenly wake up and twist their tails, where upon they would liven their pace for a while.

She used to tell us of herself and a friend, who used to come to Kashmir with her, and stay in just such a dak bungalow as we were now in. There were tales of Archy as a tiny baby too. Now, all these many years later, we were travelling the same road with my small baby but under different circumstances, by car, thank heavens, instead of by bullock cart. We could have done the whole journey in one day, whereas they must have taken a great many.

Kashmir

September 13th, 1942. I am sitting on the veranda of the little bungalow in Tangmarg. The sun is brilliant and there is a haze of heat over the forest-clad hills with the mighty range of the Himalayas on the other side of the plain. Everything is so peaceful and beautiful. The only sounds are the twittering of birds, and the rush of the distant river. Every now and then a Kashmiri horseman gallops up the road towards the little village of Tangmarg.

Ayhie with Anno and Ingrid in Tangmarg

This is such a heavenly place and I feel I could live here for a very long time. Unfortunately so far, I have not been able to attain the rest and peace I have longed for. John is so difficult to manage due to all the trauma of these past months. The experience of the war in Hong Kong and China is bound to have a deep effect on an impressionable child. It is also such a pity that he has no other children of his own age to play with. Ingrid is also still suffering from the effects of dysentery from our trek.

This makes her very irritable with fits of crying and outright screaming, which is nerve shattering for everybody around.

I feel ashamed of both my children's behaviour, and Gerd misses no opportunity of making critical remarks about them. I can understand that she resents the peace and quiet of her life being spoilt. But I confess I have been hurt by her total lack of compassion or interest in our long journey to reach here.

Unfortunately she and Sophie do not get along well at all. Acid remarks are frequently exchanged and there is an atmosphere of tension most of the time, which I find very distressing. She disapproves of the way Sophie fusses over me, when I am feeling really unwell, and that I am just putting it all on! In fact I am also suffering from dysentery.

Now Sophie too has become ill, probably from something she picked up in Calcutta, so I am thankful that we have a Kashmiri doctor in a small clinic not far from here.

Overlooking the Vale of Kashmir

When I feel too depressed, I just go out and contemplate the glories of nature all around. From here we look across the wide, wide Vale of Kashmir, so flat and covered with vast fields of rice and Indian corn and a long avenue of poplar trees slicing down the middle. On the other side of the valley stands a massive range of the mighty Himalayas, truly breathtaking in magnificence. The great Haramuk, with his rounded snowy head, makes me think of a venerable old gentleman. Then the lovely but terrifying Nanga-Parbet is the greatest of them all around here, being over 26,000 feet and one of the tallest mountains in the world. Their snow-capped peaks float above the sea of clouds and mist that is formed during the day due to the heat. It is a sight that sends shivers of happiness down my spine and my spirit finds peace again.

October 4th. Last Thursday I had to go down to Srinagar to register at the police station. I hated going, but I had to go in any case, to get money from the bank. So I decided to make an adventure of it and try to enjoy myself.

Morning light on the lake in Srinagar

Completing the required paperwork in the town, I was free to explore the area. It is a dramatic place with many of the local people living along the waterways of a great lake surrounded by enormous mountains.

The next day I was up at seven in the morning and after breakfast I set off to visit the Stavrides, acquaintances who live on a houseboat nearby. It was 9 a.m. when I reached the *Manora*, and found them both still in night attire sitting on the roof of their home. They seemed happy to see me and to show me around. It was a comfortable houseboat, beautifully furnished, and had an atmosphere of worldly sophistication.

Both of them looked typically Greek with strong facial features. He is an elderly, retired businessman, very successful, who used to be with Volkart Brothers, a world known shipping and trading firm whom Reidar used to do business with from

Hong Kong. He and his daughter Helen have lived in India for so long that when he retired, they could not bear to leave.

Helen Stavrides is a striking looking blonde with mesmerizing dark eyes. She has a passion for mountain climbing that immediately put us in a closer relationship. She told me that the love of her life had been a famous mountaineer who had tragically lost his life a few years ago while on a climbing expedition on Everest. After chatting wholeheartedly about our shared love of the mountains, we decided she would return with me to go on a climb together.

She has a thriving business of her own in Kashmiri craftwork, beautiful hook-stitch rugs and carpets, embroidered materials by the yard for curtains and bedspreads, cushion-covers etc. At the work area, many people embroider artistic patterns and flowers on gorgeous silks or fine Pashmina woollen cloth, so soft it feels like the finest of silks itself. Nearby on the smooth, shiny wood floors, the cloth is cut and sewn into lovely garments for fashionable women and famous film stars.

While I was waiting for Helen to get dressed, I had a very strange surprise. I had picked up a large book called, "Best Photographs Of The Year", dated eight years ago. I was glancing through it casually when I came upon a full-page photo of myself! I was absolutely dumbfounded, as I had never known that the friend, who took it many years ago before I was married, had sent it in for publication.

It was taken when we were out sailing in Hong Kong. In fact I seemed to be so lost in far away thoughts that I never knew he was taking a picture. He had been a most ardent suitor, but never had any chance. However, we remained good friends and he remained hopeful until I was married. That photograph conjured up carefree days indeed, but now I had to hurry back to my abominable children!

Climbing Handibal

Tangmarg, October 14th. Helen returned with me and a few days later we set off to climb Handibal, one of the nearby peaks. We started off at 7 a.m. and I was so excited that I had hardly been able to sleep. It was bitterly cold and there was an enchanting sickle of moon riding high in the sky, together with the morning star just showing over the ridge of Himalayas.

We had three escorts (the *gora-walla* groom, the guide and Chokedar) and some ponies to ride through the valley. It was lovely and peaceful, with cattle grazing on the open hillsides. A burbling river turned into a tumultuous stream, and soon we were climbing steeply through wondrous thick forests until we came out on a lovely solitary plateau. High above us still towered Handibal, round, smooth and snow covered.

The gora-walla remained below with the horses, while we continued upwards. We had to go in small spurts and then stop for five minutes, hearts racing, lungs bursting and quite dizzy. I thought I simply could not make it, but knew I would, as we had planned to return another way via the Pandan Nullah.

When we finally staggered over the sloping top of the mountain, we threw ourselves down and rested a long time. The unobstructed view was incredibly beautiful with the whole plain of Kashmir at our feet and the great Himalayan range beyond. Jagged, snow-covered peaks stretched from end to end of the vast horizon. A veritable sea of mountains, like gigantic waves approaching from infinity.

Though I have never been religious, preferring to meet my God in nature, this manifestation was a truly overwhelming experience for me. I just sat there in a trance, gazing, and would have stayed indefinitely if it had not been for the cold wind.

Helen and I ate our tiffin perched on a rock and tried to melt some snow to drink, but it was too cold. Chokedar indicated that it would be shorter to go down the same way we had come up, but I wanted to go on and on. I seemed to have become affected by a sort of mountain madness. Walking down the back of the mountain, we saw fresh tracks of a bear!

Hiking with Helen high in the Himalayas

The descent was difficult, but we were soon down in the valley again amongst little log cabins that were deserted for the winter. We crossed a small glacier where the river beneath us had formed amazing caves and tunnels. I was thrilled to be walking on a real glacier, but Chokedar was starting to worry as it was beginning to get dark.

The final part on horseback took us way up the precipitous mountainside again on a narrow path with an uncomfortably steep drop to the river below. The stars shone with extra brilliance and there was a song in my heart. It was a wonderful experience I will remember forever.

Yesterday I had a day of rest to recuperate from Handibal even though I didn't feel any ill affects or tired at all. Later, Helen returned to Srinagar, and Gerd, John and I had to take some parcels that Reidar had sent us by horseback up to the Gulmarg customs office to pay duty on them.

Coming back we saw scores of monkeys in the trees and the horses cocked their ears at them nervously. I was relieved that the monkeys had not pelted us with cones, sticks or stones, as they can be very mischievous.

The horses had a great time trying to race each other all the way, and I was amazed when Gerd told me she had never been on a horse before coming to Tangmarg. I really do want us to get along well together as she is Archy's wife, but it is very difficult at times and she makes me miserable. Only ten days until we leave, and then how wonderful to be back with Reidar again, and never have to worry about moods or think three times before I say things.

I felt so thrilled when Reidar's letter arrived telling me that we could go to Colombo together as he had received permission for me to accompany him there for two weeks! Joy, joy!

On to Bombay, our new home

The return trip to Bombay was uneventful, except for the extreme heat over the long distance. At one time the train drew up at yet another small, burning-hot wayside station and I then had banging on my door. In stepped Diana Cole, dainty and fresh, as if she had just come from a beauty parlour, instead of having waited half the night and the whole morning in a dirty little Indian railway station, with the temperature away over 100 degrees.

She immediately got into blue satin pyjamas with frills around the neck, got out her beauty box and started creaming and making up her face. She is one of the more glamorous-looking members of the "SSS" (Swinging Social Society), of Calcutta and Bombay. I admire her for her good looks and for her well-groomed and dainty appearance, under such adverse conditions. But I feel sorry for her too, having divorced her husband after 13 years of marriage, with a daughter of twelve. It is said she is frantically eager to get married again, but I must say I pity any man who takes her on for life. She is really a little bitch!

At Bombay Station, several hours later, Reidar met me. I was so excited to see him that I didn't notice he was limping. Only on arrival home did I see that he had boils on his legs. He was suffering so much with them, that after the effort of coming to the station to meet me, which caused him agony to walk, he just had to take to his bed and stay there.

He advised me to go and have a long, hot bath before doing anything else, as I looked so very, VERY dirty. When I came back to him after having had my bath, he said shaking his head "So sorry but you still haven't got all the dirt off!" So I had to go and have another one!

Poor sweet, he was in such pain, it was unbelievable how many terrible boils he had all over his legs. When one got better, another started. It was so disheartening. I dressed them many times a day, but it was five days before he could walk. Actually, in spite of him being forced to stay in bed, we had a lovely time, not seeing a soul and being just us two.

November 1942. I was so happy coming to the flat, our new home, but for how long would it be I wondered? It is a very fine flat, big and airy with large windows, four bedrooms, four bathrooms, a big adjoining sitting room and dining room. I know we are incredibly lucky and fortunate to have got any flat at all in the present circumstances in Bombay...crowded as it is with military, business people and refugees. It is a stepping off and arriving place for the armed forces to all different parts of the east. The business centre has moved here from Calcutta. Many refugees from Malaya and Burma, as well as people from the east of India feel it is safer in view of the proximity to the Japs and probable raids, or maybe even invasion, although the likelihood of that seems much less now.

Although I am truly grateful and thankful to be here, I don't think I shall ever get to really like Bombay. It is such a very big and unattractive city, with no real parks or open gardens. The strips of sand, that presumably should be called beaches, are so dirty and overcrowded. One would never dream of swimming from them.

Going further away from the city, to Breach Kandy, is nice for swimming and many foreigners do this. There is quite a fashionable club there. And Juhu Beach is glorious and it is too far for most people to get to, especially with the petrol rationing. Reidar has been granted a special extra allowance of gasoline, as he has an important position with the Norwegian Government.

Bombay (Mumbai)

After Reidar comes home from the shipping office in the afternoons, we sit and have some tea and he tells me about various happenings during his day's work. It is fascinating but often horrifying, when it concerns ships being torpedoed, or striking mines and being blown up, then all too often sinking.

Some of these victims have been able to "limp" into harbour with the most gigantic holes torn in their structures, cavities so enormous that whole houses could have fitted inside. It is miraculous that they were able to keep afloat at all.

Reidar had to go down to the docks with the captains of these wounded vessels and report on everything back to Nortraship in London. There were heavy casualties sometimes. Officers and crew have had to be taken to hospital and a thousand different but relative actions taken. Those poor captains must have been under a permanent and tremendous strain. This made them all the more appreciative of being able to come to our peaceful home where they could relax briefly, talk Norwegian, enjoy a good meal and feel at home.

When we have finished our afternoon tea all we can do is to go for a walk, there being no cinemas or such entertainment available. The only place to walk is along this Cuffe Parade, with hundreds of people walking, or sitting on every bench and along the sea wall, lolling against the railings around the gardens and buildings, or sitting in their cars parked along the curb. Everybody seeking a possible breath of fresher air from the sea and a change of environment from the problems of their day.

Unfortunately, I have the feeling of living in one tiny compartment of a colossal honeycomb, just like the other hundreds of thousands of people, living in exactly the same flats with no individuality, no privacy nor solitude, nor ever complete silence.

I know I have been so spoilt in Hong Kong ever since I have been married. First our lovely flat in Pokfulam, amongst pine trees, overlooking the sea, and then our beautiful *Skyhigh*, perched on the very top of our own little peak, with such breathtaking and incomparable views all around. Both places had such peaceful solitude, which has become so important in my life. I know I could never be really happy living in a crowd.

During the war period in Hong Kong and the months in Mr. Nemazee's house, then Macao and Kweilin, even Calcutta, all taught me a great deal, as we never had a moment's real privacy for months. So by comparison, we feel marvellously fortunate and happy here. Plus John is happy here at school and Ingeling has put on a lot of weight, no longer looking as if a feather could blow her away.

Juhu beach is a marvellous place, the saving grace of Bombay, with a glorious, great sandy beach stretching for miles and hardly any people there. John and Irene very kindly lent us their palm-leafed "shack", one of a few, built amongst the coconut palms.

There are four bedrooms and bathrooms all attractively fixed up with colourful curtains and nice floor mats. The trunks of palms form part of each room, as roof supports, giving a feeling of beachcomber living. There is a main room in the centre where one has meals and a lovely veranda, where one can sit and enjoy the peaceful view of the open sea.

Far along to the right of the beach, we were told, is a place where Gandhi comes to relax and where his disciples come to pay him homage.

School in Poona

We arranged for John to enter what we hoped would be a suitable school, in Poona. It went under the somewhat fancy name of the Shri Shivaji Preparatory Military Academy, and had been recommended to us by a number of people.

There were quite a number of English boys there of prep school age, about 7 to 8 years old, all living in a separate house from the local boys, mainly because of the food difference. All his kakhi shirts and shorts had to be made at the 'Army and Navy Store' in miniature army style. But the prices were certainly not in miniature!

I couldn't help feeling a miserable pang in my heart at leaving him there. I know this is the beginning of the end— which I dreaded from the moment he was born. I remember so clearly lying in the hospital bed with my new-born son in my arms and thinking "How long will I be able to keep him before he has to be sent to school?"

From now on he will grow more and more independent and apart from us. But I shall try everything in my power to keep him feeling we are true friends, with whom he can discuss anything. He was close to tears and biting his lip hard, but there was another small boy there, very cheeky and intelligent, a year older than John, who helped him behave like a man.

Next day Irene and I drove out to Satara, a civilian internment camp, where Irene's Italian stepfather and her mother are interned for the duration of the war. We started in darkness so as to be able to arrive for breakfast and spend the day with them. It was a lovely drive of 70 miles, though the first part was very dry and barren. Then we crossed over low hills and came into beautiful green plains and pastures. The camp itself was nicely situated and I was much impressed by the nice accommodation they had. There were rows of low, clean buildings where the internees had one or two rooms, a bathroom, a kitchen and a portion of the enclosed veranda each.

Both the Sopranis struck me as looking amazingly well, particularly Mrs. Soprani, who had been ill for so long with semi-paralysis of her legs. He is a good deal thinner than Hong Kong days, but looks well and is so nice. They seemed very glad to be where they were and dreaded the possibility of being moved into the other confined camp with all the rest of the Italians, whom they heartily dislike.

The atmosphere seemed friendly, and fairly contented. But it was sad meeting some of the younger women and young unmarried girls, who are forced to lead such a confined existence. However they looked smart and snappily dressed, with hair done nicely. They certainly were trying to make the best of the situation. I was quite surprised at the open way in which they discussed politics, in lowered voices naturally. That was rather difficult with Mrs. Soprani being so deaf, and having some super-Nazi women as neighbours with no real privacy anywhere.

I was also impressed with the food they had: plenty of butter, nice bread, cake bought from a local shop, excellent meat and vegetables, even fruit and coffee! Mr. Soprani did all the cooking and it was delicious. He keeps himself busy by making all sorts of useful things for the home. They had drinks and cigarettes and even chocolates! Of course Irene brings up most of the luxuries on her visits to them.

It was sad to leave them but I couldn't help being glad we were on our way home again. During the drive back we talked a great deal, and strangely enough I think I talked more than she did. It was mostly about her and Sophie, and of Hong Kong war days too and the affect it had upon different people.

We arrived in Bombay after a three hour car and train trip. It was a great disappointment when Reidar was not on the platform. I was immediately anxious, but Captain Svane was there and told us that he was in bed, with a bad attack of lumbago! I was so upset and disappointed to find him ill again, that I wasn't very sympathetic when I saw him, but I massaged his back three times a day and he did improve greatly. On Thursday evening John, Irene and Sophie and Joe were all congregated in the bedroom keeping Reidar company and enjoying drinks. Irene amused us greatly with one of her typical remarks. She was lying on my bed beside Reidar and put her hand on his chest to tickle him. So he said, "Don't excite the patient". Whereupon she bounced upright and leaned over to him saying with mock excitement, "Oh, let's see!" and then scornfully, "Well, you can't do anything anyway, you invalid!"

A "third" honeymoon in Ceylon (Sri Lanka)

November 21. We left Bombay by train and eventually and finally reached Danushkodin, the departure point from India for Ceylon. There was the blue open sea and vast stretches of white sandy beaches, backed by coconut palms. There were quaint-looking fishing boats pulled up on the beach and half-naked natives everywhere. Some of the small girls, who were begging and smacking their tummies for food, were very beautiful.

The crossing took two hours, most of which time I spent up in the prow of the little vessel, as usual, sitting on a coil of rope, watching the sunset. I was thinking of all the thousands of men who have watched that sea tensely day and night, for murderous submarines, floating mines, and hostile raiders or warships. I suppose they do eventually get used to the feeling, that at any moment every hour they are at sea, something might happen. Personally I think I should never be able to throw off the feeling of strain and tenseness. I don't like taking risks, for the children's sake. I have so much to live for now.

When we arrived at the shores of Ceylon it was like the scenery from a romantic film. A great orange moon rose majestically out of the sea, shedding a golden path across the palm-fringed beaches of one of the most lovely tropical islands in the world. Tremendous waves curled over white and foaming, breaking with thunderous roars upon the white sands.

The train waited out on the pier alongside the ship. We found our cosy two berth compartment and then went and had dinner in the dining car at a table for two. The window was down, so that I could lean out, right over the water, and watch the mighty swell of the sea beneath us. It was incredibly beautiful and we felt so happy. Amazing that it is possible in such a war-torn world as today!

Colombo. November 27th, 1942. Here we are, and it seems like a honeymoon, just Reidar and me! Everybody is absolutely amazed that I was granted permission to come with him, but Reidar laughingly boasts that most things turn out right for him in the end!

We had a lovely trip down to Colombo, even though the train journey was long and dirty. Reidar had obtained "A" priority when he was to travel here by plane on his own, but as I couldn't get that too (most understandably), he refused it.

I missed the children very much to begin with, but I must confess it really is such a rest and change not to have to be doing things for them all the time. This is the first real holiday I have had since Reidar and I went to Singapore in the summer of 1940.

This is such a beautiful island and the hotel is very fine. The whole place is packed and swarming with servicemen, including many "wrens" and "waafs" and "wacs" (women in the forces) all over the place.

In town it now looks decidedly dreary, as all the shops and buildings are boarded up, awaiting future raids at any moment. All along the wonderful great esplanade, between the town and this hotel, there is barbed wire, with soldiers and guns everywhere. There is regular gun practice every day. The sound of planes roar overhead and *ack-ack* anti-aircraft guns go off almost under our noses. We see convoys of ships arriving or steaming off over the horizon, all giving a very topical and alert atmosphere to this former beauty and pleasure spot.

I think of Mummy and Daddy staying in this very hotel, so many years ago when Archy came from Hong Kong to meet them here for a holiday. I remember so clearly how I used to go down to the Monaco harbour and walk out to the very end of the pier, past all the beautiful luxury yachts lying there. I sat for ages in the night, looking out to sea, wondering what the future held for me and if I would ever find myself sailing over that horizon, bound for the magic orient. Now I was actually living in my fairy-tale dream, with some alterations, including the fighting going on!

Reidar goes to the Nortraship office every morning after our late breakfast and I come to this completely deserted, lovely long panelled room, overlooking the sea. One tall, slanting coconut palm is in the foreground and the sun glitters on the ever moving waves below. It is wonderful to have the time to just sit here peacefully, quite alone and write, which is always so difficult to do at home.

We decided this was a good opportunity to get some nice presents of Ceylon jewellery for Irene and Sophie. So we have been visiting many shops and seen an enormous variety of beautiful semi-precious stones.

Reidar wanted me to have something really special from Ceylon to commemorate our third "honeymoon". Eventually, after several days of comparing shops and stones and values, we bought one lovely blue sapphire stone for a brooch and two small ones for earrings. I was so thrilled and hugged and kissed him.

Last night it was raining so hard we decided to go to the cinema. It was the first I had been to since Calcutta, three and a half months ago. The newsreel showed an amazing film about a bombing raid by the R.A.F., over Holland, where the bombers were flying so close to the ground they seemed to be at tree top level. The cameras must have been placed under the fuselage, it seemed. One could see the bombs being released at such close quarters and falling upon the target below, which was the enormous Phillips electrical works at Eindhoven.

It was quite horrifying to see the terrible devastation wrought after all the explosions. It brought home to us so impressively the bravery of those pilots. But at the same time it also made us realize vividly the horrors of the bombings over England.

December 7th. Yesterday we drove to Kandy with Captain Lampe. It is a lovely drive and what a gloriously beautiful island this Ceylon is. It is bursting with life, rich vegetation and vivid colours everywhere. Even ordinary trees and bushes have a far more intense and vibrant green than in other places. The scenery was jungly and primitive, as in some of the African jungle films.

We visited a tea and rubber factory and saw how the tea was prepared, from the first stages of green leaves drying, until it was packed in cases for export. The rubber was very interesting too. We learnt that the liquid white rubber, tapped from the trees, has to be mixed with some chemical before it solidifies. It is then washed and put through various rolling machines, dried and finally emerges in sheets of pale yellow rubber crepe for export.

Before reaching Kandy we visited the world famous Peradeniya Gardens—so beautiful, colourful and unique that even Reidar was impressed. We were shown all the spice trees and in no time found our hands full of samples of cinnamon, nutmeg, quinine, citronella, cloves, eucalyptus, beetle nut, allspice and even some poison!

The gigantic size of the trees, their lovely graceful shapes, rich colouring, romantic names and the giant creepers that wound around some of them, were all most impressive. The vanilla creeper, a perfectly symmetrical zigzag, right to the top of a beetlenut palm; gorgeous orchid and fern arbours; the riotous abundance of vegetation and fabulous colourings and designs of the flowers and leaves, all fascinated me intensely. I felt I could have spent days and weeks there just looking in wonderment at it all. What a fantastic place for the military to be billeted nearby! Yet I suppose the majority of them hardly notice the beauty of their surroundings and chiefly grumble at the heat and their remoteness from city life.

Royal Air Force Operations in the Far East

The weather became cloudy, as usually seems to happen here in the afternoons, when the clouds build up over the mountains, and heavy rain started just as we were going out for a walk. So eventually we set out on our drive back, for almost the whole distance under torrential rain, with Captain Lampe driving like a demon! It was rather nerve-racking, but I still enjoyed seeing the jungles and the rivers under such a different aspect to the morning sunshine.

December 8th. Today we went and thanked Mr. Bradley, of the government air department, for having obtained an "A" pass for me too, to travel by air to Bombay. Reidar had again been assured by everybody here that it was quite out of the question to get me a passage on any plane. Nobody, not even the general's wife, was allowed to travel by air, it just could NOT be done! Nevertheless he achieved it, and so feels extremely pleased with himself!

While we were sitting having tea on the lawn after a lovely bathe, the manager came up and announced that Brigadier Davis would like to speak to us. Where upon we were introduced to Brigadier Davis whom we had noticed before at the dances. He said he had heard that Reidar came from

Bombay and was connected with shipping. He wondered whether he knew anything about a certain firm there, who wanted to do a big contract order for the army.

Next day we received a note from him asking us not to forget we were having drinks with him and his wife that evening, in their rooms, and then going to the dance together.

We then realized that the whole purpose of the carefully arranged meeting the day before, involving army contracts for four thousand cattle being shipped, etc., was really just an excuse to dance with me! How we laughed. But we were both fed up at the prospect of having to have company at our last dance evening and tried to think up all sorts of excuses.

However it turned out all right in the end. His wife was very attractive, quite elderly and didn't like dancing. So I was kept busy. He paid me, or rather to Reidar about me, compliments which were nice because they seemed so genuine. I have become so unused to hearing such things from other men. It seemed strange, but it did make me feel that I must be improving from my haggard and weary look of before.

December 12th. Colombo, Hyderabad, Bombay. We were up before daylight. Captain Lampe fetched us in his car and we were out at the airport by 9 a.m., waiting around for over an hour. Finally our plane came in. It was so tiny we got quite a shock when we saw it taxiing up to the front steps of the airport building, like a very small two-seater car, with a third seat tucked in at the back!

Our pilot was a very large Sikh, with large penetrating black eyes. His thick black beard was somehow swept up on either side of his face and tucked under his dazzling white turban. He was undoubtedly an impressive figure, but was hardly the kind of pilot I had expected. I just wondered how we could all three fit into such a tiny plane and fly such a long way!

However the others seemed to accept it as perfectly normal. It was serviced, the mail was loaded and everything weighed down to the last fraction of a pound, us included. Then we climbed in, Reidar in the seat behind the pilot and me beside him in front. It seemed quite a tight squeeze as he was so big. We then taxied across the airfield and took off.

To begin with we both felt as if we must sit very still, so as not to "upset the canoe", so to speak. We flew out over the sea and then up along the coast, past our hotel and away above the palm-fringed sands, and coconut plantations, with the waves coming rolling in like garlands of lace along the shores.

It was lovely. The sea was a heavenly aquamarine colour and so clear that we could see the coral reefs below the surface, interspersed with bright sandy areas. There were seemingly endless lagoons and sandbars, coconut groves and more coconut groves. The land was completely flat, but far away to our right the mountains rose on the horizon.

Then we came to the tip of Ceylon where we started out across the sea towards India. We saw where the ferry terminal was and the little pier jutting out into the sea, where we had sat in the train in the moonlight having dinner over the waves three whole weeks ago!

Then we flew into rain and bad weather. The sky became very dark and menacing and our pilot kept peering from side to side, I presumed to try and keep his bearings from the sand banks of Adams Bridge below, which we were following.

It was a strange sight—a bridge of sand banks stretching from the northern most point of Ceylon to the southern most tip of India, swept by the Indian Ocean on the one side and the Bay of Bengal on the other, desolate and lonely. It looked as if it could be almost possible to make the whole crossing (which must have been some twenty miles I suppose), by walking on the sand banks and then swimming the narrow channels of water in between. But the pilot told us that there were so many sharks in those waters, no swimmer could possibly survive more than a few minutes. I suppose that was the reason we did not even see a single fishing boat around there.

The point of Danushkodi was an amazing sight too. Just a narrow strip of sand, exactly enough to carry a single railway track and at the end it widened with the pier and a few huts. There the ferry came alongside, and that was all. It looked extraordinary from the air, as if such a narrow little strip of sand would surely be swept away by the wind and the waves.

The weather became worse, and we were tossed and buffetted all over the place. I didn't feel very secure and kept wondering what would happen if we had to come down and were dumped into the sea, or even on a sand bank, although at least there we would be on solid land! Then I tried not to wonder any more. After that came swamps and more swamps—it appeared as if the whole of the southern most part of India consisted of nothing but swamps.

Eventually we reached Trichinopoly but only had 10 minutes there, giving us just time to pass customs and police, and have a bite of a sandwich. Then we were off quickly again as the weather was still bad and the pilot wanted to get going. More buffeting and tossing about. We flew at 400 feet most of the time, over a flooded land of palms and paddy fields and wastelands. It was very tiring, and the winds and rain storms were very strong.

As we approached Madras, the sky ahead looked so black that I was really frightened. It seemed as though we were heading into a solid wall of something terrible. But, thank heavens, we just managed to land at the Madras airport as the most terrible storm broke upon us.

It was 4 p.m., then and we hoped to get something to eat. It was there all laid out waiting for us. But just as we sat down, the pilot came in and said we must be off immediately, as there was even worse weather coming and he had to try to make Hyderabad before dark.

So off we went feeling decidedly apprehensive, but to our enormous relief we gradually left the bad weather behind us and it became clearer. The landscape below changed from swamps to arid plains and dried up mountain ranges with hardly any cultivation. We flew at 7,000 ft over the mountains, as the sun was setting.

Finally we came down over Hyderabad, a beautiful white city bathed in a blaze of sunset reds and golds. We skimmed in over the airfield, landing perfectly, and taxied right up to the front of the imposing airport building, feeling rather insignificant arriving in such a minute plane!

We were met by the manager of our hotel, who took all three of us to the hotel up on some hill nearby. It was nearly dark as we drove through the city, but we saw some wonderful buildings—schools, museums, palaces and private villas, all so modern and dazzlingly white. It was truly impressive, as was the view from the hotel over the now dimmed lights of the city.

The hotel was very nice and attractively decorated in a modern style. It felt rather strange though, to be the only people staying there, as the lack of tourist air travel had hit them badly. I thought of my parents' description of Hyderabad in the olden days, of the vast wealth of the Nizam of Hyderabad and his incredible collection of fabulous jewellery, locked up in the many rooms of his fabulous palace! Unfortunately we then got into a rather heated discussion with the pilot at dinner and felt a bit shaken by such anti-British views.

Next day we had to be off by dawn in our tiny plane. The country again changed, every inch was cultivated over vast undulating plains, like a gigantic patchwork quilt of various colours of greens, browns and reds, stretching from end to end of the vast horizons.

Then we came to mountains, the Ghats, and passed over Poona thinking of small son John away down below us. We were flying at 7,500 feet to pass over the mountains. They looked lovely and reminded me, in formation and colouring, of the Grand Canyon.

Finally over the coast, gliding down over the sea and beach, we circled around twice to come smoothly down on the Juhu airfield.

We were met by big John at the airport, but alas no Ingeling with Ayhie, which was of course a big disappointment. But she was awaiting us at the beach house and was very shy at first. I knew she would be as we had been away so long. But she very soon got over it and how wonderful it was to hold her tightly in my arms again.

Bombay. December 28th. Nortraship held a big Christmas dinner party for all the Norwegian sailors, seamen, officers and captains in port. Reidar, of course, had a lot of organizing to do as it was "his" party.

There were more than two hundred guests, although the crews of some of the ships that had arrived during the day were unable to get ashore unfortunately. After dinner, at long tables, came the usual long speeches in true Norwegian fashion! Then we all sang Norwegian Christmas songs, holding hands around the tree. I was with some sailors and an officer and got along very well talking Norwegian to them. We hoped it may have provided a bright spot during the present darkness and uncertainty of their lives.

January 3rd, 1943. Our wedding anniversary of eight wonderful years! We feel we have been incredibly fortunate to have got away from Hong Kong, before being interned like the others. Our marriage is still as wonderful and as happy as ever.

Reidar gave me a beautiful brooch I had seen and admired greatly when we were in Colombo—a lovely aquamarine in a stunning platinum setting. It was such a surprise. When I had gone back to the shop to look at it again, the jeweller told me that it had been sold the day after we had been there. I was terribly disappointed and extremely cross with the man, as I had said to him we would come back and look at it again. In fact I was almost rude to him. He must have had a good laugh at my indignation, since Reidar was the one who had bought it!

Joining the St. John's Ambulance Brigade

January 6th. My first real start in the St. John's Ambulance Brigade. I was dressed in uniform and felt very silly with a little cocked hat, and very 'un-individual'. At the drill I felt like the chief caricature in a Laurel and Hardy film. Not knowing the drill properly I was doing complete turns at the end of my line, when all the others were facing the other way! But to see all these women of different ages, sizes and girths trying to look trim and soldierly was really laughable. Also it seemed so out of place to have a plumpish, middle aged lady shout at us that we MUST drill properly, that we were "perfectly lousy at present", and giving orders in the clipped, sharp military style.

Afterwards I went out driving an ambulance accompanied by a fair-skinned Indian girl, dressed in a khaki *saree*, very sweet and quiet. We went to Colaba Camp, Victoria Station, police station and back. I was driving all the time and negotiated the heavy traffic by the station very well, complete with rickshaws, carts and wandering cattle, and I felt quite pleased with myself.

March 11th. Time flies. I became a *Pukka* (1ˢᵗ Class) ambulance driver two weeks after starting, very quickly, according to Irene and others. We have duties two or three times a week, plus one parade each week. Every second week we have to be on emergency duty and liable to be called out at any time, at a moments notice. It is very interesting and quite fun sometimes going in convoys to the docks, to meet ships packed with troops, or Red Cross ships with sick and wounded soldiers, as long as those poor men are not suffering too terribly. I have driven some stretcher cases with badly injured men, and I have felt terrible when the roads are full of potholes and rough spots, knowing how agonizing the bumping and shaking must have been for them.

It is exciting to see the troop ships coming alongside with their decks swarming with soldiers of many different nationalities, British, American, Polish, French and, of course, they are rather surprised to see all the ambulances driven by women. Sometimes it is amusing to talk to our "passengers", though at times it is better to be very dignified! And occasionally I have been driving some who have become mentally disturbed, and have tried to climb into the front seat with me and had to be restrained by the orderlies!

Sometimes as the American ships come along side the quays, the soldiers lining the decks shout friendly greetings to us drivers and to anybody who may be standing on the pier below. Sometimes they throw cartons of cigarettes or packets of sweets, chewing-gum or chocolates down from the decks. This creates wild scrambles amongst the coolies. But, of course, we drivers do not touch any of these goodies being thrown to us, much as we would love to, with all of these things being almost impossible to get in Bombay.

It is indeed fascinating going into the docks area, packed with so many ships from so many countries around the world, all facing dreadful dangers as they make their ways across the treacherous seas. Some of these ships I have travelled on myself, in bygone years before the war, such as the *Islami*, carrying Polish troops. The *Talamba*, on which I travelled to Hong Kong before I was married, is now a Red Cross vessel.

Sometimes, when I am on duty at the Colaba General Hospital, I walk over to where I can look out across the harbour and think and think of Hong Kong with painful longing. Will we ever get back there again? And if so how many years will it take? Surely it can never be the same again.

I can't help thinking of our lovely *Skyhigh*, the house, the garden, the unique position on top of our very own small peak, and the glorious views all around of Hong Kong. Well, we did appreciate every moment we had it. We felt almost apprehensive at the same time, being so fortunate and so blissfully happy. How could such happiness last?

All week long we look forward to Sundays at Juhu, through the continuing kindness of John and Irene. It is really marvellous out there, with so few people around due to the severe gasoline rationing. One can lie in the sun on the fine soft sand, with the cool sea breeze gently waving the coconut palms overhead, and almost forget about the crowded town and daily rush. But somehow one can never escape the fact that the war goes on and on, inexorably, interminably.

There are nearly always some other friends of John's and Irene's there and they are extremely kind to so many lonely men. Paul is exceptionally nice, and SO good looking as well, and Irene considers him completely hers!

The Indian horse races

Every Saturday we go to the races. Reidar loves it and I like it too, but not to the same extent. It is a fine course and the member's enclosure "compound" is very attractive, with beautiful flowers, green lawns and shady trees.

The pageant of elegant Indian ladies in their gorgeous *sarees* is fantastically colourful. The jewellery worn is sensational, although, apart from the pure wrought gold ornaments, I find it all rather too gaudy, especially in the afternoon. Outsized diamonds, rubies, pearls, sapphires, emeralds etc., all sparkling together in shiny heavy gold settings! The princes and maharajas, dressed in the special costumes of their own states, look equally impressive and wear plenty of jewellery too. But the finest of all on parade, I find, are the wonderful horses.

Reidar is so preoccupied with studying form as the horses are being led around the paddock before the races, then the betting, and then the race itself, that I very often lose sight of him for half the afternoon. But now I have got used to it and don't mind going around on my own, although I never bet. Minou Patel (a Parsee gentleman playboy and landlord, very wealthy, and owning several big blocks of apartments, including ours), is often my faithful follower.

Herschend has arrived from Hong Kong! Same as ever. Plump and laughing and full of himself, the unpleasant side of him again submerged. He came for dinner on Saturday with Captains Svane and Mathiesen.

It was extremely interesting to hear his news from Hong Kong. He had left in December with Jocobsen and Andersen. They had gone on a picnic in the Kowloon hills one Sunday and were kidnapped by a group of Chinese peasants. It turned out that these men were in the pay of the British. Herschend and his two friends were taken away over the hills into the back country and eventually reached a British camp.

Herschend was preparing to leave anyway, so this suited him well, but the other two did not wish to leave Hong Kong. They had taken a different route to ours, via Woo chow, with the guerrillas and stayed at British Military Mission outposts en route.

They were stuck in Kweilin for ages, like us, but they could not get on any plane to fly out. They had to take a truck to Kungming, as we had contemplated doing. It had been eight days of very rough going on terrible roads over the mountains, with the risk of being ambushed by bandits on the way, or shot at. (How amazingly fortunate we were in avoiding this awful journey with two small children.)

After being held up in Kungming for a long time, waiting for a plane, Herschend got out first, because his one good eye became infected. He had told the British Consul there that unless he could get to Calcutta soon for treatment, he was at grave risk of becoming completely blind.

Reidar had helped him by sending money and standing guarantee for them in India. He also helped to obtain entry permits for them, and got the Danish community in Calcutta and Bombay to put them up.

Herschend told us that the Norwegians in Hong Kong are still criticizing Reidar for having got out of Hong Kong as we did. In spite of the fact that if it hadn't been for him managing to get money sent into Hong Kong for the remaining Norwegians, through the British Consul in Macao, they might well have been in a starving state by now.

Herschend and other well informed people are of the opinion that we shall, most likely, see very few of the Hong Kong foreigners alive again. The strain, mental and physical, is too great and the food so inadequate, together with the fact that one can never know what the Japanese will do, when things go badly for them. They may blow the place to pieces, when they are forced to leave and take the foreigners as hostages, or just shoot them all. We have heard that they have guns on the hillside above Stanley, trained upon the internment camp below.

Norwegians now have "semi-enemy" stamped on their passes and NOBODY is allowed out of Hong Kong, neutral or otherwise. More and more do we thank our lucky stars that we got away. To live under such conditions must be utterly demoralizing and heartbreaking.

Karin Lisbeth is living in the French hospital with her little Sten, who is evidently not doing well and is very weak. Her husband is still interned in the military internment prison at Sam Shui Po and is ill. We talked of all the difficult times with Herschend, and it seemed as if it was of a different world. But it is awful to think of all our friends there, who are still trapped in that horrifying situation.

Leopard's Den, Kashmir again

Kashmir, May 12th, 1943. The rain has been pouring down steadily all day, and Irene and I have spent our time in front of the fire writing, knitting and reading. I feel a great sense of peace and inner repose here with the rustic, woody atmosphere, the smell of the log fires, the solitude and the sound of the rain pattering outside.

After a trip to Calcutta for Nortraship, Reidar left for Colombo on shipping business again, and I couldn't help feeling worried, visualizing all kinds of calamities happening. I wish he could be here with us.

The time I enjoy most of all of the day is the evening before going to bed. I sit by the blazing log fire in my bedroom, writing or reading, or just thinking. And when it is time for bed, I stand naked in front of the flames, looking out of the windows at the cold, snowy mountains gleaming in the moonlight, remote, impersonal and utterly beautiful.

For some strange reason it fills me with an inexpressible longing for something, I don't know what. Somehow that wondrous, unearthly beauty affects my innermost being. I want to somehow capture it and be part of it myself. But the feelings stay pent up inside me, causing great turmoil, and my heart beats violently with a sort of suppressed excitement.

May 19th. Alas Irene is in hospital with a fractured fibula and her foot in plaster of Paris. It was such rotten luck for her. It was a glorious day, brilliant sunshine and very warm with the snow thick and dazzlingly bright all around us. Mr. Carcary, a friend of Irene's, took her for a toboggan ride, a little way down the slope.

When they came back she insisted that she and I should go for a ride, which I thought was a lovely idea of course. So we set off, she in front steering, but after gathering considerable speed, we ran slap into a fallen tree. She put out both her feet to stop some of the impact, and I did the same, but she hurt her foot badly. We thought it was just a severe bruise or sprain at first. She insisted upon hobbling up the slope, leaning upon Mr. Carcary and me. She didn't want to look silly in front of the Princess of Bihar and Princess Nillofar (Minou's goddess!), who were there with a party amusing themselves on the gentle slopes.

Later she felt rather ill and faint from the shock, and her foot pained her a great deal, but she took it very well. Poor Irene went through a lot of pain, when the doctor pulled and manipulated her foot, and had to be sustained by Mr. Carcary's good French brandy. He couldn't help making a regretful remark, when the doctor proceeded to rub her ankle and leg with the precious liquid!

May 29th. This morning we awoke to a blanket of yellow fog, like a London pea-souper, which shut out all the beautiful mountains. Then thunder rumbled loudly and the rain came down in a deluge. I felt nice and cosy in my bed with Ingeling snuggled in beside me. I can't help rather exulting in this weather too, hoping it will last all day and tomorrow too perhaps, so that I shall not have visitors here for tea as planned. Perhaps even Ursula may postpone her visit for a day or two.

In a rash moment I suggested that she should come and stay with us for a few days. I felt so sorry for her in her present position—everybody knowing how her husband Major Charles Boxer, the local head of British army intelligence, was having such an openly, shameless affair in Hong Kong with Emily "Mickey" Hahn. After the army wives including Ursula had been evacuated to Australia, Ms. Hahn made her move on Charles. She is an American who writes for *The New Yorker* magazine. Most find her quite over dramatic and vainglorious, very snide and cynical towards others, but she definitely knows how to cause a stir, which I suppose is important as a social reporter.

I shall long remember a scene at the Hong Kong Hotel where Mickey was proudly showing off her bulging tummy, tapping it and saying, "This is Charles's doing!" She sat in the lounge dressed in a scarlet silk coat with her ridiculous monkey perched on her shoulder that was dressed in a miniature dinner jacket, addressing an audience of somewhat dumbfounded young army officers!

Soon afterwards, theirs became a very public love affair in the world news after she published their personal love letters.

Anyway, Ursula, who is good looking in a very British "jolly-hockey-sticks" sort of way, but was known to have been one of the most beautiful women in Hong Kong, later left Australia and somehow turned up in Bombay, where I met her. Hearing that she was planning to come up to Gulmarg, I issued my rash invitation.

Also we are expecting Viva Ovadia, a good friend of Irene's, in a few days. She is a very smart, and sophisticated lady from Shanghai, intelligent and amusing. I always feel a country-bumpkin in her presence, although she is really a very nice person.

We don't have a radio and only get newspapers if we go to the village, so that we are very much out of touch with what is happening with the war. That is upsetting but as we can do nothing about it, we just live in a little world of our own. I just wish I could be closer to Reidar, and I think of him constantly working so hard in Bombay and not being well.

I have been very busy typing out my Hong Kong war diary. There is more material than I had realized to copy out of my little red diary, as my writing is so minuscule and I have written in every available free space.

June 19th. All this month there has been no privacy, with Irene, then Ursula and Viva staying here. Just after Irene came back, Charles Hardcastle came to stay with the consuls. At first I thought he just liked coming up to see Irene, whom he had known and admired for several years already. But Irene told me that he had spoken to her about me, saying that I was like Hazel, his wife, in many ways. Then Ursula started calling him my "boyfriend". At first I felt this to be most unjustified, until I discovered later that he really did come to see me!

I found him interesting to talk to. He is the Chief Postal Censor in Bombay. Although he never told me any state secrets, he related all sorts of interesting experiences, including how terribly embarrassed he had been, when he opened a letter to censor, addressed to Reidar, from the King of Norway!! He was so apologetic to Reidar about this afterwards.

Then Bob Dalin, Denis Hayes and Tulle arrived. I received a telegram on the 12th from Delhi, saying that they were arriving next day "three men strong", when I had expected only two. I immediately felt scared at the prospect of having three strange men living with us and having to housekeep for them.

The afternoon they arrived we unfortunately happened to have a good many visitors—apart from Charles, who now seems more my friend than Irene's.

I hardly recognized Bob. He looked so gaunt, long-haired and exhausted. It made me more nervous than ever and I visualized packing up and leaving the next day. The other two also looked far from prepossessing. However, next morning they all looked and felt so much better, so I also cheered up a little.

Dancing at Nedou's Hotel

That evening Irene and I went out to a dance at Nedou's Hotel, invited by Charles. I would not have gone if Irene had not been so keen, saying she would not go alone. She spent the day with John Humphries at the hotel and also changed in his room. I put on my white shark-skin crepe blouse and slacks, taking my black evening skirt and shoes along to put on in the ladies room.

It was a beautiful evening and it was fun riding to dinner on horseback. It was the first time I had been inside Nedou's Hotel, and I vowed then and there that it would probably be the last. Crowds and crowds of people, gossiping women and silly looking officers!

However, we had a lovely evening altogether. I enjoyed every moment of it and somehow felt as if the years had fallen away. No more cares, no more responsibilities, children, or even husband for just one evening. Although I did keep thinking of Reidar and wishing he was there, more in the way of a sweetheart than a husband.

I danced every dance and loved it. A young pilot officer was an extremely good dancer and very keen. Charles was good too, and so was John Humphries with whom I danced once. He is a type that is so easy to get along with marvellously well, very good looking, always laughing, teasing and merry. It made me feel young again. Irene danced too, in spite of her foot. She had a wonderful time, and said she enjoyed seeing me have so much fun. Charles seemed to enjoy himself too!

When the dance ended at about 1.30 a.m, we all went up to John and David's rooms, and sat chatting for a while and having a drink. Irene was to spend the night in their sitting room and a bed had been put there for her.

Finally Charles and I went on our way home. It was a magical ride in the stillness of the night, with the moon sinking low over Apharwat and throwing long shadows from the trees. We crossed the golf course and the meadows, and finally climbed the long slope up to the house, nestling at the beginning of the dark forest. By then I was thankful to get home as it had become very cold. It was 4 a.m., but it was a marvellous evening and took me back years.

The war left one with a feeling of instability, never knowing what the future holds, and physical separation from your loved ones. It was easy to lose yourself in a romance of the moment, and sometimes that was what happened.

Kashmir. June 25th. Today I have had two letters from Reidar. One was in the same tone as the last few have been, worrying and protesting strongly about "all the entertaining" we are doing. He said that he had been ill with malaria for nearly a week. Poor sweetheart, how I wish I had been there to look after him and having him at home.

His second letter has rather knocked me sideways. I feel so sad and worried. It seems that the malaria has made him so weak, the doctor says he absolutely *must* have a holiday. So this means either coming up here for three or four weeks, or taking the opportunity to go to England for business reasons, which I know he has been thinking he should do. The difficulties of travelling to Europe in war time are so complicated, and of course so dangerous. Also it certainly would not be much of a restful holiday that he really needs.

My heart leaped with excitement when I read the first part—the idea of him coming up here is so exciting and therefore just too good to come true. He asks me what he should do? How can he ask me this when he knows the only thing I can truly want is for him to be up here with me. Yet I must not try to influence him into taking a course he might regret afterwards and feel guilty at having neglected his duty to Nortraship. It is so hard to think rationally, without letting one's emotions take over.

This morning while we were having our early tea in my bedroom, Bob came in and sat on my bed. John and Ingeling were romping all around me, burrowing inside the bed with squeals of laughter and shrieks of excitement. Then it all developed into a glorious pillow fight. Eventually Denis was dragged out of bed and involved too. It was great fun.

Breakfast at Leopard's Den, with the village of Gulmarg in the valley and Mount Apharwat in the background

Then we had breakfast out in the garden in the sun, perfect weather and perfect views all around. New dazzling white snow covered the mountains. After my household duties, we all went out for a lovely ride around the Outer Circular Road and back by the Inner one. Ingeling was on her own little pony with the supporting ring around her, and faithful little gora-walla in attendance. I felt so touched that they all seemed genuinely content to go for this ride, to keep me and my children company.

Ingrid on her own little pony

In the afternoon Bob came for a walk with me, John and Ingrid, up at the back of the house and in the woods. He told me quite a lot about himself that I had not heard from Irene. I knew he works for the Swedish Match Company, in Bombay, and that he has an attractive wife, who is in Sweden now, having a cure for goitre. That must be a terrible affliction, as it is so disfiguring. It takes a long time to cure, and often leaves its mark permanently. So he was not sure when she would be able to return to Bombay, but he did not seem to mind very much. He said her character had changed as well as her looks. When she became ill, he found her very difficult to live with during the last months before she left for Sweden.

In fact, he is rather dreading her return. It is really a blessing they have no children. In the mean time he certainly seems to be enjoying his bachelor life! He is so good looking, in a rugged Scandinavian way, and so charming in manner, and fun to be with. No wonder the women fall for him, including both my special girl friends.

I put him straight early in our friendship about me, telling him, "Nothing doing, I am very much in love with my own husband", and he laughs and says he accepts that situation but if I happen to change my mind please just let him know!

Denis, on the other hand, is a very different character, very English and formal in his behaviour, and not outstanding to look at. But he is just such a nice person altogether, and I find we have much in common on our views of life in general. He is not married but said he would like to be, if he could only find the right girl.

I sent my long telegram to Reidar, but hardly had I got back from the village post office than another arrived from him. The doctors had insisted upon him coming up here, and he would leave as soon as the permits were in order! What JOY on my part at this heavenly surprise! The thought of him actually being here with me has always seemed to be too wonderful to come true.

He himself has thought that the height may be bad for his heart and when I argued against that, he says, "Alright, I will come up there sometime just to prove to you that I will die of heart failure!"

Bear hunting

July 2nd. We are on a camping expedition at this moment and I am writing sitting in a tent. It has been raining. Outside the great trees stand dark and dripping. There is a wonderful fresh, damp, earthy smell coming up from the ground. I have been here three days—glorious, marvellous, memorable days for me. I have always longed to be able to go camping in some beautiful, faraway place, to sleep outside with just nature all around, remote from cities and people.

So when the "three men strong" went to camp, for their bear hunting expedition, they asked me to join them. I simply couldn't resist.The first day, Irene and I rode out there through glorious woods, across two beautiful clearings, carpeted with wild flowers—Canterbury bells, forget-me-nots, daisies and buttercups, green ferns and great boulders of rock strewn about. It was as if giants had been rolling stones down from the steep and wild mountainside.

Then we plunged into deep, dark woods again, where bears and leopards prowl at nights, as we were told by the *gora-wallas*. We crossed many small mountain streams, gurgling across our path. There were indescribably lovely little glades, brilliant green with soft ferns, where the sunlight filtered through the giant trees. I felt like pulling off my clothes to run through the trees, lie amongst the ferns, and splash in the sparkling cold water of the mountain brooks.

Eventually we came out onto a lovely *marg*—an undulating, green meadow dotted with cattle, horses and water buffaloes. On one hillside were many little log cabins, for shepherds and their flocks, with their roofs slanting right into the mountainside. Then, far up in the furthest corner, tucked away at the beginning of the great forest, we saw four tiny white tents.

By that time I was in such a state of excitement and wild happiness that, in spite of Irene's foot, I just had to gallop. We let the horses race over the green slopes and up the final one, shouting madly at the top of our voices. At the camp I felt like dancing and rolling on the ground with joy. Tulle looked on in mild amazement and the others just laughed. I felt so happy and free, so bursting with life and vitality.

The bear hunting party setting camp

We had lunch seated on logs. It was served by the helpers provided by the camping outfitters, plus our own bearer from the house. Afterwards I was far too restless and went climbing up to the forest, over the carpet of soft pine needles, through spicy-scented undergrowth. Up and up I went, past dead trees lying like fallen giants here and there, victims of violent storms. I did not feel tired at all, but just drawn irresistibly towards the forest above. I had been told that there were bears living in this wood, so I was a little frightened and didn't go in very far.

I noticed Denis much further down the hill collecting logs for our campfire. I sat down on the soft-sweet smelling earth and he came and joined me. We sat and talked, of woods and wildlife and nature. He knows a lot about woodcraft and I found it very interesting listening. Afterwards I helped him pulling down logs, even some small dead trees. It was quite strenuous but fun.

When Irene decided that she was going back to the house, Bob and I tried to persuade her to stay but she wouldn't. So we walked with her some of the way and then on the way back joined hands and ran over the soft green grass, until my head was dizzy and I had no more breath. Bob put his arms around me, which felt so natural, but then I remembered Reidar and moved apart.

When we got back to the camp Tulle was just starting out to go and keep a whole night's vigil up in a *machan*. It was the spot where a leopard had killed a horse the night before. I didn't envy him going to spend the night, lonely, cold and uncomfortable, sitting up in a tree, waiting and watching until his eyes ached, and all the shadows and sounds assuming strange shapes and proportions.

We had our dinner sitting around the blazing campfire. Later I brought out my fur rug and spread it on the ground. I lay looking up at Apharwat, treeless against the darkening sky, as a multitude of sparkling stars appeared. The Kashmiris were in their tent talking and eating. Denis and Bob sat on a log near the fire, silently smoking. I felt as if I was in a wonderful dream, trying to imprint every detail on my memory, to be treasured forever.

I went to bed quite early and was thrilled to be lying on a bed made of spruce twigs, fragrant and soft, looking out onto the fire. It blazed up brightly and crackled, sending out showers of sparks. The firelight illuminated the great trees and branches with a red glow, making dancing shadows across the dark forest until I fell asleep.

Later I awoke and realized it had become very dark. The fire had died down to a pile of glowing embers. The *chokedah* who was supposed to keep it going, to scare off any wild animals, must have fallen asleep himself.

As I was looking at the triangular opening of the tent flap, I realized there was an animal standing at the foot of my bed sniffing my fur cover. I could only see its black silhouette against the glowing embers of the fire. It looked like a wolf. I tried to scream for help to frighten it away. But I was so terrified it was going to attack me, that I simply could not utter a sound! My sudden movement on waking must have scared it, as it disappeared into the darkness. So did my fear. I jumped up and ran out to see what kind of an animal it was, but it had vanished already.

The chokedar came quickly and threw more big logs on the fire. Both Denis and Bob slept peacefully throughout the incident. The next morning when I told them about it, how frightened I had been—neither of these mighty hunters coming to my rescue—they looked rather embarrassed!

We had our early morning tea sitting on the logs near the fire. It was really cold. Tulle came back from his night watch, not having even seen a sign of any animal and he went to sleep until lunchtime. Meanwhile Bob, Denis and I went up into the woods behind, up and up until the trees stopped. We came out on top of the smooth, steep, grassy knoll, where some stunted and twisted pines grew, and some wind-swept evergreens. Bob had taken his gun, but only shot a pigeon, thank goodness. The view was spectacular all around.

Camping on Ferozepore Nullah

I left the two men and ran on, through a belt of trees to the second mountaintop. There I took off all my clothes, and danced on the glorious soft springy turf, feeling part of nature.

July 17th. Reidar has been here since the 10th. The day before he arrived, I spent settling into our little log cabin up at the back of the main house, making it cosy, as it had been empty for so long. It touched me how concerned the three men were that Reidar and I should be comfortable there.

After lunch and a colossal amount of fidgeting and impatience on my part, we set off for Tangmarg. We were armed with a basket containing hot coffee and sandwiches, to revive Reidar after his many hours of travel. I was very worried in case it rained for Reidar's trip up the mountain by *dandi* (a sedan chair with poles carried on the shoulders of four men).

We sat and watched the road, while it grew colder and colder. Suddenly a car came along and my sweetheart was sitting in the front seat. I just leapt down the bank, and hugged and hugged him. He looked dreadfully tired. It reminded me of our arrival in Chungking. We walked the little distance up to the village, and he said that was the furthest he had walked for weeks. We got him into a *dandi* and gave him coffee and sandwiches. Then Bob rode off back to Leopard's Den, being very tactful, to see that the fires were lit in our little cabin.

That ride up to Gulmarg was so awful! Right from the start and throughout the whole way up the hill the *dandi-wallas* shouted at each other, hit each other and argued at the tops of their voices. Before we had gone one quarter of the way, Reidar started asking if we had reached the top already.

He looked so drawn and pale that I was afraid he was going to pass out at any moment. I rode beside him and tried to keep up some light and cheerful conversation, to keep his mind off the present situation. At times he responded but most of the time the strain was awful. It grew darker and colder. He was dressed in shorts, but thank goodness Bob had given us his overcoat, which Reidar wrapped around his knees—or rather I did for him as he seemed too weak to do anything.

It was almost dark when we reached the top and crossed the golf course. When we came to the stream, Reidar had to get out to cross the log bridge and walk over it. He swayed so much, I was terrified he would fall in. I kept telling him, "It's not so much further now", but in the end he became suspicious of these promises, as it always seemed to be, "only about ten minutes more".

However we eventually saw a tiny glimmer of light away up against the blackness of the far side of the valley. Up and up the final steep slope we went, the *dandi-wallas* still arguing together, me trying to be encouraging and Reidar completely silent. He told me afterwards that he was cursing that he had ever attempted to come up here. But he had made up his mind that he was going to come, just to prove to me that he couldn't take it.

However once he got into our little sitting room, so warm and cosy, sitting by the blazing fire and a whiskey soda in hand, he already felt much better. We had dinner side by side on the sofa in front of the fire and then went to bed, by that time it was amazing how un-tired he felt!

For the next three days he stayed in bed. He didn't feel his heart troubled, but only a little trouble in breathing at times. The weather all this time has not been very bright and it has rained on and off every day. But I must admit to being rather pleased, because it has been a little difficult suppressing my bouncing wandering feelings, to stop myself longing to dash up into the woods at all odd hours, or go up on the mountain tops.

It is so unbelievably wonderful having my sweetheart actually here with me that it makes me feel guilty even thinking of such things. So when the rain patters down upon the silvery wood shingles, I just gaze out of the windows thinking how lovely it all looks. He worries too about restricting me from doing many things, and I should hate it if I gave him cause to think for one moment that I wanted to be elsewhere rather than with him.

We are so happy in this tiny cabin and it is fun having our little daughter come bursting in to see us, when we have our early morning tea. She is so full of fun and laughter, sparkling with mischief and happiness.

John and Ingrid enjoying the outdoors

The men here are all captivated by her. Even at this early stage of her life, she is a true female and very flirtatious. Yesterday when we were all having breakfast in the garden, Ingrid made her appearance after she had been dressed and hair prettily brushed by Ayhie. She went around the table, greeting everyone most graciously, then suddenly stopped a little way off, seeming to think, then lifted her dress up and exclaimed, with an expression of mock surprise and consternation, "My Gosh—no panties!" She then ran into the house, amid general applause at her performance!

Ursula is back in Gulmarg again, but not staying with us. However I thought she might enjoy going for a picnic with the men, as Bob seemed a little lonely for feminine company. I told him she was good looking and fancy-free and he was very enthusiastic. So I wrote her a little note, telling her to come on a picnic, and Bob would light a fire to cook their lunch. Well, Bob certainly lit a fire! They have been together practically all the time since then. I am glad for both of them that my plan was a success!

Reidar recovering from his travels

July 20th. Today has been a lovely day, weather and all. Reidar gets better each day and can do more without getting too exhausted. We went for quite a long walk this morning along the track to Ningle Nullah. Reidar rode back and already feels more at ease on horseback.

Father and son enjoying each other's company

After tiffin I rode to the village with Denis. His ideas on life are so much the opposite to Bob's, more serious and solid. I am so in love with my own husband that I am in no danger of falling for either of them. But it is nice knowing that they both are half in love with me and respect me for not succumbing. Denis keeps saying he wishes he could find somebody like me to marry. Bob, being married already, makes no pretensions as to his desires!

On our way back, we met Reidar, who had come to meet me. Denis rode on ahead most tactfully and I dismounted and we walked home together. We were followed by a duck all the way. It waddled solemnly after us, stopped when we did, sometimes settled down patiently to wait for us. When we were kissing and hugging each other for too long it would waddle a little way ahead, then stop and look back at us with its head on one side and quack plaintively! Bob and Denis suddenly appeared through the trees ahead of us and were most amused at our escort.

The news about the war is good now—about the British, Canadian and American troops advancing on Sicily, having bombed Rome, also American activities against Japan. But it seems as though we shall have to wait for the war to finish in Europe first before Japan can be dealt with finally, and we can return to our beloved Hong Kong. It is incredible how cut off and isolated we are here from what is going on in the rest of the world, having no radio or telephone.

Reidar got a telegram today from Reeves in Macao, saying that the owners of the ship, *Masbate*, had no more money to support Captain Jorgensen and crew, who have been holed up there ever since the war came to Hong Kong. So Reidar is going to try and arrange a remittance to them somehow.

Camping on the slopes of Domercote

August 7th. Reidar and I have been camping! Way up in the mountains, on the inside slopes of Domercote. It was so wonderful and so beautiful up there. I was thrilled, even if it was for just one night.

When we started out Reidar was full of skepticism. We started off on horseback and there was a wonderful warm fragrance of innumerable scented herbs and shrubs baking in the sun, mixed with the perfume of pines. It was lovely through the quiet woods and the soft, green undergrowth. Reidar became quite chatty so I felt more cheerful.

Then the path suddenly started to climb and I saw we were headed for a pass on the top ridge of the mountain. My spirits plummeted as I wondered how Reidar was ever going to make that steep climb. But he took it marvellously.

We stopped on a little *marg* where I persuaded him, much against his will, to lie down and rest a while. Even more against his will, I massaged his back a little as it was aching across the shoulders. Then we set off on one of the steepest climbs I have ever done on horseback. I would have got off, only I did not want Reidar to walk, so I had to pretend it was all perfectly normal. We almost had to clasp them around the neck at times so as not to slide off their backs.

Reidar took it all in a most matter of fact way, with a slight air of resignation, but also enjoying himself and pleased with his achievements. We did have to get off eventually and climb a good bit on foot. I kept imploring him to go slowly, but he said he felt fine. Finally we emerged onto a beautiful little *marg*, having taken two hours and a half on the climb. As darkness was approaching, we agreed that this was the place to stop.

Our mountain slope, with a stream below, abruptly fell away into a deep valley. Beyond was the great flat plain of the Vale of Kashmir, majestic Handibal with his head in the clouds, and then Nanga Parbat, the third highest mountain in the world, still unconquered by man. I have looked at this giant through binoculars at the stark ferocity of those rock faces, falling in sheer drops for thousands of feet on to tremendous glaciers. It fills me with awe. This was a fabulous place to camp.

The men pitched the tents and I helped as much as I could. Then I asked them to help me collect spruce boughs for our beds from a few scattered, stunted trees growing fairly near. I arranged them carefully as I had seen the men do at our other camp and Reidar lay on the soft short grass and rested, but said he felt fine.

Later we went for a stroll before dinner, up the gentle, grassy incline and amongst the stunted mountain trees. Suddenly we came upon the head of a cow, still covered with fur and obviously fairly recently killed, which reminded us of the story a shepherd had just told the servants, of a bear having killed a cow the night before in some woods nearby!

The night was not so good as there were so many mosquitoes. We had a big fire burning to keep away any wild animals, but it must have died down at one time as jackals, or some other animals, stole the food out of the servant's tent. The chokedar and servants also said they were freezing cold because we were in such an exposed position.

The next morning the clouds gathered, slowly rolling up the valley and blotting out Gulmarg. After breakfast we walked slowly up to the top of the crest behind the camp. It was lovely, hot and sunny, so we gradually shed our clothes by the wayside, until we were finally walking about on the top with nothing on at all. No shoes even, as the grass was so soft and springy. But the mist came and enveloped us, blotting out the fabulous view for a while, then lifted again. It was beautiful looking down through it. We felt so happy and thrilled to be up there, 12,000 feet high on a Himalayan mountain, just Reidar and me, with no clothes, that suddenly we found ourselves lying on the soft grass and making love. It seemed the right thing to do.

Later, the weather started to look very threatening in the distance and they all said there was going to be a very big storm, which did indeed happen. But it started when we had nearly reached home again, thank goodness, and carried on with great force for 24 hours. We were most thankful not to have been caught up in the mountains then. But we were both so thrilled with the whole experience that we didn't really mind having to come home earlier than intended.

I don't think it is right to walk in deep snow high up on the mountains, all alone. I suppose that is because of the terrifying experience I had not so long ago, when I was going for a climb up in the mountains with just a Kashmiri guide and the chokedar from the hut. I was very anxious to reach a small frozen lake that I had been told lay higher up the mountain. It was a glorious day and the sun was really warm.

When I told the men I wanted to go further up, pointing to where I thought the lake was, they seemed very reluctant to go. So I said they could wait for me, as I was only going such a little way further up, crossing a smooth open slope. I right away found the snow much deeper than I had anticipated. I sank in over my knees and sometimes even up to my waist, so that each step was an effort. But I was determined to keep on, as the ridge beyond where the lake lay seemed fairly close.

When I reached the middle of this open slope, I stopped to enjoy the glorious scenery all around me. The slope was at a fairly steep angle, carrying on down until it abruptly vanished over a precipitous gorge. As I stood there looking and thinking how amazing it was that I should be completely alone on this spectacular, pristine, snow-covered mountain slope, suddenly there came a terrifying, earsplitting great crack and the whole slope seemed to subside. I was absolutely petrified with fright and was sure I had started an avalanche.

All Bob's warnings came flooding back and his lessons about how to understand the snow under so many different circumstances, particularly when the sun had been shining on a south-facing slope, it would melt the snow lying on the rock faces and cause avalanches, which is what had happened that day.

I stayed riveted to the spot, not daring even to breath with my heart banging painfully against my ribs. I waited for the slide to begin, but nothing more happened. I was too frightened to move for a long time, but eventually I turned, very softly and gently, and crept back across the slope putting each foot into the footprints I had made coming over. The relief on getting back safely was quite overwhelming, and that experience a lesson never to be forgotten.

Bombay again

October 30, 1943. Juhu Beach. Reidar was called to London by Nortraship on business. So he had to go, but despite the problems and danger of such a trip in war time, I think he was almost glad to go and to be able to personally meet the various top people in Nortraship, with whom he has been working and communicating by letter and coded telegrams only, for the past two years.

Also he was anxious to see about Wallem & Company's affairs, now being looked after by Lambert Brothers in London. But it was awful saying goodbye to him, knowing that I am not going to be able to hear a word from him until he returns, and nobody can tell when that will be.

He was not told by what route he would be flying, just that it would be in a military transport, and that he must not, on any account, try to communicate with me, or try to tell me where he is. Obviously they will be taking a very round-about route, as a flight across Europe would be out of the question now. So many planes have been shot down even far out of the war zone. I can hardly bear to think of it. It is such a long time already since he has been gone and not a word. One can only hope that no news is good news.

So, here I am at Juhu staying in the Ritchies' comfortable shack with John and Ingrid, and of course Ayhie. I love the quiet nights, with just the soft whispering splash of the waves, and then the early mornings, calm and cool and so peaceful. Then the children go off with Ayhie to watch the fishermen bring in their nets along the beach, and I am left in my much appreciated solitude for a little while.

Sophie and Ingrid at Juhu

There is also a terrific strain and tension in the relations between Irene and Sophie, because Sophie had been for a very long walk with Pip after dinner, much to Irene's annoyance, and evidently Pip is one of her latest boyfriends.

Irene

But this sort of thing happens so frequently. So many of Irene's special friends fall for Sophie, which is not surprising, as she is lovely to look at, very flirtatious, and a fancy-free young widow. Although Irene is also very lovely and very flirtatious, she has a husband and at times, I must confess, I am amazed at the amount of freedom he gives her and does not seem to be jealous of any of her numerous admirers.

Bob's week of leave happened to coincide with my stay out here and on Monday he came around quite early. We sat and had a long talk about life and public opinions etc., and the way people always seem to think the worst. This was because it worried me that people would hear that he was staying at Juhu also, while I am here alone. People are bound to gossip, particularly as it is Bob. He was very nice and decided to stay in town until the public holidays of Divali started.

Reidar shares a drink with Clark Gable

November 1943. Wonderful, wonderful! Reidar is back after being away for two whole months, without being able to communicate with each other. That was a depressing state of affairs. But one just had to switch off imagining all the awful things that might happen while travelling on such a perilous journey these days. Thank goodness I did not fully realize the dangers of his trip to London and back, but from what I know now, it was truly hazardous.

The journey to London took ten days, as it was impossible to fly direct. He had to first stop for some days in Cairo, then on to Lagos, Nigeria, across North Africa, where he waited again to be fitted into a military plane bound for Lisbon. I learnt afterwards that this was the most dangerous part of the journey, as so many planes were being shot down on this particular route.

After another few days in Lisbon, he finally reached London. That was a pretty terrible experience too, with air raids night after night, and having to find one's way about the vast city, completely blacked out at night. It was better not to go out if possible, but sometimes he had to.

He was surprised that a very fine suite in Claridges Hotel, on the top floor, had been available, but was told that nobody wanted to stay there any more, because of the bombing! And indeed night after night the sirens screamed and all the hotel guests would grab warm clothes and go down into the cellars, hoping the "all clear" would sound before too many hours. It must have been truly nerve-racking and exhausting, never being able to get a proper night's sleep.

Finally Reidar decided that he would not go down to the cellars, but stay in his comfortable rooms with a book and a bottle of whiskey to pass the time! However, after the warning sounded and the other inhabitants of the top floor had gone down, he opened his door and peered along the passage, only to see his neighbour doing exactly the same. So they exchanged greetings and kept each other company, sharing the bottle of whiskey in a very friendly manner. Reidar later discovered that his new friend was Clark Gable!

Despite the difficulties of getting about London, he managed to see many important people and attend to Wallem & Co. business, as well as all that he had to do for Nortraship, which was very interesting as well as taxing. But he was gratified by the reception and appreciation he received from the "high ups" in Nortraship. He was very glad he had been on this demanding visit, though he still is not allowed to mention the specific route that he travelled.

The Allies gain ground against the Axis Powers

1944 marked numerous Allied victories against Germany in Europe, and US and Commonwealth force victories against Japan in Asia.

On June 6th, Western Allies invaded northern France at Normandy in the largest seaborne invasion in history. Known as D-Day, the operation began the invasion of German-occupied Western Europe, leading to the liberation of France from Nazi control. The Soviet army beat back Germany on the Eastern Front. By the end of the year, Germany is fighting desperately and Allied victory looks certain.

Meanwhile in the Pacific theatre, American forces continue to drive back the Japanese, and later intensive bomber attacks are launched on Japanese home islands.

Anniversary celebration

Bombay, January 3rd, 1945. I have returned to writing in my diary after a year of relative calm in our lives during 1944, except for continuous good and bad news of the war, and the various trips Reidar has taken for Nortraship to Colombo, Calcutta and other places for the shipping command. Meanwhile I have been busy managing the house, children and still working as an ambulance driver.

Today is our tenth wedding anniversary! I am sitting at this moment in my ambulance at the Indian Military Hospital, on duty for the morning. It is quite chilly, but nice to have a little break from the usual hot weather. I am hoping that the other two girls on duty won't come over and chat to me!

This morning, with the early tea in bed, my sweetheart gave me the most beautiful bracelet of heavy gold links, with sapphires and diamonds. It is typical of the jewellery one sees so much of here, worn by Indian highborn ladies, modern and sophisticated. I am thrilled with it, and Reidar confessed that he had been hugging himself in anticipation of my reaction for months already. What a truly wonderful husband I have!

The thoughts uppermost in all people's minds – what does 1945 hold in store for the anxious world? I don't feel very optimistic about the war being over very soon, but Reidar and I plan to go to England in the summer, and wonder when our return to Hong Kong will be and whether it will ever be the same.

Bob's suicide

Bob came to see me yesterday morning. It was several weeks since our last meeting, when he told me how much he was dreading his wife's arrival from Sweden. She is supposed to be cured now from the goitre she had been suffering from for the last couple of years. It had completely changed her character, according to him.

I have never met her, but have heard from his friends that she was pretty and bright and a great favourite with the Swedish community in Bombay. They were all very grieved when she became ill, and, eventually, had to return to Sweden for treatment for her malady.

He told me that several of his friends and colleagues in the Swedish Match Company were very censorious about his way of life and all his girlfriends, since she left Bombay. But he also told me how very difficult life with her had become, as her illness developed. They had terrible rows and their lives became truly miserable, until she decided that the only course was, at that point, to go back to Sweden and seek a cure.

Well now, seemingly, she has been cured and is anticipating picking up their lives together as they used to be when they were first married. But, his great trouble now is that he has lost all his love for her. This gives him a terribly guilty feeling, not just for the fact that he has had so many girlfriends since she left, but because now he is expected to be overjoyed by her return.

When he had murmured to one or two of his friends that he doubted he would be able to live up to these expectations, they had been very critical of him. Even the head of the firm had been implying that he would simply have to "reform or else...". All this has been hanging over him as the day of her return approached and his dread increased.

When he arrived yesterday I could see that he was in a highly emotional state and he poured out his heart from its very depths. He was truly distraught, saying over and over again that it was no use, no use. He had tried desperately, but simply could not feel anything but revulsion for her.

He was convulsed with sobs and kept saying that he knew all his friends and his boss were bitterly against him. They were critical of the gay bachelor life he has been leading while she was away, and showed their disapproval in no uncertain way. They expected him to change completely now and become a model husband.

But his wife is still so changed, her looks have improved to a certain extent he says, but not her character. She has become totally antipathetic to him to the extent that he simply cannot bear living in the same house with her.

He was pacing around the room, telling me all this, shaking his head and groaning, "What can I do, how can I find any way out of this mess? If I ask for a divorce, I know I will be kicked out of the firm and I suppose I deserve it. It is so awful but I simply cannot go back to her."

At one point I went over and put my arms around him to try and calm him down, and begged him to stay with us for a few days, until he could sort himself out a bit. Since Sophie has gone to England we have a spare room and I know Reidar would agree with me and want to do anything possible to help him, as he likes him so much. I felt just staying away from that whole situation for a few days might help him to see things more clearly, and also being able to talk to Reidar, who is so wise and calm.

But he wouldn't listen and eventually he left, saying he wished he could stay and find refuge here, but No, he had to find his own solution. When Reidar returned from the office and I told him all about it, he said he wished I had been able to prevail upon him to stay.

This morning I received a telephone call from Bob's secretary telling me that Bob had committed suicide. He had shot himself! It is such a horrifying shock it is difficult to believe. Such a sad, sad waste of a fine life.

If only I had been stronger and able to persuade him to stay. It just might have made a difference. Why had his secretary, whom I have never met or even heard of, telephoned to tell me? The finality of his solution is shattering.

March 12th, 1945. Sophie has gone to England. She said she was so scared setting off for the first time on a long voyage all by herself. So I told her how I always loved going off by myself and was always ready for adventure. After that she too was "all set for adventure!" Naturally, being such a lovely girl, she will always find people to help her.

After she had left, Harry, another admirer came and told me about his pent-up feelings for Sophie. I am wondering what will happen when they meet again in London soon. I think that Sophie is obviously hoping that Harry may turn out to be like my Reidar, an older and reliable man, who loves her devotedly. He is older but a dour Scott, and not demonstrative enough for her as Reidar is towards me. However, he begged me to give her a special message from him, to give him "the green light" when he got back to England.

Voyage to England

April 9th, 1945. We are leaving for England! Our cabin was not far from that of the children, but I hated being separated from them at night as one was permanently worrying about torpedos or hitting a mine. Of course we had "boat drill" every day and everybody was obliged to carry their life jacket everywhere they went, getting into big trouble if they did not. This was a nuisance as the children particularly, and many others too, were always forgetting them.

We were travelling in a convoy of about a dozen ships, escorted by three destroyers. I think most of the passengers must have spent a great deal of time looking out to sea, in all directions, just in case some enemy craft could be spotted but thank heavens, we never did see any.

V.E. Day

By early 1945, Allied forces attack Germany on its own soil from all directions. On April 12, President Roosevelt dies and is succeeded by Harry Truman. On April 28, the Facist leader Benito Mussolini is killed by Italian partisans. His body is hung upside down for public viewing and to provide confirmation of his demise.

Shocking the world, on April 30, Adolf Hitler commits suicide during the Battle of Berlin. His body is burned by SS officers to avoid capture.

A week later, on May 8th, Nazi Germany surrenders unconditionally its armed forces to the Allies. Known as "Victory in Europe Day", it marks the end of World War II in Europe. Upon the formal defeat of Germany, celebrations erupt throughout the world.

Allied Victory in Europe headlines

May 8th, 1945. We got to Gibraltar the very day that "Victory in Europe" Day was declared and of course there was wild jubilation and celebrations.

But it was not all joy, because rumours were flying that two German submarines were in the vicinity of Gibraltar and would almost certainly decide to get rid of their last torpedoes, trying to sink any allied vessel nearby before having to give themselves up. However, thankfully, this did not happen and we eventually reached Tilbury Docks safely.

After the hassle of dealing with all of our baggage and transportation, it was amazing to drive through London to see the horrifying bomb damage all about, and yet people in the streets full of hope.

At last we reached the Savoy Hotel. I was too tired to worry about my scruffy appearance entering such a posh hotel! I had no idea that Lambert Brothers, Wallem's shipping agent in London, had booked us there and would certainly have asked to be booked at a more modest establishment had I known beforehand. We found that two super luxury suites had been held for us, one for Reidar and me and the other for Miss Sykes, Reidar's Iraqi secretary, and the children. After a long, hot bath, JoJo and Ingrid, each in an enormous double bed, lay propped up by a bank of big, puffy pillows, looking like two innocent cherubs!

We can now finally start to plan ahead. After victory in Europe, we wonder when the Japanese will be defeated, and when we can go home to Hong Kong.

Meanwhile we have to find a place to stay in England. And Reidar is also very anxious to get over to Norway as soon as possible to see all his relatives there. Alas, his mother and father died during the German occupation, but he has his four brothers still in Bergen with their families to visit.

Though our travels to get here have been long and arduous, we are immensely relieved and thankful that all of us are now in good health and eagerly looking forward to the future, wherever it will take us.

Our Return to Hong Kong

The fall of the Japanese Empire

In March, 1945, American bombers struck Tokyo with incendiary bombs, killing over 100,000 people, and during the next five months bombed 66 other Japanese cities, levelling them and killing between 350,000 and 500,000 Japanese civilians.

By the end of July 1945, the Imperial Japanese Navy was incapable of conducting major operations and an Allied ground invasion of Japan was imminent. The Allies reiterated the demand for unconditional surrender of all Japanese forces, stating "the alternative for Japan is prompt and utter destruction", yet Japan generals continued to declare their intent to fight on to the bitter end. It appeared that Japanese defeat would require a massive ground assault on Japan's mainland, dragging out the war and incurring many more losses on both sides.

On August 6th, 1945, the United States stunned the world by detonating an atomic bomb over the Japanese city of Hiroshima, killing between 90,000 and 160,000 people. However Japan continued to resist. Three days later, August 9th, the Soviet Union declared war on Japan and invaded the Japanese puppet state of Manchukuo (Manchuria) to defeat the largest Japanese fighting force. That same day, the United States dropped a second atomic bomb on the Japanese city of Nagasaki, where 40,000 to 80,000 perished.

The combined shock of these events caused Emperor Hirohito to announce the surrender of Japan to the Allies and Japan formally sign the surrender agreement on September 2, 1945, bringing the hostilities of World War II to a close.

Estimates for the total casualties of World War II, in Europe and the Pacific combined, suggest that approximately 75 million people died, including about 20 million military personnel and 40 million civilians. Many millions had suffered and perished in the German concentration camps and the Japanese prison camps.

After nearly a decade of imperial expansion, resulting in destruction and suffering worldwide, the German and Japanese Empires were reduced to ashes.

Hong Kong is liberated

The Japanese occupation of Hong Kong lasted for three years and eight months. Now who should rule Hong Kong?

Chinese Nationalist Chiang Kai-shek assumed he would take control of the whole of China. Earlier, U.S. President Franklin Roosevelt insisted that colonialism should end, and promised Soong May-ling that Hong Kong would be restored to Chinese control.

However, the British moved quickly to regain power and their Royal Navy, with permission from US President Truman, sailed into Hong Kong to re-establish the British government's control over the colony and accept the Japanese surrender on August 30, 1945, which was declared as "Liberation Day".

Meanwhile Chiang Kai-shek was quickly trying to occupy as much territory on mainland China as possible, including to re-establish the former capital of Nanking, before the arrival of the Communists.

Liberation Day ceremonies in Hong Kong

We read the headline news of the terrible bombs that were dropped on Hiroshima and Nagasaki with mixed emotions. This horribly violent act had forced the Japanese to surrender. World War II was over and now we could go home.

Reidar was among the first to be sent back to Hong Kong. My brother, Archy, was sent to Shanghai at the same time. Ships were of paramount importance in order to bring food and every kind of supply to the whole population that was in such desperate need. Food was so scarce that many were starving.

Hong Kong was still in a state of chaos after the war, with so many buildings destroyed in the city and all over the island. The waterworks, electricity and sewage systems were all dangerously disrupted, and motor transport was almost nonexistent. And after so much Japanese bombing, housing was also very limited.

Reidar had gone back to Mr. Nemazee's house to stay with Mehdi, his cousin/housekeeper, who was still surviving there on his own. Under these terribly difficult conditions, no women or children were allowed back to the colony until the following year when there was considerable improvement.

But, when Ingrid and I got back—after a very long sea voyage of many weeks on a Norwegian cargo vessel, and being delayed in Singapore for three weeks on our way—it was a great shock to find my poor Reidar struggling to recover from a dangerous bout of typhoid fever. He looked like a walking skeleton, but was fortunate to be alive at all. The conditions in Hong Kong during this period had been so bad that many people had succumbed to sickness and died.

The reconstruction of Hong Kong depended heavily on the import of raw materials and supplies to rebuild the city and create livable conditions. The organization of this effort required Reidar's expertise in shipping logistics for the process to move smoothly and quickly.

World War II had also been devastating for Wallem and Company controlled ships, both in the Pacific against the Japanese, and elsewhere against German submarines. More than 20 Wallem ships were lost by seizure, torpedoing and bombing. Many crew were lost at sea or captured as prisoners of war. In the torpedoing of one ship alone, the s.s. Storviken, 37 of the 42 crewmen perished as they waited days for rescue on their makeshift raft, while third mate, Finn Kjellevik, was tortured aboard the Japanaese submarine that sank her. These were employees and friends that Reidar had felt responsible for during the difficult times.

As conditions in Hong Kong improved, Reidar invited staff members who had survived the war back to their old posts. The company was back in business.

Eventually, after many months under Mr. Nemazee's always-hospitable roof, we were able to return to our beloved *Skyhigh* again. It had had to be almost completely rebuilt, except for the ground floor where the thick foundation walls had saved our lives. We were overjoyed to be back again and could hardly believe that our dreams and prayers had come true.

Iris and Reidar back at Skyhigh once again

Hong Kong's post-war recovery was swift. By November 1945, the economy had recovered so well that government controls were lifted and free markets restored. The population returned from 600,000 during occupation to around one million by early 1946, and two million by 1947, fueled by immigration from China of people fleeing the current civil war between the Nationalists and the Communists.

Colonial taboos also broke down in the post-war years as European colonial powers realised that they could not administer their colonies as they did before the war. Reforms brought new racial and social integration to Hong Kong's society. Welfare programs also improved. Chinese people were no longer restricted from certain beaches or from living on Victoria Peak. A certain level of democracy was introduced to the colony to gain Chinese support for continued British rule, however it was difficult to maintain as Britain had to tighten its control on Hong Kong when the Communists continued to gain territory on the mainland.

By 1948, the Nationalist Koumintang government had retreated from Nanking to Canton, the mainland's closest city to Hong Kong, leaving all of northern China in Communist control under Mao Zedong's People's Liberation Army. Soon after, Chiang Kai-shek's Nationalist government and National Revolutionary Army retreated to the island of Formosa (Taiwan), where he imposed martial law and ruled for 30 years until his death in 1975.

The change of power to Chairman Mao's Communist Party of China in their People's Republic of China prompted free-market businesses on the mainland to move their operations to Hong Kong, creating another boom on the island.

We were amazed at how quickly Hong Kong was growing. New people poured in and new buildings shot up, each one taller than the next. Vast new apartment buildings climbed the steep hillsides of Victoria Peak. The streets became daily more crowded with rushing traffic and hurrying people, and thousands more *punters* (gamblers) thronged the racecourses. Life had become so hectic and social, with work and parties and more parties.

Reidar and Iris leading in the winner Norse Queen

Reidar and I were caught up in it completely, and we enjoyed being a part of this incredible period of growth and energy. But eventually the pace became overwhelming and we became tired of it. In fact, Reidar had always promised me that he would retire at an early age to enjoy a more relaxed lifestyle.

At 55 years old, he decided that he was finished and we planned our final departure from our wonderful home at *Skyhigh*, still the highest house perched on the top of Hong Kong and overlooking the vast landscape of China.

Reidar and John going for a drive

Since he was a young man, Reidar was focused and driven to succeed at business. He had left his family in Norway to seek his fortune away from home in America and later in the Far East, working seven days a week for years to achieve his goals.

During Iris and Reidar's time in Asia, the political environment in China had various important effects on the shipping business in Hong Kong: early years of economic stagnation; a boom resulting from Shanghai's capture by the Japanese and the exodus of Chinese business from there that followed; a collapse during the Japanese invasion of Hong Kong; and after the years of WWII and China's civil war, an incredible boom from businesses fleeing communist China to its only remaining free-trade zone.

In 1948, Reidar was awarded the Royal Norwegian Order of St. Olav, Knight of First Class, by King Haakon VII of Norway for his services during the war coordinating Norwegian shipping for Nortraship in the India-Ceylon area, as well as establishing the Seaman's Mission in Hong Kong for travelling sailors.

Wallem & Co. continued its operations in shipping, including acting as the broker for Sinofracht (the official ship chartering company of the Communist government of the People's Republic of China), and soon extended its activities into aviation, insurance and trade.

In 1954, Reidar retired after 33 years at Wallem & Co. and living in the Far East. In April of the same year, the South China Morning Post *newspaper wrote, "Well-Known Residents Leaving: Wednesday will see the departure from the Colony of two of its very popular residents, Mr. and Mrs. Reidar Johannessen, who during some 30 years in Hong Kong have become noted not only for their fine Norse Stables, which have produced champion ponies of every class, but also for their time and money they have given unstintingly to any worthy cause. The senior partner of Wallem & Co., he has been a member of the Hong Kong Port Welfare Committee, the Board of Governors of the Matilda and War Memorial Hospital, Chairman of the Executive Committee of the Hong Kong Society for the Protection of Children, a Director of the Anti-Tuberculosis Association, a member of the Board of Directors of numerous prominent local companies..."*

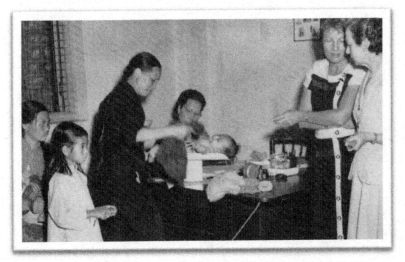

Iris at the Society for the Protection of Children

The young man from Bergen, Norway, who had started as a junior clerk in a shipping office, had risen to the top of the shipping business and became referred to as a "tai-pan" (Chinese for "top class" or "big shot"), foreign-born businessmen who head large "hongs" (major companies).

It was nearly 100 years ago when Reidar began working with his boss Haakon "Typhoon Wallem" in Shanghai, and soon after when he set off to open the Hong Kong office. Today, Wallem & Co. is still based in Hong Kong and has 47 offices in 18 countries, and continues to be one of the most important and experienced shipping companies in the world.

Epilogue

Norse Hill, Jamaica 2001.   After leaving Hong Kong in 1954, Reidar and I could now enjoy travelling about the world as we pleased. Life again was a great adventure together, as we explored many new places and cultures.

We bought a very beautiful villa in the south of France at Roquebrune-Cap Martin, which softened the sad wrench of leaving our lovely *Skyhigh*, home in the clouds.

Iris in front of the Villa del Mare

The *Palazzo del Mare* (which we later changed to *Villa del Mare*) was built by a prince of Montenegro. It was situated on a steep hillside about one hundred feet above the sea with a glorious view across the water to Monte Carlo and the Tête de Chien cliff towering in the background.

However, after six years of living in that beautiful villa, Reidar and I came to the conclusion that it could never feel like a real home for teenage children, and the whole atmosphere in that part of the world was too unnatural and super-sophisticated.

So we took a trip to Jamaica on the strong recommendation of a good friend of ours who had been colonial secretary there long ago. We ended up buying a lovely site in a very beautiful part of the island's remote north shore in San San Bay.

Norse Hill, San San, Jamaica

We built our home, which we called *Norse Hill,* and created a wonderful garden around it. Here everything I planted grew brilliantly. Tall bamboo, ginger, bougainvillea, hibiscus, tulips trees, grapefruits, avocados, papayas, allspice, vanilla bean creepers and endless others made the gardens a magical place.

Norse Point, San San Bay, Jamaica

Far below, we also built a small beach house we called *Norse Point* on the shore of San San Bay, a short swim to a beautiful little island. Our children loved it there and so did many of our friends who came to visit.

Exploring the fjords of Norway

The summers were always spent with the family in Norway at our house on the island of Lepsoy near Bergen, fishing and exploring the endless fjords and forests.

Ingrid and John in Rio de Janeiro, Brasil

At the same time we kept a flat in Brasil to visit John and Ingrid who were both living in Rio de Janeiro. The attractive lifestyle of Ipanema and Copacabana beaches was hard to resist during the 1960's, and they both wound up falling in love there and getting married.

Life was very pleasant for us at this time, as Reidar and I could do as we pleased, and we were always together and loved each other profoundly. Every since we were married, he had given me so much kindness, consideration and thoughtfulness in every way, and was always patient with me with so many of my silly ways. His wonderful generosity, of things great and small, was always with so much love and thought behind it. What had I to give him in return? To me, it seemed so inadequate, but it was all that I had – myself and all of my love .

Ingrid, Reidar and Iris at their home in Jamaica

My beloved Reidar died in Jamaica, on January 3rd, 1970, on our 35th wedding anniversary. Soon after, I placed his ashes in the same snow-covered grave as his parents in Norway. Somehow everything about our *Storhaugen* seemed so different without him, deadened further by the great blanket of snow and ice all over the land. My tears fell in a torrent of sorrow, as everything seemed so meaningless without my Reidar.

It seemed to me as if the whole world had become dark and full of shadows—there was nothing ahead to aim for. My life was like a ship without a rudder, drifting on a sea of loneliness with the winds of fate carrying me I knew not where.

My only haven of refuge was my dear, wonderful children, both starting young families of their own. However I spent most of the next six years drifting about the world, trying to escape myself and my suffering.

I travelled and travelled...to the great pyramids of Egypt, to the Inca ruins of Machu Pichu in the Peruvian Andes, to the monuments of ancient Greece, Rome, Turkey, and the Middle East. I climbed the steps of the Aztec pyramids in Mexico and saw the sun set behind the strange statues of Easter Island. Yet the beauty and magic of these wonderful places that had always fascinated me could not fill the hollow feeling in my heart.

More fulfilling to me were the visits to see John and Patricia at their homes in England and Wales, and later John with Barbara in Portugal (after Patricia had passed away). I also visited Ingrid and Bill who were moving around the world from Colombia, to Brasil, to France, and later settling in to San Francisco and northern California where they built a vineyard and winery.

Iris with her children and grandchildren at Norse Hill in Jamaica

I had the great pleasure to be with my four darling grandchildren, whom I could squeeze with big hugs, grateful to feel an important part of their lives, but without the responsibility to clean up after them!

Then Fate intervened for me as Burke Knapp came into my life. When Reidar and I had first met him and his wife, we had both liked them very much, and Reidar had even offered Burke and his family the loan of our house in Jamaica for a holiday.

But Burke was always too involved on World Bank affairs as Senior Vice President for this to happen. So we eventually lost touch, until the sudden arrival of his telegram asking if "we" could come for a visit. I had expected his wife, but it was his daughter who came, and only then I learnt of his divorce.

And that was the beginning of a new life for me. Now it seems almost unbelievable that I have been married to Burke for nearly 35 years. He is a dear, wonderful friend...although we have our many differences.

Iris and Burke in the Gobi Desert, Mongolia

At first, we lived together in Washington DC when he was still head of the bank and meeting with the world's leaders. Then later we moved to San Francisco Bay to our home in Silicon Valley, near Stanford University where he had studied. All the while, I continued to go back and forth to my home in Jamaica where I had my beautiful garden and where I felt truly happy.

Iris in her garden at Norse Hill with San San Bay in the background

Even though I love Burke, I could never really adjust to the hustle and bustle of city living, so in 1995, at 86 years old, I decided to move back to Jamaica permanently by myself. Burke enjoys his visits to Jamaica, but is much too active and social to stay for more than a few weeks. Our situation works well for us however, as we can visit each other when we please, but we live our own lives as we desire. For this I am very grateful.

My children, and my grandchildren who now have families of their own, enjoy coming to visit me in Jamaica on a regular basis. What a gift it is to know one's great-grandchildren and have them running around and asking me amusing questions about my life!

How life can change. When I was young, my brothers Archy and Vean and I felt very little affection from my mother, and my father was always very far away. We were distanced from all other family. My parents barely knew us, and never met their grandchildren. Yet today to have such an extended family all around me is the greatest wish one could ask for.

I am 99 years old. Much to my amazement, I still have my health and have yet to lose my mind. Burke has been living in a comfortable social "retirement community", while I continue to live independently.

I have lived a thrilling life throughout an entire century. I have experienced wonderful times, having friends and family to share them with, as well as the tragic events of the war that cost so many lives and was so utterly destructive. There were times of prosperity, and times of being penniless, and periods of pure joy, happiness and a true love.

Now I just wish I could turn a switch and disappear. I am ready to move on to the next adventure.

Iris at 99 years old reading from her 1940's war diary

Afterword

Iris Hay-Edie Johannessen was born in Cornwall, England, in 1909. She died in California in 2009, living a long, eventful and adventurous life.

As a young girl, she grew up in unusually grand residences in the south of France, in Tennyson's castle *Château de l'Aiguetta* in Eze Village and in the *Villa Lumiere*, built by the inventors of the cinema, in Cap d'Ail, Monte Carlo. Neither could be called a home, as she and her brothers were sent away to boarding schools at a very young age. Their father was away for years working in the Far East and their estranged mother was completely involved in her own social life. During this period, Iris suffered greatly from loneliness and her mother's opression.

Château de l'Aiguetta is the largest castle on the Cote d'Azur, at 4,000m2 on 16 hectares of land. It was purchased by the Monte Carlo Casino, later fell into ruin, and then was renovated again to a grander scale.

Château de l'Aiguetta, Cote d'Azur, France

Her "escape" to England, and later to Hong Kong, changed her life in every way. Without money or plans, Iris became a

385

gypsy-like world-traveller, very unusual for a single woman in those days. Before she was 25 years old, before passenger airplane transport existed, she had travelled extensively on her own by train and by ship, through Europe, the Middle East and the Far East, as well as circumnavegating the globe and driving coast-to-coast across the United States in the rumble seat of a open two-seater Plymouth.

Her writing in her diary reflects the fascination she experiences with each place she visits, offering very colorful descriptions of the landscapes, cultures and curious people she meets along the way.

In Hong Kong she reunites with her brother Archy, and soon after marries her "true love". Reidar and Iris build her first real home and call it *Skyhigh*, the highest house on the island on top of Victoria Peak. John and Ingrid are born there, but just two years later in 1941, *Skyhigh* is bombed by the Japanese during the Hong Kong invasion. Everything is lost.

Figuring their low chances of survival in a Japanese internment camp with two young children, they make their perilous escape through China, over "the Hump" of the Himalayas and eventually to India where Reidar plays an important role in Nortraship, the exiled Norwegian government's shipping fleet.

After the war, they returned to Hong Kong to rebuild their home. Reidar rose to be a "taipan" (chinese for "magnate") in the shipping business which grew substantially in Hong Kong and Asia after the war. Iris became involved in charity work and the Far East social scene.

In 1954 Reidar retired and they sold *Skyhigh* to the Hong Kong and Shanghai Bank, to be the chairman's home with major renovations to fit the opulence of the number one VIP of Hong Kong.

The Skyhigh property now with four modern homes built

From there, the property went through various well-documented and widely-publicized changes which rocked the real estate world with new levels of ostentation and "sky high" prices. It became the world's most expensive property, setting a Guiness World Record. Later, torn down and subdivided into four ultra-modern homes, and together (all within the original property) they would be valued at over US$500 million.

The current view from the Skyhigh property over Hong Kong

Leaving Hong Kong in 1954, Iris and Reidar moved to France and bought the *Palazzo del Mare* on the shores of Cap Martin, overlooking Monte Carlo. In 1960 they sold it to an American banker, later it was purchased by a Saudi billionaire, and then exchanged again to be made a residence-fortress by President Mobutu Sese Seko of Zaire, known as one of the most corrupt leaders in history who had embezzled over US$10 billion of his poor country's money.

What became of Iris' brothers? After the war, Archy returned to work in Hong Kong, but his wife Gerd felt that life there was not suitable for their four children, so she moved with them to Ireland where she began a successful hand weaving workshop as a textile designer. Archy continued to work with Mackinnon Mackenzie in Hong Kong for several years, but missed his children so much that he decided to take early retirement and rejoin his family in Ireland. Meanwhile, their younger brother Vean lived the rest of his life as a quiet and reclusive gardener on Vancouver Island in Canada, his self esteem permanently marked by the mistreatment from his mother.

The shores of the Caribbean Sea became Iris and Reidar's final settlement together. They built an estate high in the jungle under the Blue Mountains and overlooking San San Bay, on Jamaica's remote north-east coast, which they named *Norse Hill*, as well as a small beach house called *Norse Point* across from picture-perfect Pellew Island. In the 1960's, this area of Jamaica was a quaint hideaway to many prominent figures and their friends and neighbors included Baron Hans Heinrich Thyssen-Bornemisza, Molson brewery owner Senator Harland Molson, Prince Sadruddin Aga Khan, Lady Price, and actor Errol Flynn and his actress wife Patrice Wymore Flynn.

Over the next 40 years, Iris developed a spectacular botanical garden at *Norse Hill*. It became her passion, and Jamaica was a paradise for her. They shared ten wonderful years living together there, until 1970, when Reidar passed away.

Their children, John and Ingrid, had families of their own, and later Iris married Burke Knapp, who helped to fill the void she felt in her heart. With her family and friends scattered throught the world, Jamaica became the gathering place for all to enjoy their holidays together.

A century old, blessed with good health, a sound mind and sense of humor, Iris was the cornerstone and spirit of her family. She leaves her diary for her descendants and those interested in reliving her adventures and the extraordinary events - that she witnessed and carefully documented – of an era that shaped the "Far East" into the powerhouse that Asia is today.

Iris Hay-Edie Johannessen
1909-2009

Her view from Skyhigh of Hong Kong in the 1940's

CPSIA information can be obtained
at www.ICGtesting.com
Printed in the USA
FSOW03n1349090816
23523FS